DEAD HANDS

DEAD HANDS

A Social History of Wills, Trusts, and Inheritance Law

Lawrence M. Friedman

Stanford Law Books
An Imprint of Stanford University Press
Stanford, California

© 2009 Lawrence M. Friedman. All rights reserved.

No part of this book may be reproduced or transmitted in any form or by any means, electronic or mechanical, including photocopying and recording, or in any information storage or retrieval system without the prior written permission of Stanford University Press.

Printed in the United States of America on acid-free, archival-quality paper

Library of Congress Cataloging-in-Publication Data

Friedman, Lawrence Meir
  Dead hands : a social history of wills, trusts, and inheritance law / Lawrence M. Friedman.
      p. cm.
  Includes bibliographical references and index.
  ISBN 978-0-8047-6036-2 (cloth : alk. paper) —
  ISBN 978-0-8047-6209-0 (pbk : alk. paper)
  1. Inheritance and succession—United States—History. 2. Inheritance and succession—Social aspects—United States. I. Title.
KF753.F75 2009
346.7305'2—dc22

2008042353

Typeset at Stanford University Press in 10.5/15 Adobe Garamond

To Leah, Jane, Amy, Paul, Sarah, David, and Lucy

CONTENTS

Acknowledgments ix
1 *Introduction* 1
2 *Distribution after Death* 15
3 *The Last Will and Testament* 58
4 *Breaking a Will: Will Contests and Their Social Meaning* 82
5 *Will Substitutes* 100
6 *Dynastic and Caretaker Trusts* 111
7 *Control by the Dead and Its Limits: The Rise and Fall of the Rule against Perpetuities* 125
8 *Charitable Gifts and Foundations* 140
9 *Death and Taxes* 171
10 *Conclusion* 179

Notes 185
Index 217

ACKNOWLEDGMENTS

I WOULD LIKE TO THANK a number of people who helped me with the research for this book. They include David Oyer, Lucy Oyer, Sari Bourne, Scott Shackelton, and Renee Stowitzky. I also want to thank two anonymous reviewers for their comments, and most especially, Joanna Grossman for going over every page of the manuscript and saving me from the most egregious errors. As usual, too, I owe an enormous debt to the library staff of the Stanford Law School. I'd like to mention specifically Paul Lomio, Erika Wayne, Kate Wilko, and George Wilson. My assistant, Mary Tye, was a big help too; and of course, I have to thank my family for their everlasting support.

CHAPTER 1

INTRODUCTION

On August 13, 2007, Brooke Astor, at the ripe old age of 105, died at her estate, Holly Hill, in New York. Brooke was, by all accounts, a warm and winning human being; she was often called New York City's "unofficial first lady." She was also a very rich lady. She had inherited a massive fortune from her third husband, Vincent Astor. She became well known for her charitable activities; she gave away more than $200 million. Money, she said, "is like manure"; it "should be spread around." In 1998 the Presidential Medal of Freedom was awarded to Brooke Astor.[1]

But in her last years, ill and demented, she sank into the dim world of those who suffer from Alzheimer's disease. Her one son, Anthony Marshall, acted as her guardian, managing her affairs. His management, however, had somewhat scandalous results. Marshall's own son, Phillip, accused him of abusing the old lady and pillaging her estate. Anthony, it was claimed, lined his own pockets, while Brooke Astor slept on a couch that smelled of urine and lived on pureed peas and oatmeal; her beloved dogs, Boysie and Girlsie, were locked in a pantry. The court removed Anthony from his position of trust. The court named Annette de la Renta, an old friend, as guardian of the person—in charge of Brooke Astor's life and health; a bank became guardian of the estate—in charge of her fortune. And when Brooke Astor finally died, an unseemly quarrel broke out over the estate; the scandal even touched the lawyers who were involved.

Squabbles over the money and bodies of old people, and over the estates of the dead, are nothing new. They have been around for centuries. In 1889, for example, the city of Pasadena was abuzz over what the newspapers called the Banta will contest. Isaac Banta, who died in Ohio, had left behind considerable property in California. His legacy also included a nasty fight, between his daughter and son-in-law on one side, and the rest of his family on the other. The son-in-law, Pierce (according to the family), had gotten hold of this old, feeble man and plied him with alcohol and laudanum. The old man was a virtual prisoner; Pierce, moreover, had poisoned his mind against his near and dear ones and induced Banta to give the bulk of his property to Pierce. Testimony on both sides was as different as night and day. One witness argued that Banta was "perfectly rational," and in fact an "exceedingly shrewd businessman."[2] Another, Frank Wilson, called him "crazy as a loon" and told a story about a trip to the mines, during which Banta jumped out of a wagon "and ran off into the desert"; they had to bring him back forcefully, singing and carrying on in a way that seemed totally insane.[3] In the end, after a long parade of witnesses, the jury sustained the will: they declared that the old man was sane after all, and that there was no fraud, no undue influence.[4] There was talk of an appeal to the California Supreme Court; the family, however, rather meekly agreed to a settlement a month or so later. Pierce resigned as trustee of the old man's property, but essentially he won the case.[5]

The struggle over the Banta estate was unusual. Every year, thousands of estates pass through probate (which is, briefly, the legal process of settling the estate of a deceased person), without a whisper in the press. The Banta case was extreme; yet old age, decay, family quarrels, and money passing from one generation to another—these are normal, everyday affairs. They do not, ordinarily, involve courts and lawsuits, let alone newspapers. The machinery, as a rule, runs smoothly. In some ways the legal system plays an obvious role in this process; in other ways it is silent and almost invisible. Some concepts that are relevant here are so fundamental that we take them for granted: the concept of family, or private property, or marriage. Yet these are legal concepts as well as everyday ideas; and the probate process presupposes them.

Even when the role of the legal system is obvious, it does its work as a matter of routine. But what is routine is by no means unimportant. Routine is the heart of social action; a person's heartbeat is routine; the work of the lungs is routine; the work of brain, stomach, legs, and kidneys is routine. So too of many actions and habits of daily life. And so too of the rhythm of life and death—and the passing of wealth and property from dead hands to living ones.

This book is about both the routine and the unusual in that branch of law we call the law of succession. In simple language, it is about the way property changes hands when a person dies, and about related processes that go on, as the legal phrase has it, "in contemplation of death." It is about cases like Isaac Banta's, but also about the untold thousands—or millions—who leave some sort of legacy behind when they die: people who matter to the people who survive and mourn them, but otherwise hardly make a ripple in the vast ocean of the law.

The whole edifice of the law of succession, legally and socially, rests on one brute fact: you can't take it with you. Death is inevitable, fundamental, and definitive. When people die, everything they think they own, everything struggled, scrimped, and saved for, every jewel and bauble, every bank account, all stocks and bonds, the cars and houses, corn futures or gold bullion, all books, CD's, pictures, and carpets—everything will pass on to somebody or something else. A certain amount can be spent on a funeral or a fancy coffin. A person can ask for, and get, an elaborate headstone and can buy a policy of "perpetual care" for the grave. People can, if they wish, be buried still wearing their favorite ring or a wedding band, or dressed in their favorite clothes. But these are incidentals. Fundamentally, when the body flatlines, a person's iron grip on "assets," all rights of ownership, all powers and authority supported by custom and law, dissolve, turn limp and flaccid; and the wealth, no matter how great, slips out of the person's hands. There are people who have paid good money to have their bodies frozen in perpetuity at death. The hope is that medical science will figure out a way to wake them up in the future. The Reanimation Foundation, of Liechtenstein, will set up and manage a trust fund for such people, so that they won't be revived as paupers.[6] The ancient pharaohs, and many great kings and princes, erected huge pyramids and tombs for themselves. They buried themselves in luxury, wrapped and mummified in elaborate coffins, surrounded by gold and silver objects and all sorts of finery;

they believed they could transport themselves and their goods into another world. In the long run, all this wealth and grandeur passed into the hands of looters and grave robbers; and much of what the looters missed, archaeologists dug up and put behind glass in museums. In the end, even the mightiest pharaoh probably took nothing at all to the other side.

This rite of passage, this transfer of goods at death, has tremendous social and legal importance. The transfer takes different forms in different societies, and in different times. There is no single name for the process. Here, as I said, we call it *succession*—a shorthand way of summing up social processes and institutions and their legal echoes, which govern the way property moves from generation to generation and to the living from the dead. "Succession" includes the law of wills, the law of intestacy, the law of trusts (for the most part), the law of charitable foundations, the law concerning "death taxes," and even some aspects of an arcane field of law that lawyers call the law of future interests.

Obviously, when you die, you lose control in any literal sense. But human law can, and does, open the door to a certain amount of post-mortem control. The dead hand rules, if we let it, from beyond the grave, at least up to a point. The simplest way this is done is through a *will*, in which you have the right, if you follow certain formalities, to specify who gets what when you die. In our society, property is not abandoned like a corpse to the vultures. The will sets out a scheme for disposing of the property when you die; or, if there is no will, a body of rules of law, the law of *intestate succession*, gives you (by default) an estate plan. This book, to a considerable extent, is about the rights and powers, the scope and limits, of the dead hand: control of property, or lack of control, when a person dies.

Succession, as I have already said, is a social process of enormous importance. In a rich country, the stock of wealth that turns over as people die, one by one, is staggeringly large. In the United States, according to one estimate, some $41 trillion will pass from the dead to the living in the first half of the twenty-first century. This figure has been disputed, and an argument rages among economists as to the exact amounts—all the way from "only" $10 trillion to the high estimate of $41 trillion. But no matter who is right, clearly we are dealing with immense amounts of money.[7]

Anything that involves trillions of dollars is important in and of itself. But the social impact of inheritance is more than a matter of money. More broadly, it is also a matter of what money buys and what money brings about. In our society—and in many societies—money determines social class, social structure. George Marcus and Peter Hall, in their study of "dynastic families," have pointed out the supreme importance of law and legal institutions to these dynasties; law and legal institutions determine whether or not these dynasties will persist.[8] But institutions of succession are significant far beyond the world of the great families. What DNA is to the physical body, processes of succession are to society—that is, to the social body. An elite, an upper class, is a class that inherits. A lower class is a class that inherits nothing. There may be a certain amount of regression to the mean—that is, over generations, great fortunes tend to become somewhat diluted. But this occurs, if it occurs, pretty slowly.[9] And yes, there is social mobility. Poor children can grow up to be rich adults. A certain number of heirs squander their money and sink into the mud at the bottom of society.[10] Still, on the whole, the poor stay poor and the rich stay rich; and inheritance is a large part of this story.

In short, succession is one of the most vital and fundamental of all social processes. And of legal processes too. Estate planning is a lucrative business for lawyers—and a necessary business for their customers. Thousands of lawyers make their living, or part of their living, by drawing up wills and trusts, handling estates of the dead, and helping rich and very rich people avoid or minimize death taxes. There is plenty of material to guide and instruct these lawyers—a big literature of practical knowledge. The social science literature is much skimpier. Economists have nibbled at the edges of the subject. Sociologists have hardly looked at it at all.[11] There are occasional studies of such things as inheritance of farms in rural communities.[12] Anthropologists have told us something about succession—though mostly about the customs and habits of tribal people in exotic places. There are a handful of studies of the probate process, sampling wills and estates here and there in the United States. Some of these are historical,[13] or old enough to be treated as historical.[14] But historians, like the social scientists, have hardly even started to exhume the detailed history of succession laws. There are a few honorable exceptions—very notably, a pioneering study by Carole Shammas, Marylynn Salmon, and Michel Dahlin, which looks at patterns of testation over the first 200 years of the United States.[15] Other, smaller studies focus on patterns of testation in particular places and at particular times—for example, Cuyahoga County, Ohio; or San Bernardino County, California, in the 1960's.[16] There are other scattered studies and collections of data; but on the whole, the literature is hardly as rich as one might like. Of course, for the general public—for the intelligent lay reader—there are guides (how to make your own will; what every man and woman should know about probate; and so on), but very little looking at succession as a social process, as an area of life with cultural meaning and importance. This book is a modest attempt to fill some of the gaps, by recounting some aspects of the social history of the law of succession.

The story is important in its own right, as I said. It also has significance for those interested in theories about the relationship between law and society. Big changes in the law of succession necessarily reflect big changes in society. At one time, for example, no married woman could make out a will disposing of land her parents might have left to her. Her husband had total control. In modern society, of course, such a rule would be impossible. In fact, the old rule has been dead for a century and a half. The social and economic position of women, including married women, has changed enormously since, say, 1800. This much is obvious.

But some smaller, more technical changes in the law have, in a way, even more theoretical interest than big changes. This is an area of law (not the only one, of course) where the average citizen knows very little, and cares very little too, about it—that is, until somebody in the family dies. Then, all of a sudden, the rules and practices can become extremely important. It is also, in some ways, a very technical field. It is a field that rarely makes the headlines. There is the occasional big will contest, cases like Isaac Banta's, or more recently, the sad sagas of Anna Nicole Smith and Brooke Astor. Otherwise, there is media silence. That affirmative action or abortion are the stuff of politics and sociology is painfully clear. But what about the politics and sociology of the rule against perpetuities? Or doctrines about mistakes in wills? What are the forces that mold and shape an area of law insulated from the media, an area that works in routine and quiet ways?

Necessarily, this book leaves out a lot of details. Some treatises on the law of wills, or on the law of trusts, run to many volumes (and pretty dreary volumes at that). Here we will have to bypass some interesting highways and byways in the law. I include little or nothing about dependent relative revocation, or ademption by extinction, or anti-lapse statutes—meaning no disrespect to these noble doctrines; or about an enormous body of doctrine and case law about the rights and duties of trustees. This book is selective; it touches only on certain salient aspects of the law of succession. These are, on the whole, aspects that bear most directly on the book's theme: the social meaning and impact of the law.

Probably every society has inheritance rules. There were rules about inheritance in Greek and Roman law and in the laws of Egypt. There are references to inheritance laws in the Old Testament and in the codes of the ancient Middle East. There are rules of inheritance and succession in preliterate societies. Every modern country, of course, has rules and norms about inheritance and succession. For the most part, I concern myself chiefly with the United States; there are some references, too, to England, which was the source of many of the American rules and practices, and the source of the very vocabulary of succession.

American society is exceedingly wealthy. The United States is a member of a lucky and exclusive club—societies that are democratic, rich, and highly developed. Most countries in Western Europe, along with such countries as Japan and Australia, are members of this club. In these societies too, the populations tend to live long, healthy lives—lives much longer and healthier than those of their ancestors. These are also primarily middle-class societies. Millions of people have money in the bank, own a house or an apartment, possibly too some stocks and bonds. A small but crucial fraction of the population is made up of people and families that are really rich. These are the ones who leave behind big "estates" when members of the family die off.

At the time of the American Revolution, most people in what became the United States lived on farms and farmed for a living. In the southern part of the country, there was, to be sure, a kind of aristocracy: rich planters, men like Washington and Jefferson, who owned large tracts of land, with gangs of African slaves to do the work. In the North, most people lived on what we would now call family farms. With few exceptions, there was nothing in the North like the southern plantations—or, for that matter, like the English landed gentry, the class of people described by Jane Austen or the Victorian novelists, people who had servants and country estates, and who lived (and lived very nicely) off the rent paid by tenant farmers. English inheritance law had been molded, or had evolved, to suit the interests of the landed gentry. American inheritance law, on the other hand, had different tasks; it had to meet the needs and wants of a big class of smallholders, families that owned small tracts of land.

The idea of the yeoman farmer, and his family, was a crucial element in the theory of American democracy. Private ownership of land by masses of people was a fact of life. It was also a critical pillar of ideology. Americans tended to think that their way of life was the best and most advanced, a way of life that represented the highest form of civilization, and that anything else was deviant. There were, of course, crucial differences between North and South. In the nineteenth century, many Yankees found the southern way of life repulsive, in particular the institution of slavery. Southern aristocracy thought the North, with its "wage slaves," was a corrupt and inferior society. Later, both North and South were repelled by Mormon polygamy and were deeply suspicious of the power of the Mormon Church over the lives and the fortunes of the faithful. And Americans in general had no understanding of the land tenure systems of the Native peoples (and no sympathy with these systems), often with tragic consequences.[17]

Americans in the nineteenth century were, on the whole, very proud of their form of government. But it was a system that astonished (or horrified) visitors from Europe. It inspired Alexis de Tocqueville's classic study, *Democracy in America*, which described and analyzed the bold new experiment in popular government. Today we are much less impressed with American democracy in the days of de Tocqueville. There was, to begin with, chattel slavery. Millions of African Americans were slaves, tied to the land, paid nothing for their labor. Even free blacks were not really free; they were second-class citizens, and everywhere, not only in the South, they faced discrimination and legal disabilities. The treatment of the Native tribes was, to our way of thinking, shameful and at times genocidal. And then there were laws and customs that relegated women, especially married women, to a subordinate place in the social order. Under the doctrine of "coverture," when a woman married, her husband gained control of her assets; he gained outright ownership of personal property in many states. All those "chattels, which belonged formerly to the wife, are by act of law vested in the husband," as Blackstone put it. The "very being and existence of the woman is suspended during the coverture." As far as land was concerned, the husband had full rights to the "rents and profits" during the marriage.[18] For her part, she could not buy or sell land, or dispose of land by will. Legally speaking, a "feme covert" (married woman) was not much better off than an idiot or a newborn baby.

Most of the settlers who lived in the American colonies came from the British Isles. The rules of inheritance and succession that formed the living law of the colonies were unmistakably colored by English law and experience. Even the terms and the forms were English. But it is also true that the colonies tended to go down their own paths. England was very far away; conditions in the colonies were very different from conditions in the mother country. Powerful social forces were driving society apart on the two sides of the Atlantic. Probably most important was the sheer abundance of land. England was a very hierarchical society. At the top of the pyramid was the king; below him were the nobles and the landed gentry. They owned virtually all of the land. The bulk of the population worked the land as tenant farmers, paying rent to the landowner. Any attempt to transplant a system of this type was doomed to failure in, say, a colony such as Massachusetts Bay. Here there seemed to be enough land for everybody—for every family, at any rate. (The claims of the Native peoples to the land were largely ignored or discounted.) Already at the time of the Revolution the American law of succession had parted company with English law in a number of significant ways, most strikingly in the northern colonies. I will come back to this point.

One aspect of English law that did carry over was the idea of a probate process. In English law, and in American law, an elaborate procedure had to be followed when a person died and left property behind. (In continental Europe, the rules and procedures tended to be much simpler.) First, the will (if there was one) had to be filed, and there were procedures for getting it admitted and approved officially. This part is the probate process, literally speaking. (The Latin root in "probate" is the same root found in "prove.") The term "probate," however, is applied colloquially to everything else that happens between the filing of the will, at the beginning, and closing the estate and distributing the property at the end.

The essence of the process is this: somebody has to be appointed to manage the estate until it is finally distributed. This is the "personal representative." The personal representative is either an *executor* or an *administrator*. The executor is a person (or corporation) named by the deceased in his will. Where there is no will, the court has to appoint someone to do the job; and this someone is called the administrator.[19] Usually this is a close relative of the deceased.

The personal representative takes charge of the property, draws up an inventory of the assets, pays off claims, files any necessary tax returns, sells property that has to be sold, and does whatever else has to be done while the estate is under his care. When these jobs are finished, the personal representative files some sort of accounting with the probate court in charge of the estate, hands the property over to the heirs, and then bows out.[20]

A lot of this work is necessary; somebody has to do it. But in the United States the system is more cumbersome and expensive than it needs to be. It is much more laborious and bureaucratic than in European countries, and even, today, in England.[21] The problem in our system is that, in most places and for most estates, the administrator may need the approval of the probate judge for each step of the way. This means filling out forms and presenting them in probate court. If, for example, the executor or administrator wants to sell off some stocks and bonds, or the decedent's diamond ring, or a painting of his grandmother, there has to be court approval. Some states have tried to fix this problem, by allowing "independent administration"—that is, letting people give the executor or administrator a fairly free hand, for the most part, in managing the estate. So, for example, under the Texas Probate Code, a person can specify in his will that nothing has to be funneled through the court except the "probating and recording of [the] . . . will, and the return of an inventory, appraisement, and list of claims of his estate."[22]

People tend to exaggerate the costs of the probate process.[23] To be sure, there are fees to be paid; and the personal representative has a right to collect a fee. But these costs are not much of an issue, especially for really large estates. Estates below a certain threshold can escape the fuss and bother of probate, and escape the process altogether. For the smallest estates, local statutes basically prescribe who gets the assets. If a man has a wife and children and an estate of a few thousand dollars, whatever he says in his will does not really matter. The statute will decide the fate of the whole estate. In California, for example, if the net value of the estate is less than $20,000, the family can file a petition to the probate court asking for the estate to be given over to the "surviving spouse and minor children, or one or more of them."[24] This, I suppose, is one of the few advantages of dying without much money. There are also, in many places, simple provisions for these simple estates—laws under which, for instance, a widow can get title to a car without much fuss. Of course, rich people too can avoid probate—by setting up living trusts or through some other device (I will come back to this point). And rich and poor can bypass the probate process in other ways—by holding the family home in joint tenancy, for instance.[25]

SOME GENERAL THEMES

Certain leitmotifs run through this book. Most basic is the simple proposition that the social meaning and nature of succession law is variable, and that it has changed over time. Changes in family structure, changes in the nature of the legal order, demographic change, and changes in social norms and attitudes have all left their mark on the law of succession.

First, with regard to family structure: here the law has traveled one particular path. It has shifted emphasis from what we might call the *bloodline family* to the *family of affection and dependence*. Historically, the husband was the head of the family, and inheritance favored his bloodline, especially the male bloodline. When a member of the English landed gentry died in the Middle Ages, his lands went to his heir—his oldest son. There were some protections for the grieving widow during her lifetime; but she had no say over what would eventually happen to the property. At least this was the case when the landowner died without a will. The rules were a reflection of gender roles. They were also designed to maintain a class of landed gentlefolk. The idea was to keep the land intact, as a single "estate," and not to split it into many bits and pieces. Other kinds of property were not terribly important at the time. Nobody in the Middle Ages owned stocks and bonds.

The modern family does not look very much like the upper-class English family of the Middle Ages. The family has changed, and so has the law. There have been many legal changes over the past century and a half or so, and the big winner in these changes has been the surviving spouse—widows and widowers, but especially widows. The traditional patriarchal family has given way (in part at least) to so-called companionate marriage. Women and men have equal rights in the workplace and in the family—theoretically and, more and more, in reality. Marriages are much more a matter of individual choice. Families are involved, of course, but neither custom nor law allows a parent to veto the marriage choices of an adult child.

What we have now is the family of affection and dependence. The common law, for example, did not recognize the adoption of children. A person either had children the usual way; or was childless. Adoption laws date from about the middle of the nineteenth century in the United States (in Great Britain, adoption was not recognized by law until 1926). All modern probate codes generally treat adopted children the same as "natural" children. Inheritance law always focused on the family; but the image of the family today is the image of a close-knit group, living together, with strong emotional ties or ties of blood, marriage, or adoption. In this society, children are sometimes estranged from their parents, and brothers and sisters may not be on speaking terms; but in general, the law assumes a kind of deep-seated affection. And this is especially true of a person's life-partner. There is a strong tendency (though not without resistance) to recognize "domestic partners," gay or straight. There is also a strong tendency to wipe out the inheritance rights of distant relatives, the so-called laughing heirs.

All of these tendencies appear most clearly in *intestacy laws*: the rules that govern what happens to an estate when the deceased has no valid will. A surviving spouse also has protection of some sort against a deceased spouse who has tried to use the will to cut his or her partner out of any share of the estate. Children, on the whole, do not have this kind of protection. This is so despite the fact that children are the very core of the family of affection and dependence. In this regard, the common law is quite different from the civil law systems in such countries as Germany or France. In America it is possible—and in fact quite easy—to disinherit all of your children. I will try to explain this (apparent) paradox later on.

Intestacy laws are important; but a will can override almost all of the intestacy rules. Patterns of testation, however, show the same sort of evolution as the intestacy laws. As preference for the bloodline family weakens, preference for the family of affection and dependence gets stronger. Studies of the wills that people make show this very clearly. In wills today, the surviving spouse (widow or widower) is much more likely to get a bigger share of the estate, and gain a much higher degree of control, than was true in the eighteenth or nineteenth century.

Family structure has also changed in ways that have an impact on succession. Traditional marriage has given way to companionate marriage. This was surely a factor in the rise of the family of affection and dependence. In the nineteenth century divorce was uncommon; but death at an early age was not. Today more marriages are dissolved by divorce than by early death. Marriage, in the (cynical) old saying, is the triumph of hope over experience; and divorced men and women often try and try again. It is common, then, for people to have children from two or three marriages. This makes a difference in the context of inheritance. Should intestacy laws, for example, distinguish between widows who are mothers of the dead man's kids and widows who are only their stepmother? Also, in the contemporary world, there are all sorts of nontraditional families—couples who live together without getting married and same-sex couples, for example. And there are children that have both womb mothers and egg mothers. Or who are conceived after their father's death, from frozen sperm. All of these circumstances have an impact, or a potential impact, on laws of succession.[26]

Second, in this age of elaborate record keeping, computers, data bases, and vibrant bureaucracies, the will has become much less important than it was in the past. Historically, the will was a vital document, not only for disposing of a person's estate, but also for proving who owned what and who had a right to property (especially land). Today the will has been at least partly dethroned. Modern law and practice recognize a whole cluster of will substitutes—devices that can and do take the place of a will. Most important, perhaps, is the so-called living trust. The rise of these will substitutes has had a big impact on the law of succession. Many of the old—and rather rigid—rules that governed the law of wills have weakened, or have been eliminated. A later chapter explores how and why this has happened.

Third, demographic and cultural changes have also had a powerful impact on the law of succession. In the nineteenth century, people lived, on the whole, much shorter lives than they do today. Hence people tended to inherit from their parents, if there was anything to inherit, at a younger age than they do now. John Langbein, for one, has made this point, and spelled out the consequences of modern longevity.[27] If a man lives to be 80 and leaves everything to his wife, who lives to be 90, their children will be gray-haired and possibly even retired by the time they inherit. Brooke Astor lived to be 105, and her son was over 80 when she died. As a consequence, today, for many families, lifetime transfers are more important than inheritances. Parents with money pay for college, and for trips abroad; they may help with a down payment on a house, or with funds for the grandchildren. There are, of course, other consequences—people live longer and healthier lives; but a fair number of them, alas, perhaps live a bit too long. They outlive their ability to take care of themselves and their property. They need help; and there are various legal (and nonlegal) ways of getting it for them. This is an important subject, but I do not take it up in this book.

One study showed that roughly one family out of five gets a "wealth transfer" (a gift or inheritance) in any year (the latest year in the study was 1998). The figures were not broken down in such a way as to distinguish between gifts and bequests. Poor people get small transfers, but these small transfers may mean a lot more to them than the big transfers some rich people get.[28] For millions of people, though, these transfers are extremely significant. As I pointed out earlier, the whole social system rests, in a way, on transfers of wealth between generations. Most newborn babies and toddlers have no money of their own, and everything they have—their clothes, their strollers, the mashed babyfood they eat—comes by way of transfer from an older generation. Even the few babies that (legally speaking) "own" property or other assets which they inherited from some relative obviously have no way to control their wealth; they have to depend on what parents, guardians, or other adults decide.

One last factor of legal culture has to be mentioned: attitudes in society toward wealth and the wealthy. These attitudes are politically and socially of great importance. And they change hugely over time. America was born in revolt against a system of inherited, dynastic wealth. But by the late nineteenth century it had grown its own crop of dynasties. Legal rules that once disfavored dynasties—and, one should add, dynastic institutions like the Church of Rome—gradually gave way in the law of succession to rules that *favored* dynastic wealth. Indeed, some of the most arcane and mysterious rules find their explanation, ultimately, in their impact on dynastic wealth. Attitudes toward wealth also help explain the fall and rise of the charitable foundation, as well as the rise and fall of estate and inheritance taxes, a story that in our times is still unfolding.

CHAPTER 2

DISTRIBUTION AFTER DEATH

ONLY LIVING PEOPLE can "own" something. Once a person dies, ownership lapses, and the goods and assets pass into other hands. There are several ways in which society can deal with the property of a dead person. One way would be to cut off any rights the dead person might have had and leave the asset up for grabs. Or the state could confiscate the property and use it for whatever purposes it chooses. Or, to mention a third possibility, legal rules could dictate what becomes of the property—who gets what, and in what proportions. Fourth, we could let the dead person decide and honor whatever requests or arrangements he or she might have made.

In fact, our system has elements of all four, though the last two probably dominate. Leaving things "up for grabs" is never the rule for property. But this is something that follows from the way our society defines property. Anything that, at death, is up for grabs is simply not classified as property at all. Property in general is not an easy concept to define. Every society has its own conception of property. Willard Hurst defined property as the "legitimate power to initiate decisions on the use of economic assets."[1] This definition is as good as any. But no definition covers all societies at all times. To take a simple example: if the mayor of a city dies, her right to the office lapses; she could not sell it while she was alive, and she cannot leave it to her children in her will. There will have to be a new election unless there is a deputy mayor or some other arrangement for choosing a successor. The office of mayor, in other words, is not "property." But in medieval England, many offices *were* property, and could be inherited and possibly even sold.

Our legal system—and our social system—has its own conventional definition of property, which excludes, for example, public office. The economic and social system is based to a large extent on the concept of private property. Assets—things of value—can be "owned" by individuals. This means that people have a full bundle of rights over their assets. The bundle of rights includes the right to buy and sell these assets and, what is germane to our subject, to dispose of the assets at death, as a general rule. Of course, two or more people can share ownership rights. Husbands and wives can have joint bank accounts. In some apartment buildings, tenants "own" their apartments, but there is a kind of collective ownership of lobbies and other common areas. Other buildings are "co-ops." In modern societies, social collectives—families or clans—do not usually "own" property. In many societies in the past, and in quite a few preliterate societies, family, clan, tribal, or village ownership was the rule, not the exception.

California and a number of other states, mostly in the West, are "community property" states. This system was unknown to the common law. It has a civil law background. It survived in such states as Texas and California, which were once part of Mexico. These states follow the Spanish version of community property. In most states what a wife earns is hers, and what a husband earns is his. Legally, they are separate entities. But in a community property state husbands and wives form a "community": half of what he earns belongs automatically to her, and half of what she earns belongs automatically to him. It is possible for them to keep their incomes and properties separate, but they must make specific arrangements to do so, in writing. Property owned *before* marriage, even in community property states, continues to be "separate property."

To be sure, husbands and wives, even in states without the blessings of community property, can and do file joint income tax returns. In this way, they treat themselves as if they were, in effect, residents of a community property state. It is worth mentioning how this came about. When the bite of the income tax law began to affect masses of taxpayers, it turned out that married people who lived in, say, California, paid less tax than married people who lived in, say, New York. This is because the Californians could claim that each of them earned 50% of their joint earnings. Splitting the income this way often put a family in a lower tax bracket than a family with the same joint income in New York if, for example, the husband made heaps of money and the wife stayed home with the kids and had no independent income of her own. This created great dissatisfaction among huge numbers of taxpayers. Some states toyed with the idea of switching to a community property system. Politically, the pressure had an impact on the federal income tax law: the law was changed so that married people in every state got the same treatment they would have received in California and other community property states.

In this society, women have the same property rights as men; but this was not always the case. Indeed, in some systems, a wife (never a husband) was little more than a piece of property, owned by her father or her husband. Sometimes there were even rules for disposing of wives when the husband died. This idea clearly seems connected to the notion that a husband has a monopoly over his wife's sexuality. "Traditional morality" plainly implied such a right. In theory, it was reciprocal: the man was supposed to have sex with his wife, and with no one else. In practice, the "double standard" meant that this duty was much less pronounced than *her* duty. In any event, this exclusive right to a woman's body is not usually thought of, in our society, as a property right; and it clearly lapses when he dies.

But this was not always or necessarily the case. The Old Testament describes a system of so-called levirate marriage. If a man died childless, his wife was not to marry outside the family; instead, her husband's brother was supposed to marry her (Deuteronomy 25:5). There was, however, no compulsion; if the brother did not feel like marrying his sister-in-law, he could refuse, and the Bible sets out rules to govern the ceremony of renunciation. In India there was the notorious practice of suttee (or sati), where a widow would—supposedly of her own free will—mount her husband's funeral pyre and join him in death. Long after suttee was formally abolished, the custom persisted in some rural areas. In general, the position of the widow in Indian society was not an enviable one. It is graphically described in the movie *Water*, directed by Deepa Mehta; the movie takes place in 1938, in a city where widows live in seclusion in an ashram, dress in white, have their hair shaved off, and are forbidden to remarry. This custom, which seems so barbaric to us, implied that the husband owned his wife's body and that his "rights" persisted after death.

Western societies recognize no such right, of course; certainly not today. But the so-called double standard implied that husbands had a good deal more freedom, sexually speaking, than wives did; and the double standard did not necessarily lose its grip when a husband died. A man who hated the thought that his wife might marry (and sleep with) somebody else could put in his will a clause that gave the widow nothing more than a life income, and specified that this right would lapse if she ever chanced to remarry. This kind of provision, common in the nineteenth century, is rarely found today.[2]

In no society does the state or government simply grab everything at death and redistribute it. Not even the most extreme socialist or Communist societies have done this. They all allowed some amount of private ownership, and some freedom to pass goods on after death. The modern state does, however, claim its share, in the form of taxes on estates and inheritances. At times, and in some societies, this share could amount to a sizable chunk of the estates of people of wealth. American law never went quite so far. There were, however, substantial "death taxes" in the twentieth century. The political will to tax estates has ebbed considerably. I take up this subject in more detail in Chapter 9.

The third way is the way of the *intestacy* laws. These are rules—laws—that specify who inherits if the deceased dies without leaving behind a valid will. These rules differ from place to place in many details and have changed a lot over the years. But the general idea is everywhere the same: close relatives are preferred over those who are not so close. In no state today would the law favor your Aunt Minnie over your son or your mother. The system also prefers descendants to ancestors: your mother's right to inherit would usually be trumped by your daughter's. We also take it for granted that a person's relatives on both sides of the family are equally entitled to a share. No American state prefers a mother's brother to a father's brother, or vice versa; this equality is the essence of the American kinship system. Many societies—in Africa, for example—have different traditions and laws.

By definition, intestacy laws apply to people who do not leave behind a will. But even those who do are subject to some restrictions. In almost all of the American states it is not possible (or at least not easy) to cut a wife or husband off entirely.[3] But for the most part, property owners in the United States enjoy the privilege of the fourth way, which we call *freedom of testation*. This is the dead hand's right to decide how property will be handled after a person dies. This is, in theory, the basic principle of American law, and of common law systems in general (a little less so in civil law countries). But the law does require a certain amount of formality—execution of a will, or some equivalent. There are also some limits and restrictions on freedom of testation, which I will deal with in due course.

As this brief discussion makes clear, the American system is a mixture of various ways of distributing property at death. Strictly speaking, nothing you "own" is up for grabs; but this simply follows from the way society defines ownership. Succession taxes, the intestacy laws, and freedom of testation are all real aspects of our law of succession. But the mixture of the various elements, and the ways in which they relate to the social context, vary over time and space, and are the main subject of this book.

THE DEVELOPMENT OF INTESTACY LAWS

A single simple idea lies behind the intestacy laws of today. If a person dies without a will, the property goes to a surviving wife or husband, to the children and grandchildren, and if there are none of these, then to closest relatives. Nobody else has any claim. In broad outline, this has been the practice for centuries. The proportions and the emphasis, however, have changed with the passage of time.

Two changes are of particular importance. The first is the merger of rules about real estate and rules about personal property. The second is the growing share of the estate that goes to a surviving spouse, at the expense of other possible heirs. This trend is connected to the trend mentioned in the Introduction: the shift from emphasis on the *bloodline* family to the *family of affection and dependence*.

Historically, English law made a sharp distinction between real and personal property. Real property meant primarily land and whatever was attached to it—houses, for example, or trees and growing crops. Personal property was everything else. Rules of inheritance were quite different for real and personal property, and so was the terminology. A will disposed of land; a testament disposed of personal property. Land descended to heirs; personal property was distributed to next of kin. A will devised land and a testament bequeathed personal property. Of course, people today do not make these fine verbal distinctions; nor should they. Some of them survive, but simply as matters of verbal convention. (People often label their will "Last Will and Testament.") Rules about inheritance of real estate are essentially the same as rules about inheritance of personal property.

In England, under the old common law, primogeniture was the basic principle that governed the inheritance of land. Estates in land passed to a man's eldest son. A small group of landed gentry and the nobility owned virtually all of the land in England; land was the basis of political and economic power. One function of all legal systems, whatever the society, is to preserve things more or less as they are, and to allow change, when change happens, to proceed in an orderly (and often quite slow) way. The English system was designed to preserve a system ruled by the nobility and the landed gentry. The point of primogeniture is fairly obvious. It tends to maintain, intact, the holdings of great families. If the lands of an earl or a baron, say, had to be carved up among all of their brood, land tenure would become more fragmented. Breaking up an estate "into smaller, and still smaller patches" would (it was thought) create a "redundant and starving population, destitute alike of the means, and of the enterprise requisite to better their condition."[4] In any event, just as the titles earl, duke, and baron descended to an heir (the eldest son), so too did the landed estates. Daughters inherited only if there was no son. Second sons and third sons could go into the church or the army or marry an heiress. Daughters had to find some sort of suitable marriage.

Primogeniture applied only to real property. An entirely different rule, embodied in the Statute of Distributions, governed personal property. Personal property such as jewelry, cash, and securities was divided equally among the children. But before modern times, in England, personal property was not particularly important to the wealthy. Land and income from land was the thing.

From a very early date, American rules about intestate succession deviated quite sharply from the rules that applied in England. The northern colonies for the most part rejected primogeniture. They adopted the rule of *partible inheritance*—that is, equal shares for the children. In the seventeenth century in Massachusetts, and in some other colonies, the oldest son received a double share.⁵ But otherwise, equality among the children was the rule.

There are various theories about the origins of partible inheritance. Some scholars have tried to find its source in local English customs. Primogeniture was the general rule of the common law; but some parts of the country followed their own and different systems. If you rummage about among these customs, you can find examples of partible inheritance; in the county of Kent, for example, there was a system called "gavelkind," in which land descended to all the sons in equal shares. It may well be that some English customs lent support to the colonial system. But it cannot be the real reason for so radical a departure from English practice. Primogeniture made little or no sense in New England, socially and economically, if only because of the sheer abundance of land. Primogeniture may have been useful to landed gentry; but it was of no relevance to a system of smallholders. As James Kent put it in the early nineteenth century, what made primogeniture pointless was the "extraordinary extent of our unsettled territories, the abundance of uncultivated land in the market, and the constant stream of emigration from the Atlantic to the interior states."⁶

The northern colonies quite generally rejected primogeniture. It lasted much longer in the South. In the southern colonies, where the weather was warmer, a system of fairly large estates grew up—a plantation economy, with (as time went on) large gangs of slave laborers. Conditions in the South were, in other words, more like English conditions than was true of Massachusetts or Connecticut with their small towns and family farms. More like England, but hardly identical. There was no slavery in England, and there was no equivalent in England of an inland empire of unclaimed land.

Colonial conditions had already undermined—and to a degree replaced—English inheritance law. After the Revolution, the process continued. The states were eager to create a "republican" system of land tenure and inheritance.⁷ Primogeniture came to an end, even in the South. Many states, too, abolished the "fee tail." Land owned in fee tail descended to "heirs of the body" forever. This meant that no present owner could sell the land; it could only pass to a descendant in his bloodline. It was, in short, tied up in the family, and there it remained as long as there were heirs who could inherit it. But even in the late Middle Ages clever men found ways to get around these limitations; and the courts went along. Practically speaking, then, an owner *could* sell or give away land in fee tail. Fee tail was thus nearly obsolete. Quite generally, the new states rejected the very idea. "Estates tail" were turned into fee simple estates—that is, estates over which the owner had full dominion and control.[8] This was in line with the general principle, very strong in the new republic, that land should be at all times "alienable," that is, available for sale on the market. This translated into a widespread distaste for "dynastic" systems of land ownership—a notion that had a profound influence on a number of aspects of the law of succession (and indeed, on the laws of property in general).

A second fundamental change was the increase in the rights and powers of widows and widowers (in legalese, the "surviving spouse"). In the common law system, a man's widow did inherit a third of his personal property. But for the gentry this was not particularly important; land was the basis of power and wealth. Rents paid by tenant farmers supported the gentry on their country estates and gave them the money to buy their townhouses in London. A man's real estate, when he died, was expected to remain in his bloodline. The widow was a stranger to that bloodline. When her husband died, she did not inherit his land; instead, she had to be satisfied with what was called "dower."[9] This was the right to enjoy the income from one-third of her husband's landed property. This right lasted as long as the widow lived. When she died, her interest died with her. As to where the property would go after her death, she had no say. The heirs were the children or other blood relatives. Adoption was not recognized in English common law. Blood was all. You were either a natural-born child, or you were nothing.[10]

Common law dower applied only to widows. Widowers had their own inheritance right, which was called "curtesy." This was the widower's right to enjoy, for life, the income and rights to *all* of his late wife's estate. But there was a catch: a widower had this right *only* if a child had been born from the marriage. If the marriage was childless, there was no "curtesy." The widower did not have to be *survived* by a child; if a child had been born alive, he was entitled to curtesy. Blackstone notes the common idea that "it must be heard to cry; but that is a mistake. Crying indeed is the strongest evidence of its being born alive; but it is not the only evidence." He also adds a quaint proviso: the child must be "born during the life of the mother; for, if the mother dies in labour, and the Caesarean operation is performed, the husband in this case shall not be tenant by the curtesy."[11]

In practice, in England, the rights of married women were more complicated than one might imagine from reading Blackstone. Under the doctrine of "coverture," all land that a woman owned passed into her husband's control as soon as she married him. But families with land often created elaborate devices ("settlements" or "separate estates") to get around the doctrine of coverture. The idea was to set up a kind of trust, before the marriage. Legally and officially, the trustee had title to the property, not the daughter. As soon as the trust was created, the property was no longer hers (in a sense); in any event, it did not pass into her husband's grip. Landed gentry in England often used these devices.[12] They were also often used by rich landowners in the United States. Suzanne Lebsock has documented this fact in her study of Petersburg, Virginia, in the first half of the nineteenth century; she found almost 600 separate estates in the town, between 1821 and 1860. In each case there was a "written conveyance of property . . . to a trustee. . . . to hold . . . for the separate use of a . . . married woman."[13] Settlements and separate estates were useful in getting around the hurdle of coverture. But they were tricky too; they needed skilled lawyering, and courts were sometimes finicky about the forms and the rules.

Common law dower had other peculiarities. For one thing, it defeated the rights of creditors. If a man died, leaving behind land—but also a mountain of debts—the widow took her dower rights regardless. Also, the widow had rights not only to land that her husband actually owned when he died; she could also claim dower in land he *used* to own, if he had sold it or given it away without her consent. This rule was meant to give the widow some additional protection. This "inchoate" right was one reason why, in the nineteenth century in the United States, the dower system struck legislators (and voters too, no doubt) as fatally flawed. The "inchoate" character of dower was a "cloud" on titles. There was always a danger—small but real—that when you bought a piece of land some old lady would appear out of nowhere and claim her rights of dower. Public policy in the nineteenth century strongly disfavored any rule, doctrine, or institution that seemed to clog an active land market. The same factor was at work in rules about trusts, charitable gifts, and other legal practices that threatened to "tie up" property and take land off the market.

In the laws in force in the first part of the nineteenth century, the idea of the bloodline was still quite clearly influential. Under the statutes of New York state in 1829, the "real estate of every person, who shall die without devising the same," would go first to his "lineal descendants"; next to his father; then to his mother; and then to his "collateral relatives."[14] If a person died without children, in other words, his father inherited his land. But if the land was inherited from his mother, then it went back to her. The statute provided that relatives of the "half blood" (for example, half brothers or sisters) inherited "equally with those of the whole blood."[15] On the other hand if, for example, a man inherited his land from his mother, then his half-sisters and -brothers who were children of his father, but not of his mother, would be excluded from inheritance rights.[16] Under this statute, a widow got nothing but her dower. In some states, Michigan, for example, the law as of 1846 gave the widow the real property "during her lifetime," but only if there was "no issue" (lineal descendants); she inherited outright only if there were absolutely no "kindred."[17]

The Decline of Dower

Dower was the widow's main source of sustenance under classic common law. But dower did not provide much actual protection for widows. A one-third interest in a family farm was not likely to be worth much or produce a lot. It was one thing to give dower to the widow of an English earl, quite another to the widow of a farmer in Illinois. It was even less helpful, for the most part, if the widow lived in New York City. Change in the nature of the family itself—change in the role of wives and mothers within the family—probably also contributed to the decline and fall of dower.[18] In any event, in the middle of the nineteenth century the states began to think seriously about getting rid of this ancient system. In 1852, Indiana simply abolished dower and replaced it with a share of the property, real and personal. This share was not a lifetime interest, but a "fee simple," that is, a widow owned the property outright and could do with it whatever she pleased.[19] Kansas, in 1862, gave the widow the right to choose between dower and an absolute share (one-half) of her husband's land and other property. Naturally, she would always choose the absolute share, *unless* her husband died insolvent, in which case dower was the better choice, because it defeated the rights of the creditors.[20]

Today, practically speaking, dower no longer exists, certainly not in its original form.[21] Instead, states give the surviving spouse (widow or widower) the right to a fixed share of the estate—usually a third or a half. There is a strong trend to be even more generous. In Oregon, if a man dies leaving a wife and children, and the wife is the mother of the children, she gets everything; and the same for a widower. If the children are from a different wife or husband, the surviving spouse gets half. And if there are no children at all, the widow or widower gets the whole estate.[22] In Florida too, if there are no "lineal descendants" and a person dies intestate, the surviving spouse gets everything. If there are such descendants, the widow or widower gets the first $60,000 of the estate and half of the rest; but if the "lineal descendants" are from another marriage, the surviving spouse gets half the intestate estate.[23] More and more states are changing their laws to give the surviving spouse a larger share of the estate, and all of it if there are no children. Or, in some cases, at least all of the first $50,000 to $100,000, to make sure the widow or widower is adequately supported. Marriage may be a weaker reed than it used to be, but you could not prove it through the intestacy laws.

Widows and widowers are protected not only when their spouse dies without a will; they are also protected against deliberate disinheritance. If the will leaves a widow nothing, or less than she would be entitled to without a will, then this widow can "elect" to renounce the will and take the legal share. In other words, you cannot simply flat-out disinherit your spouse. Or, to be more accurate, you cannot disinherit your spouse by cutting her out of your will, unless she agreed to this in advance, for example, by signing a premarital agreement. Can you cut off a spouse in some other way? Could you set up a trust during your lifetime in which the wife or husband has no share at all, and transfer all your property into the trust, leaving you with nothing in your "estate," when you actually die? Are there other tricks for cheating a life partner? This is a complex subject; the short answer is that it is probably possible, but it is not as easy as one might think. A leading case, decided in 1937, concerned the estate of Ferdinand Straus of New York, head of an insurance brokerage firm. His first wife died in 1927, and he then married a much younger woman. The marriage was, to put it mildly, not a success; and Ferdinand clearly made up his mind that this woman was not going to get his money. Although the will left her a good share, this was something of a joke (or meant to be): the will was a hollow shell. The "estate" was worth less than $1,000, even though Straus was a wealthy man. This was because, shortly before he died, Ferdinand transferred almost everything he owned to trustees; he retained the right to change the trust if he wanted to; but in the meantime it held all of his worldly goods. The trust made no provision for his wife. The court said the gift to the trustees was "illusory"; it was nothing but a "mask for the effective retention by the settlor of the property." Consequently, the wife could claim her statutory share from the assets in the trust.[24] In most states, there are statutes and case law that aim at protecting a widow or widower against Ferdinand's type of trick, and some other arrangements with the same general goal. But the protection is far from complete.[25]

A surviving spouse can claim a fixed share of the estate in most places, But not in all. In Georgia, for example, the surviving spouse can be cut off entirely; the spouse is entitled to a year's support, and nothing more.[26] In the community property states, such as California and Texas, property acquired during the marriage becomes part of the "community," and thus belongs half to the wife and half to the husband. As to community property, then, the surviving spouse supposedly does not need special protection; she already has it. At least this is the theory. Each spouse can dispose of his or her half of the community property (plus any property that is not community property), but no more. The surviving spouse can, of course, get a bigger share if the dead spouse wants it that way. And in California, for example, if a man dies intestate, his wife ends up with *all* of the community property—she already owns half of it; and under the law she gets the other half as well.[27] In short, although the law is complicated, its basic thrust is to try to ensure a sizable chunk of the estate for a surviving spouse.

Another development of the mid-nineteenth century was the decline and fall of the ancient doctrine of coverture. A married woman (a "feme covert") had basically no property rights. Like dower, coverture could be a nuisance as far as the land market was concerned. Suppose that a woman's husband deserted her and disappeared into the wilds of the frontier—not a rare occurrence. She would find it very hard, perhaps impossible, to mortgage the property, sell it, or deal with it in any way. That could, of course, be a serious problem for her. It could also be a problem, say, for a neighbor who might want to buy the land. One solution, in the first part of the nineteenth century, was for an owner to go to the state legislature and ask the legislature to pass a private statute that would allow her to sell the land.²⁸ Sometimes this happened. But this was, of course, a fairly cumbersome process. And it dealt with specific people and situations, not the general problem.

The broader solution was to get rid of the doctrine of coverture. This was the job of the so-called Married Women's Property Laws. The earliest of these was passed in Mississippi in 1839; it dealt mostly with the rights of married women to own and dispose of slaves.²⁹ Many of the other early laws also dealt with the issue in bits and pieces. They also met with a certain amount of hostility from the courts, which were, after all, exclusively clubs of men. But by the end of the century the old rules of coverture were just about gone. Inheritance was always an aspect of these married women's laws. The Maryland statute of 1842–43, for example, gave married women the right to become "seized or possessed of any property, real or of slaves by direct bequest, demise, [or] gift." The statute was probably mostly concerned about ownership of slaves. But it did give the wife "the right to make a will." In her will, she could leave her property to her husband, or to somebody else with his written consent. Interestingly, the witnesses to a married woman's will were supposed to examine the wife privately, out of the "presence and hearing of her husband," to find out if she was making the will "freely and voluntarily and without being induced thereto by fear or threats or ill usage by said husband."³⁰ The later statutes were far less tentative. By 1900, married women could quite generally make out wills and dispose of their property. And everywhere, the surviving spouse—male or female—had become the chief heir in intestacy.

MODERN INTESTACY LAWS

Today every state has an intestacy law. They differ in many details, but the patterns are quite similar. A widow or widower gets a big share of the estate. In some states, if there are no children, he or she may get everything. If there are children, spouse and children will share in the estate. If there are no children and no spouse, the estate will go to parents or brothers and sisters. If the dead person has no spouse, children, parents, or siblings, then whoever is closest in blood will take the estate. (Many states now have a cut-off: no relatives more distant than grandparents and their descendants can inherit.) But if there are no qualified relatives, or no relatives at all, then the estate "escheats"; that is, the money goes to the state.

Of course, everybody has *some* relatives; nobody came into this world without any family connections, and nobody leaves the world without some family either. But there are people who, practically speaking, have no relatives, or, to be more exact, no relatives that anybody can find and identify. This may be a consequence of our mobile society—a society with immigrants and rolling stones. Young men leave home and wander off to make a fortune. Sometimes they make this fortune, but along the way they never bother to marry, have children, or cultivate any family connections. Imagine, for example, an immigrant who comes to the United States as a young man from some town in Eastern Europe, makes money, and dies intestate at the age of 95, a lonely bachelor. Suppose he never talked very much about where he came from; or perhaps he was an orphan or a foundling, raised in a foster home or an orphanage. It may be next to impossible to know who, if anybody, is related to him. If there is no will, but considerable money, claimants—distant cousins of all shades and sorts, or alleged cousins—will come out of the woodwork, and a distasteful squabble over the money is bound to follow. One notable example, which I will mention again later, was the estate of Howard Hughes, the eccentric billionaire; a last will did show up, but it was most likely a forgery—at least the court so held.

In a few very rare cases, the fight rests on a different basis. A member of the family is dead, or thought to be dead; then, lo and behold, someone appears and claims to be the long lost son or brother, making a claim either under a will or through intestacy. One of the most sensational trials of Victorian England involved the estate of a baronet, James Tichborne. The heir, Roger, was lost at sea in 1859. When Roger's father died, the estate and the property passed to Roger's brother Alfred. But Roger's mother was convinced he was still alive. And sure enough, a claimant appeared, out of the wilds of Australia. Lady Tichborne insisted that this was truly her missing son. To less prejudiced heads, however, the idea seemed preposterous; the man seemed to be an obvious imposter. The claimant, it turned out, was one Arthur Orton, a butcher's son. A sensational trial made it quite clear that Orton was simply lying. In the end, he went to jail for perjury.[31] Ida Wood died at 93, in 1932. She was rich and eccentric. She spent the last thirty years of her life as a recluse. She left no will. More than a thousand people claimed a share of her estate.[32] Henrietta Garrett died in Philadelphia County in 1930, leaving no will and an estate of more than $17 million. In this case, there were more than 26,000 claims.[33] No doubt some of these claimants really thought they were entitled to part of the estate. But often, as in a case involving the estate of Georgiana Wendel, many claims were simply fraudulent—forged documents of one sort or another.[34] In general, if a dead person is rich enough, and there are no obvious relatives, the smell of big money will almost surely attract a crowd of buzzards who will lay claim to the estate.

A mobile society may contain many unattached people, people without obvious family connections—mostly but not exclusively men. Most people in the United States have families, and indeed strong families; but there are fewer and fewer so-called extended families. There are many societies in the world where third cousins are considered close kin, where blood relationships, no matter how thin they might be stretched, are vitally important. Needless to say, the United States of America is not one of these societies. Millions of Americans hardly speak to their brothers and sisters, let alone cousins. Under traditional intestacy laws, blood relationship was all. The nearest relatives would inherit, even though there was nothing "near" about them, even if they had had nothing to do with the deceased, had never met the dear departed, and perhaps never even heard of him or her. There are firms of "heir hunters" that make a living finding "heirs" of this kind, for a fee, or a share of the proceeds, or who simply buy claims from such "heirs" and then rush into probate court.[35]

In a California case, Denis Griswold died intestate, in 1996, leaving a modest estate, which consisted of separate property (not community property).[36] He was survived by a widow, but no children. His widow claimed the whole estate; but suddenly one Francis V. See, a "forensic genealogist," appeared and entered a claim on behalf of two other people. See told the following story: Griswold had been an illegitimate child. His biological father, Draves, admitted that he was Griswold's father. He was ordered to pay some child support, which he did. Meanwhile, young Denis's mother married a Mr. Griswold, and they brought him up as their son. Life went on for Draves too; he married and had two additional children, Margaret and Daniel. Griswold had never met his half-brother and half-sister; at some point, he did find out that Draves was his biological father, but he never met him, or even looked for him. The case report does not tell us how Francis See found out about this family saga; but somehow he did, and he got in touch with Margaret and Daniel. They "assigned" their interest in the estate to See, who no doubt gave them some money or a promise of money. It was See, then, who appealed when the trial court denied the claim. And, on appeal, this heir hunter won his case.

Heir hunting, as this case shows, at least sometimes pays off. A number of companies specialize in this business. One company that advertises online, Josh Butler & Co., boasts that it can "locate almost anyone for any good reason." If the customer is "not completely satisfied, we are owed nothing. Period. No fine print. Nothing is due in advance."[37] Still, not only is the wild scramble for the dead man's wealth unseemly, it also seems not quite right for distant relatives to inherit, solely because of some remote tie of blood. This is the so-called "laughing heir"—too distant to feel any grief, and laughing all the way to the bank. At one time the "laughing heir" was a real possibility, in every state. No longer. In about half of the states the closest blood relative still gets to inherit, no matter how remote the relationship.[38] But in the other half of the states there are now laws that aim to get rid of the "laughing heir." Many of these states have followed the lead of the Uniform Probate Code. They have drawn the line at first cousins (descendants of a person's grandparents) and (if all first cousins happened to be dead) descendants of first cousins. Nobody more remote has the right to inherit. Descendants of great-grandparents are out of luck.[39] Obviously, such statutes bite into the work of "heir hunters." Courts in many states seem to look askance at these companies, too, on various legal grounds.[40] Not that these firms will go out of business, even if they lose the job of finding lost heirs. The Butler company, for example, also looks for "class action members," patent holders, landowners, corporate shareholders, and, somewhat intriguingly, "witnesses to history."

In their emphasis on the nuclear family, intestacy laws recognize the wife or husband as the main focus of inheritance. Law (and society) more and more tends to treat marriage as "an economic partnership." That is, when he and she say "I do," they are considered to be entering into an "unspoken marital bargain," an agreement to share and share alike in "the fruits of the marriage."[41] That (assumed) bargain means that we do not ask whether the marriage was happy or unhappy. The law does not care whether they ever kissed, held hands, or had sexual intercourse. It does not even care whether he and she were living together at the time one of them dies. A wife who has filed for divorce but has not yet gotten it is still a wife and gets her share of his estate if he dies. (After all, if the divorce had gone through, she would probably have gained some of his assets as part of the settlement.)

Does it matter how long the couple was married? That depends on where they live; state laws matter. Robert Neiderhiser, on September 11, 1976, appeared at the Fort Palmer United Presbyterian Church in Westmoreland County, Pennsylvania, together with his fiancée, Naomi Nicely. The Reverend William Jacobs began the ceremony. Robert and Naomi repeated their vows to each other. He slipped a ring on her fourth finger and said, "With this ring I thee wed, In the name of the Father, and of the Son, and of the Holy Spirit, Amen." The minister began a prayer. Suddenly, Robert slumped to the floor. The Reverend Jacob quickly pronounced them man and wife, as Robert collapsed. A moment later he was dead. Naomi was now a widow. Or was she? Naomi was appointed administrator of Robert's estate, but members of his family challenged her appointment. A Pennsylvania court held that the two were indeed married and that Naomi was entitled to administer his estate.[42]

In other states, the rights of a widow or widower *might* depend on the length of the marriage. This is, for example, true of community property states. The longer the marriage, the more likely that *most* of the estate will be community property, meaning that each spouse would own half of it. If poor Robert Neiderhiser had dropped dead in California, Naomi would not have received a cent of community property. There was no time to generate any such property. Under the latest version of the Uniform Probate Code, which a number of states have adopted, a surviving spouse has rights to part of the "augmented estate" of the deceased, depending on how durable the marriage. (The "augmented estate" includes the kind of transfer Ferdinand Straus tried to use to disinherit his young wife.) If husband and wife were married a year but less than two years, the survivor gets only 3% of the augmented estate; if they were married 15 years or more, 50%.[43]

In Arkansas, if one spouse disinherits the other, the survivor can renounce the will and take a share—but they have to be married "continuously for a period in excess of one year."[44] One interesting case involved the rather rocky marriage history of Carolyn and Lloyd Shaw. Carolyn and Lloyd were married four times—each time to each other. They were also divorced three times. The fourth marriage lasted exactly thirteen days, at which point Lloyd died. He had left Carolyn nothing. Thirteen days is far short of a year; but the two had been married, in total, more than fifteen years, if you counted the three prior marriages. This the court refused to do, and Carolyn ended up with nothing.[45]

The intestacy laws are rather rigid, generally speaking. This was true in the early nineteenth century, and it is still true today. The statutes lay down rules about the devolution of property; and these rules are concrete, specific, and in the normal case inflexible.

Mary Anne, a wealthy widow, dies intestate. She leaves behind two daughters and two sons. All of them are adults. One of the daughters is married to a millionaire. The other daughter works at a low-paying job, has two children, was deserted by her husband, and has very little money. One son moved to Australia twenty years earlier, and he made a lot of money in the computer business. Mother and son had always had a rocky relationship; and the mother never approved of the woman he married. After moving to Australia, he never wrote or called his mother. The other son has quite a different story. He never married. He always lived with his mother, and when she became old and feeble he took care of her day and night. This son, moreover, is in bad health; and because he quit his job to take care of his mother, he has almost no resources of his own. In other words, some of the children need money; some don't; some deserve money, and some don't. Mary Anne also had a sister, who is unmarried and suffering from Alzheimer's disease. Mary Anne had been supporting her sister for years. But Mary Anne never made out a will. The law will slice her estate into four equal parts, no matter what. Each child will get the same amount. The sister gets nothing. What people need or deserve makes no difference. American law is quite clear on this point.

There are, to be sure, some minor rules, which do take "merit" into account. None of them apply to Mary Anne's estate, and most of them are not particularly important. Probate codes typically provide, for example, that if you murder someone (a parent, for example), you cannot inherit from them. This applies both to wills and to intestacy. There are some differences in details and about certain side issues. For example, do the statutes apply to manslaughter? Reckless homicide? What if the killer was found not guilty by reason of insanity?[46] The California statute talks about someone who "feloniously and intentionally kills the decedent."[47] What happens if you and the person you killed had a joint bank account? Can you collect the money that was in the account?[48]

Fortunately, homicidal heirs are not an everyday occurrence. Not many people kill the source of their money.

Under the statutes, if the heir is convicted of murder, this most definitely shuts off the money. But the reverse is not true. That is, an acquittal does not *necessarily* open the door to inheritance. The standard of proof in a criminal trial is the famous formula "guilty beyond a reasonable doubt." A civil suit is much less stringent. A dispute over inheritance is a civil case, not a criminal case. This means that a plaintiff can win if, on balance, the "preponderance of the evidence" tilts more in favor of plaintiff than defendant. This difference is not mere theory. In *United States* v. *Burns*,[49] Monette Burns shot and killed her husband, Emmet. The couple had broken up, and the night that Emmet died she was with another man. Her story was that she killed in self-defense. After her husband "violently attacked her," she got a "loaded automatic pistol from her dresser drawer." When her husband (she said) lunged at her, she "fired four shots in quick succession into his body." A jury acquitted her of the criminal charges. But when she sued to collect on a government insurance policy she lost the case. The acquittal did not convince the government, or the court, that she was entitled to collect.[50]

A recent statute in California also disinherits anyone who can be shown "by clear and convincing evidence" to be guilty of "physical abuse, neglect, or fiduciary abuse of . . . an elder or dependent adult."[51] This is, alas, a more common situation than outright murder. Apparently no other state has passed such a statute. It is not yet clear how and when the statute will apply, and whether it will make much difference in practice. The chances are it will not. In any event, murder and physical abuse are the only real exceptions to the rule that the courts did not judge whether heirs actually deserve the money.

At one time, there was at least one more exception. An old Indiana statute provided that "if a wife leave her husband, and live with her adulterer, she shall be barred forever of her dower."[52] This law harked back to an even older English statute frequently copied in the states. (Note that the statute said nothing about an adulterous husband; the double standard was in full flower.)[53] In Connecticut today there is a unisex version of a similar idea: a surviving husband or wife loses the statutory share of the dead spouse's estate if the survivor, "without sufficient cause, abandoned the other and continued such abandonment to the time of the other's death."[54] But this statute is exceptional. In general, courts refuse to go into questions of moral or immoral behavior. Shirley E. Scott died intestate in California in 1947. She was survived by her husband, Henry. Henry was not exactly a model spouse. He deserted Shirley and took up housekeeping with another woman. No matter, said the court. A spouse is a spouse. The intestacy laws make no exception for worthless, philandering husbands. It was "immaterial" whether inheritance laws meshed with ideas of "justice, morality or natural right. The matter is in the plenary control of the state legislature."[55]

One court, in South Dakota, did stretch a bit in the opposite direction.[56] The dead man, Walter O'Keefe, died at the age of 101. He left no will. Two nephews and a niece survived him. The nephews had been rotten toward the old man; they took advantage of him, and helped themselves to some of his assets. The estate sued the nephews and won the case. They were ordered to pay back the money they took, plus $25,000 in punitive damages. This money, of course, went back into the estate. But under the intestacy laws they were entitled to two-thirds of the estate (including the reimbursement money). The niece—their sister—protested, and the court agreed with her. They did not deserve to get two-thirds of that part of the estate which consisted of money they had stolen and been forced to pay back.

But even in this case, the court ruled that the two wicked brothers *were* entitled to two-thirds of the *rest* of the estate—two-thirds of whatever else the old man left behind. Their villainy was legally irrelevant. And in a Connecticut case, decided in 1989, a court flatly refused to pass judgment on an intestate heir.[57] In this case, Kenneth Hotarek and Suzanne Benson were married; they had a son, Paul. When Paul was 2 years old, the marriage ended in divorce. Suzanne left and never saw her son again. The boy died tragically in an auto accident at the age of 15. It took a private investigator even to find Paul's mother and tell her that her son was dead. Meanwhile, Paul's estate collected a substantial amount of money as a result of the accident. The father tried to prevent the mother from sharing in this money, because she had "failed to provide any financial support to, maintain any interest in, or display any love and affection for her son." But he lost the case. She was one of her son's lawful heirs. The law was the law.

This might seem unfair; and indeed the Connecticut court, after making its decision, uttered the usual pious platitude: "if the law is to be changed," it is up to the legislature to make the change, not the court; and the court did urge the legislature to do its duty—at least for situations as extreme as this one.

Of course, the legislature did nothing of the sort. Even if the legislature had considered the issue, which is doubtful, it would be most unlikely to change the law in this direction. Doing so would mean giving courts the job of deciding, in particular cases, if heirs deserved to inherit or not. Many heirs are clearly not deserving. In fact, this is almost always the case when a person dies intestate, and the nearest kin are distant cousins who live somewhere else, had no contact with the deceased, and could hardly be expected to shed any tears over his death. Perhaps the dead man had a kindly neighbor who ran errands for him, sat with him when he was sick, and was genuinely unhappy when he died. No matter. The word "friend" does not appear in any intestacy law. Nor does "neighbor." The laws that cut off the so-called laughing heirs do recognize, however, that while blood is thicker than water, some blood is thicker than others.

Illinois has taken a small step in the direction of rewarding heirs who deserve more than other heirs. A husband, wife, parent, brother or sister, or child of a "disabled person" who was "dedicated" to the care of this disabled person, "by living with and personally caring for the disabled person for at least three years" can file a claim against the estate. The claim can take into account the caregiver's "lost employment opportunities, lost lifestyle opportunities, and emotional distress." For taking care of a completely disabled person, the claim is fixed at $100,000. But the claim is independent of a claim for nursing care.[58] This is a rather narrow and idiosyncratic piece of legislation. Whether it will lead to more of this kind of statute remains to be seen. It is not by any means unthinkable that the law might give courts power to decide who *needs* the money most. As we will see, some common law countries have done precisely that. And for very small estates, the same is basically true in the United States as well, as we will soon see.

Protecting Widows and Widowers

Intestacy laws apply only when there is no will, of course. But the law has a kind of intestacy law even for people who *do* make out a will—as far as spouses are concerned. A man cannot disinherit his widow, and a woman cannot disinherit her widower—at least not easily. The surviving spouse gets a share, even if there is a will that leaves her little or nothing. This is the so-called "forced share" or "indefeasible share."

In most states, too, if you leave a modest estate, you might as well die intestate. In California, for example, if the value of the estate is $20,000 or less, the whole estate can be set aside for the surviving spouse and any minor children; the law, however, gives the judge a good deal of discretion. The judge can consider the needs of the survivors, the intent of the deceased, and "any other relevant considerations."[59] A surviving spouse and minor children are also entitled to a "family allowance" during the time the estate is tied up in probate; and there is a grab bag of other family rights, including, quite often, a homestead right—that is, a right either to remain physically in the homestead or to commute the value of the homestead into money. The right to keep on living in the "homestead" goes back to an old widow's right, called "quarantine," which had nothing to do with infectious diseases; based on the Latin word for forty, it was the widow's right to stay in her home for forty days after her husband died.[60] In Ohio a "surviving spouse" can stay in "the mansion house free of charge for one year."[61] In many states there are elaborate homestead provisions; the homestead is usually exempt from the claims of creditors. In California, for example, the surviving spouse and minor children are eligible to claim the homestead benefit. But the order setting property aside as a "probate homestead" has to be "for a limited period," and never "beyond the lifetime of the surviving spouse" or the years when the child or children are minors.[62]

Children as Heirs

One striking feature of the American law of succession is that it allows a parent, by will, to cut children off without a penny. Most countries in Europe and Latin America simply do not allow this. In those countries you cannot totally disinherit your children; they have a claim to a specific share of the estate. In Italy, for example, the children get half the estate, divided equally, even if the parent by will tried to leave them nothing. One American state, Louisiana, which has a civil law background, has also, historically, protected the inheritance rights of children. No child could be disinherited unless the parent had a very good reason. (These reasons were listed in the statute—they included, among other things, failure to ransom a parent who had been taken hostage, probably not a very common situation.) But in recent years, even Louisiana has abandoned this civil law position; a parent can disinherit his children, except those who are 23 years old or younger, or who suffer from severe "mental incapacity or physical informity."[63]

The Louisiana story is worth a somewhat closer look. In 1921, the tradition of "forced heirship" was even given constitutional status. A delegate to the constitutional convention of Louisiana in that year, Sidney Herold, was one of the delegates who firmly believed in this move. In a speech, he mentioned what he considered the "current problem of the maldistribution of wealth" and in particular the "unhealthy accumulation" of wealth. Forced heirship "helped to prevent the passing of great estates into single hands." It allowed the "agency of death" to perform "its normal function—it releases the grasp of the possessor over worldly accumulation." It was, in short, a tool against "the dead hand."[64]

As a result, a provision in the Constitution of Louisiana laid down the rule that no law could be passed abolishing the principle of forced heirship. As the quotes make clear, at least some delegates connected the Louisiana way with the trend toward getting rid of rules against primogeniture, entails (that is, estates tied up in families), and long-term trusts in land. This seems like a fairly archaic bogeyman. In any event, the Constitution of 1974 continued the provision protecting forced heirship. But the legislature seemed to believe it had a right to tinker with forced heirship, so long as it was not actually abolished. A law was passed eliminating forced heirship, except for children under 24 and those who could not take care of themselves. In 1993 the Supreme Court of Louisiana declared this law unconstitutional.[65] The Constitution was then amended to limit forced heirship as the statute had done: that is, to children 23 or younger, and children who, because of "mental incapacity or physical infirmity," were not self-sufficient. The current law, then, gives parents a right to disinherit, except for some classes of children who have a strong moral claim for support. In any event, Louisiana voters (and legislators) have quite obviously changed their mind in one crucial regard; they no longer think forced heirship helps prevent "maldistribution of wealth." Of course, people might still be against "maldistribution," but think that forced heirship was not the way to get to that goal. What seems more likely is that, in Louisiana as elsewhere, the political and moral appeal of measures to prevent "maldistribution" are not what they used to be.

Although minor children might have a claim to some support during the probate period, adult children have no claim at all. How can we explain this? What is the social function of this rule? Does it conform to what most people want? Yes and no. We will come back to this point. One thing to bear in mind is that people rarely disinherit *all* of their children. The rule lets them do this; but more important, it lets them treat children in very unequal ways. A parent who has ten children can nonetheless decide to leave everything to one son or daughter, and nothing, or almost nothing, to the rest.

Clearly, among the landed gentry, this permitted favoring the "heir," that is, the oldest child. The idea of an "heir" of this sort meant nothing to, say, your typical Illinois farmer in the 1830's. But this farmer could, nonetheless, make excellent use of the rule. As Hendrik Hartog has pointed out,[66] the rule was of enormous practical value in the days before the welfare state. The farmer, as he got old and feeble, could promise to leave the farm to the son, or daughter, who would take care of him in his declining years. The historical record shows that this was not mere theory, but a common occurrence in rural areas. Inheritance of the farm was an important bargaining chip.

In the past, most states gave children a wee bit of protection against disinheritance, in the form of "pretermission" statutes. This meant that a parent could not disinherit a son or a daughter simply by ignoring the child in the will. The testator had to say something explicit: "I leave nothing to my son Caleb," or "I leave $1 to Caleb." Unless you did this, the child got a share of the estate. This was often the child's intestate share—that is, what the child would have gotten if the old man had died without a will.

The estate of Larry Hillblom found out all about pretermitted children, to its grief.[67] Hillblom, a cofounder of the air courier service DHL, was a very rich man. His various businesses were worth more than half a billion dollars. Hillblom had some nasty personal habits. He roamed about Asia, paying teenage girls for sex. He particularly wanted unprotected sex with young virgins. Hillblom, who made his home in Saipan, died at the age of 52, when his seaplane went down in the ocean. He was declared legally dead, but the body was never recovered.

Hillblom's will left his fortune to a trust, to be used to support medical research, mostly at the University of California. The will said nothing about children. Soon young Asian women from several countries began popping up, with kids, all claiming they had sex with Hillblom, bore him a child, and were entitled to share in the estate. When the news got out, as one account put it, "attorneys armed with photos of Hillblom canvassed the seedy bars of Southeast Asia," looking for more women who could make a claim.[68]

But how could anybody prove that the child in question was Hillblom's? Hillblom's body and its precious stock of DNA were at the bottom of the sea. One thought was to use a mole, removed from his face in San Francisco. A battle raged over the mole, which the hospital refused to release; in the end its release was ordered—and then it turned out that the mole was from somebody else's face (an embarrassing mistake). Next, a "forensic mathematician," whose business card claimed "Aphorisms, Inferences and Conclusions from Thin Air," entered the picture. He "designed a computer program to look at the genetics" of the children. Some of the children had DNA profiles "that could only be explained if they had the same father," which made it very likely that Hillblom had produced them (the mothers, after all, were strangers to each other and had little in common except sex with Hillblom).[69] Later, for a million dollars and part of a French chalet, Hillblom's mother provided a blood sample. This confirmed that four children were indeed siblings and therefore were fathered by Hillblom. More legal maneuvering followed, but in the end, a settlement was reached. Each of the four children got about $50 million; the foundation got the rest, still a substantial sum. Lawyers for the various parties, to be sure, reaped a rich harvest as well.

Hillblom could have avoided all of this, most likely, if he had specifically disinherited any children he might have fathered, or left each one some token amount. In many states today, even the feeble protection of statutes on pretermitted children is gone. Children left out of a will get nothing, even if the will makes no mention of them. The statute only protects a child "born or adopted after the execution of . . . the decedent's testamentary instruments," as the California Probate Code puts it (§21620); and even this is not an absolute rule. If the decedent made it clear that his "failure to provide" was intentional, or if he left the money to the "other parent of the omitted child," the afterborn child will get nothing.[70] The most, then, that can be said is that in some states it takes a slight effort to disinherit a child, but a parent who really wants to leave nothing to his children can do it fairly easily.

Even assuming that the American rule was once useful, is it an anomaly today? Specifically, does it fly in the face of public opinion? On the whole, the answer is probably no. Most people *want* to disinherit their children, not because they hate them—they probably love them dearly—but because they want everything to go to a surviving spouse, who is usually the children's mother (men tend to die before women). In a classic study from the 1950's, Cohen, Robson, and Bates found that over 90% of their sample (from the state of Nebraska) thought the law should prevent a person from disinheriting minor children; the percentage dropped considerably if the child was an adult and well off; but even here it was over 50%.[71] They thought this showed that the law was out of step with community attitudes. But the way they framed the question influenced their answer. They began by assuming that the husband or wife was dead, that the survivor "willed all of [the] . . . property . . . outside the family," and that this could mean that "the child might have to depend on some outside source for the necessities of life."

This does seem like a bad idea. On the other hand, *if* you have to choose a single rule, in an inflexible system, the American rule—even though it lets an evil parent leave his money "outside the family"—seems like a fairly good plan for the average family. Very rich people can provide for spouse *and* children; but everybody else would be better off leaving the money to the children's mother or father. This is *especially* true, whatever people may think in Nebraska, when the children are babies or even teenagers. It is never a good idea to leave money directly to minors. Until they become adults, you might need a clumsy and expensive guardianship. In modest estates, a widow or widower probably needs all the money to take care of the children; if the money went to them directly, they'd actually be *less* well off in the short run because of the costs of the guardianship.

Did Cohen, Robson, and Bates really measure "community attitudes"? If they had framed the question differently, they might have received different answers. Suppose the question had been: "A man dies at the age of 55. His widow is 50. She is a housewife. He leaves behind about $100,000. He has two children—a son of 16 and a 12-year-old daughter. Which is better: giving the estate to the widow, or giving her half, and the rest to the children? If you give half to the children, a guardian will have to be appointed. And when they reach 18, the money is theirs, to spend entirely as they wish." I would guess that most people would say, give it all to the spouse.[72]

But would they? In an Illinois survey, published in 1976, a sample of the population was asked, What percentage of the estate would you give the spouse, if a spouse and minor child survived? Fifty-three percent said they would give everything to the spouse, but the rest would give half or more (!) to the child.

If the child was an adult, only 41% would give everything to the spouse; but another 18% would give the spouse more than half. If the child were by a previous marriage, less than 20% would give the wife everything (this is no surprise), provided the child lives with the deceased; the new spouse tends to get a bigger share (but not all) if the child lives with the former spouse.[73]

These surveys can be misleading; so much depends on how the questions are framed. And people who answer survey questions, unlike lawyers and the clients they talk to, do not spend much time thinking about the issue and its ramifications. The few studies of actual wills suggest attitudes somewhat at variance with the surveys. The size of the estate makes a difference. In Bucks County, Pennsylvania, in 1979, if the estate was less than $120,000, 63% of the testators left everything to the surviving spouse. If the estate was larger, fewer testators did so.[74] Almost all married men make provisions in their wills for their wives. Most married women leave something to their husbands, but on a slightly smaller scale. This was the case in the San Bernardino study of the 1960's.[75]

At one time, men who died often seemed reluctant to leave money outright to a widow. Many men preferred to set up some sort of a trust, to last for her lifetime, or until she remarried. This practice reflects the old preference for the bloodline, and also the idea that women had no head for managing money and other property. It may also reflect, as I mentioned, a kind of reluctance to accept the idea of a wife remarrying. In the nineteenth century, these trusts were far from rare; but they are no longer the norm.[76] Trusts that only last until the widow remarries are extremely rare. Lifetime trusts for spouses still exist today. They are actually quite common, but only if the testator is seriously rich. Here the form of the trust is influenced by technical details of the federal estate tax. We will deal with this issue later.

The rules about wills and intestacy, then, insofar as they make it easy to disinherit children, makes more sense than appears at first glance. But these rules make less sense today than when Cohen, Robson, and Bates asked their questions in Nebraska. There was a high rate of divorce in the twentieth century, and it continues in the twenty-first; the rate is higher than it was fifty years ago. The formal rule seems pretty fair for traditional families. It fits rather poorly if the deceased was married more than once, and had children with several husbands or wives.

A bitter family quarrel, and a possible lawsuit, is particularly likely when the deceased was an extremely rich old goat who married a young wife, and then left her his vast fortune, cutting off his children by his earlier marriage(s). Seward Johnson, who was immensely rich, had a flock of children (whether they were dutiful children is another question) from a prior marriage; in old age, he married a young woman, a Polish immigrant who worked as a housemaid, and left her virtually all his money. A monster lawsuit ensued, in which the children tried to "break" the will (more on this later).[77] In Italy, of course, the children would have a legal right to half the estate, which might have satisfied them. There was plenty of money to go around.

In one bizarre Kansas case (2002), Marshall Gardiner, who was rich, feeble, and old (85), married a certain J'Noel Ball. He died a year later, without a will. J'Noel claimed the widow's share of the estate, and the rest of the family resisted. They had rather unusual grounds for contesting the widow's claims. J'Noel, it seems, was a transsexual. She had been born male, and sex-change operations had turned her into J'Noel. It was at this point that she married Marshall Gardiner. Legally, she insisted, she was now a woman, not a man. But the court disagreed. In Kansas, at any rate, only a biological woman, a woman from birth, could become a widow. Transsexuals were out of luck.[78] Obviously, not many disappointed relatives will have this sort of case against an estate.

When the rules of intestacy are rigid, this means that the statutes have made certain definite choices. Rules are on the books that seem to fit *most* situations, though clearly not all. It is certainly possible to design a system with a lot more give and take. If a man or woman died without a will, the law could give power to the probate judge to divide up the estate in a way that took into account the actual family situation. And even if there was a will, the law *could* give a judge power to shift assets around, as needed. Would this be a good system? It would certainly be a complicated one. At present, there is a no-nonsense system, where the rules are clear-cut and disappointed family members have very little hope of arguing against them. In this sense, the situation is relatively efficient. Lawsuits are fairly rare. As we will see, there are not many practical ways to contest a will; and "breaking" a will is never easy. Disappointed heirs, for the most part, simply have to swallow their disappointment.

If we allowed a judge or some other decision maker to tailor inheritance to the needs of each family, litigation might increase, at least somewhat. The whole process might become slower, more cumbersome, and more contentious. How much of a problem this would be is impossible to tell. The evidence we have, from studies of probated wills, suggests that most testators try to be fair to their families. Of course, the raw files tell us nothing about the actual family situation. A woman leaves her estate in equal shares to her three daughters. Perhaps one daughter is a Cordelia, the other two a Goneril and a Regan. We have no way to tell.

Other countries in the common law family have been more willing than the United States to try a new path. In 1938 the British Parliament passed a Family Provision Act.[79] This gave courts the right to order "reasonable provision" out of an estate, despite what a will provided, for four classes of people: the wife or husband of the dead person; a "daughter who has not been married, or who is, by reason of some mental or physical disability, incapable of maintaining herself," a minor son, or a son who is also "incapable of maintaining himself" because of "some mental or physical disability." Apparently, between 1938 and 1952, some 2,000 persons applied to the court for relief.[80] This means about 150 people a year in England. The figure suggests that the act has some use, but is hardly vital to the scheme of inheritance. After all, the law did not apply to very small estates, which already went entirely to the immediate family. Very rich families were unlikely to need the law. It was, in short, a device for middle-class families, and "fortunes of a few thousand pounds."[81]

Later, Parliament enacted the Inheritance [Provision for Family and Dependants] Act of 1975.[82] This broadened the earlier act by giving judges power to allot money from an estate to wives and husbands, former wives or husbands who were single, children, and anybody else the deceased was supporting. Any of these people could petition for "reasonable financial provision" if the will or the intestacy law did not take care of the situation. The judge could take into account needs and resources, any "physical or mental disability of any applicant," and "any other matter . . . which . . . the court may consider relevant," including the "conduct of the applicant." This law obviously gives a judge a great deal of latitude. In one case in 1983,[83] old William McGarrell left his daughter nothing; the estate went to charity and to the husbands of two nieces. The daughter was a married woman with four children, living on a very tight budget. For some years, she had helped her father with housework, and he had lived with her and her family for a while. But there was some suggestion that he resented ending his days in an old people's home. The judge thought she had a "moral claim on the estate" and that the will did not make "reasonable financial provision" for the daughter. The court ordered that she should "receive one quarter of the net estate of the deceased."

A similar law is in effect in Australia and has had a similar effect. In a 1991 case,[84] the dead man, George Lambeff, had made out a will that left his whole estate in trust for his two sons. He left nothing to his daughter, the plaintiff, a child of his first marriage. The father had in effect abandoned this daughter, and she lived with her mother and stepfather, who were reasonably well off; she had a decent job with an insurance company. She was, in fact, better off than her two half-brothers, who had "little in the way of assets and . . . families to support. . . . They are, however, both young and fit." The daughter had done all right in life, but might have "done better with proper support." The judge thought that her claim should succeed but that "in all the circumstances the provision should be modest"; he ordered her to get $20,000 out of the estate.

Reported cases are always anomalies in some way. Thousands of estates pass through probate without providing grist for the law reporter's mill. The cases that invoke these statutes are surely extremely rare; not many actions are brought, and fewer still get appealed and enshrined in the books. Potentially, to be sure, these laws could totally overturn the ethos of the law of succession. In the Australian case, the court carefully examined the life circumstances of Lambeff's two sons and his daughter. The court came to the conclusion that the daughter had to share in the estate even though her father had nothing to do with her, had no wish to have anything to do with her, and would have had a perfect right, under earlier law, to leave her absolutely nothing—which is what he did. Here the court blasted a huge hole in the intestacy laws—and in the idea of freedom of testation. Nothing in American law up to this point goes quite this far. Nor is anything of this sort likely to happen.

As we will see, American succession law *is* changing—but not in this direction, except for small estates. If anything, American law is trying harder than ever to make sure that the dead hand gets what it wants. Australia, despite macho myths about the outback and rugged self-reliance, is actually closer to England, and the modern welfare state, than the United States is or is likely to become.

Escheat

In the United States, the favored heirs under intestacy laws—no surprise—are spouses and children. If the dead person has no spouse or children, the next in line typically are parents, brothers, and sisters. If these are lacking too, then the estate goes to uncles, aunts, and cousins. The basic idea is that a person's closest relatives inherit when he dies. There are formal ways of measuring "closeness" in deciding such questions as whether a second cousin once removed beats out a third cousin. The statutes spell these out in some detail.

What if there is absolutely nobody eligible to claim the estate? In this case, the estate "escheats"; that is, the state steps in and takes the money. In states that have chopped off the rights of "laughing heirs," this can happen with some frequency. In other states, in theory, it should never happen, since everybody has *some* relative. But even in these states, a person can die in such obscurity that nobody has a plausible claim to blood relationship. At this point, the property is likely to escheat.

Issues of escheat rarely get to court. One that did arose in South Dakota.[85] Robert Jetter and his brother, Martin, were farmers and ranchers in Haakon County. Neither brother ever married or had children. They were very successful in their ranching efforts and made a lot of money. They made out very similar wills. Each brother left everything to the other brother and added the words: "I hereby generally and specifically disinherit each and all persons whomsoever claiming to be my heirs-at-law." The wills said nothing about what would happen to the money when the second brother died. Martin died first, then Robert. Because Robert's will left everything to his brother and disinherited all other "heirs-at-law," the state claimed the money. But Robert did have relatives: children of a half-brother, and also relatives of the Jetters's mother. The state argued that none of these people had any rights because Robert had specifically cut them out of his estate. That left nobody; hence the escheat. The relatives, naturally, disagreed and claimed the money. They argued that Robert had, in effect, left his estate to nobody. The will, in short, had a huge, gaping hole in it: it failed to say where the money would go on the death of the second brother. The result (the relatives said) was as if Robert had died without a will. And when that happens, the nearest relatives inherit. The court bought this argument and gave the money to the relatives (though two judges dissented). The real moral of this story is not about escheat; it is about choosing your lawyer wisely. The country lawyer who drew up these wills for the Jetter brothers could hardly have done a worse job. The wills he drafted did not provide for a contingency that a child could spot in a minute. After all, one of the brothers was sure to die first, and the wills did not cover that situation in any sensible way.

Freedom of Testation

Freedom of testation is supposed to be the guiding principle of modern law. In essence, you can leave your money to anybody you choose to leave it to. The intestacy laws are only for people who haven't bothered to express their choice by will. This is a fundamental principle of law. It is also, apparently, a fundamental social norm. At least people say so; whether they mean it is another question. In a 1977 study, a sample of people in five states were asked whether the law should "limit inheritance" to relatives, "friends of long standing," and "organizations to which an individual has had a long-time connection," or, contrariwise, make no restrictions at all on the way a person distributes what he owns. Almost everybody—89%—opted for no restrictions. But in the same breath, when they were asked if a person "should have the right to give most of his estate to the care and maintenance of his dog or cat for as long as that animal shall live," 54% said no. If you ask the question in the abstract. people are extremely keen on freedom of testation; in concrete situations, perhaps less so.[86]

And in fact, millions of people in the developed world do not actually have freedom of testation. Or they have it to a very limited degree. To begin with, married people cannot disinherit a spouse—at least not easily. In most countries you cannot disinherit your children, though in common law countries, generally speaking, you can. These are very big limitations. Also, as I pointed out, even in the United States, freedom of testation is (like so many other things in society) mainly for the rich. Ordinary people do not get to taste its joys. If your estate is small enough, your immediate dependents will swallow it up.

Is there freedom of testation for pension rights? Many pension plans include death benefits of one sort or another. These pension plans often give the worker the right to choose who gets the death benefit. Sometimes, the pension rights either die with you or go to your immediate family, a wife, a husband, children, and the like. At times, this is not something you can override or overrule. Under plans guaranteed by ERISA, the federal law that regulates pensions, you cannot name anybody other than a spouse, except with the consent of the spouse. Many plans, too, will specify what happens if you die without naming a beneficiary. This is, in short, a kind of intestacy.

What is surprising is how many of these intestacy laws or situations there are. As long ago as 1958, Allison Dunham published an article with the intriguing title "Sixty Different Succession Laws in Illinois."[87] Most legal scholars would have thought there was only *one* succession law in Illinois, but Dunham showed they were wrong. Illinois had no fewer than forty, and federal laws that covered people in Illinois added another twenty. These were mostly pension laws—for teachers, members of the police department, and so on. The federal program of old-age benefits (Social Security) is probably the most important of the federal laws. It does not leave any room for "freedom of testation." The benefits end when the ex-worker dies. There are provisions for minor children. Widows (and widowers)[88] can continue to collect money. But there is nothing for adult children, or for that matter, for anybody else, except a surviving spouse. If an unmarried worker dies before retirement, and before any payments are due, nobody will ever collect anything, no matter how much he or she has paid into the system. If an unmarried, childless worker dies at 72, the payments simply stop.

But many other pensions and pension plans do have death benefits, and do grant a kind of freedom of testation. And, as in Dunham's day, there are many statutory plans. I have not gone to the trouble to count them, but probably there are still just as many succession laws in Illinois. And elsewhere. To take just one example: if a public defender on the payroll in Connecticut dies in office, the surviving spouse will receive a "monthly allowance" based on the dead defender's salary. If the defender dies without a surviving spouse, or if the spouse dies "before the youngest child . . . reaches the age of eighteen," the child's guardian will collect the money as long as the child is a minor.[89] Presumably, nothing gets paid to a defender who dies childless and without benefit of spouse.

Marriage and Inheritance

Intestacy laws, as we have seen, are tilted strongly in favor of a widow or widower and the dead person's children. Widows are more common than widowers. Women live longer than men and tend to marry men who are older than they are. Usually, it's perfectly clear who is a widow or widower, and who is a child and who is not. But in both categories there are significant gray areas.

On one point, historically, the law was quite firm. A woman who wanted to inherit from a man she lived with had to be a legal wife. And for him to inherit, he had to be a legal husband. In most states today, it is easy to know who is and who is not truly married. Married people get a marriage license, and they go through a ceremony before a judge, a justice of the peace, a clergyman, or in rare cases a ship captain or the like. They may have gone to some tawdry "marriage chapel" in Nevada or had a big church wedding and reception, pulling out all the stops. In any event, the marriage leaves behind a clean official record.

But marriage was not always quite so clear-cut. The so-called common law marriage was, in most states, a legally recognized and perfectly lawful marriage. A common law marriage did not need a marriage license, minister, or justice of the peace; it did not need witnesses or any of the trappings of a ceremonial marriage. A common law marriage needed only one thing: mutual agreement. If a man and a woman simply said to each other, let's be husband and wife, then they *were* husband and wife. This romantic conversation could take place in total privacy. If so, how did anybody *know* it had ever taken place? As a practical matter, if a man and woman *acted* as if they were married—lived together, behaved like married people, went to church, and that sort of thing—the law would presume or infer that they had made an agreement to *be* married. And that would be quite enough in a state that recognized common law marriage.

In the nineteenth century, most states recognized such arrangements.[90] This was a striking departure from English law. Lord Hardwicke's Marriage Act, enacted by Parliament in 1753, made this kind of marriage impossible. For a legal marriage, "Banns of Matrimony" had to be "published in an audible Manner in the Parish Church, or in some Publick Chapel" three Sundays in a row. Marriages were to be performed by the clergy and "solemnized in the Presence of Two or more credible Witnesses," and then entered into a register.[91] But Lord Hardwicke's law never took hold in the United States.

Why did the states—or most of them—accept as valid so loose and informal a way of getting married? Clearly, one important point was inheritance of property. If a man and woman lived together and had children, and if the man died without a will, the woman could inherit only if she was a wife, and the children could inherit only if they were legitimate children of the dead man. Indeed, most of the litigation on the common law marriage came up after one or both of the "spouses" was dead; and the issue was almost always money or some other inheritance. In the early nineteenth century, clergy were in short supply in some parts of the country. More to the point, record keeping was primitive and unreliable. What the common law marriage doctrine really meant was this: if a man and a woman live together, act as if they are married, and if the community *thinks* they are married, then the law will act as if they really *are* married. It will assume that, at some point, before they took up housekeeping and started sleeping in the same bed, they had whispered or shouted the magic words at each other.

That such a romantic little private ceremony ever actually took place seems pretty unlikely. And judges were not so naive as to think it did. Nonetheless, they embraced the idea of the common law marriage. For one thing, it protected the honor of the couple. They were not living in sin, but in holy matrimony. More to the point, the doctrine had a clear, strong impact on the disposition of property. A common law wife was a wife, a real wife, a legal wife; and this meant that she inherited from her husband, whether or not he had a will. It also meant that the children were real children, legal children, and not bastards, with no right to inherit from their fathers. The United States was a country in which tens of thousands of ordinary people owned land or other property. This made the question, who exactly is a wife (or husband), much more salient than (say) in England, where property was concentrated in a very few hands.

The common law marriage, however, fell into disrepute in the late nineteenth century, and even more so in the twentieth century. For one thing, it seemed much less necessary. Record keeping got much better. Getting married was cheap and easy. There was no shortage of clergymen or justices of the peace. In addition, common law marriage became a downright nuisance in an age of pension laws (for Civil War veterans, for example, and their widows), and later on, under the Social Security law. Government would have to decide whether women were really common law wives or just plain mistresses. Also, in the heyday of the eugenics movement, the states wanted better control over marriage. Laws were passed calling for blood tests and forbidding people who were mentally ill or defective or had loathsome diseases from marrying. Common law marriage, because it was so informal, would make nonsense of these laws and frustrate the policy of preventing "defectives" from getting married and having children.[92] By the late twentieth century, only about a dozen or so states still recognized common law marriage.[93] One state, New Hampshire, had codified the doctrine, or to be more accurate, had provided by law for something fairly similar to common law marriage. Under New Hampshire law, a couple that had been "cohabiting and acknowledging each other as husband and wife," and who were "generally reputed to be such, for the period of 3 years, and until the decease of one of them," were to be deemed "legally married."[94]

This was however, exceptional. In most states, the common law marriage died—rather slowly and gradually, to be sure, but steadily nonetheless. In the early twenty-first century, the number of states that recognized the doctrine continued to shrink. For example, after January 1, 2005, no common law marriage was to be valid in Pennsylvania.[95] Yet in the late twentieth century, dramatic changes in sexual attitudes and behaviors had brought another turn of the wheel. "Cohabitation"—unmarried people openly living together—became extremely common. Some of these couples were in long-term relationships, and some had children together. Then there were also many same-sex partnerships, and a great many of these too were long term and monogamous; and sometimes these couples too had children living with them in their household. Did cohabiters, of whatever sexes, have inheritance rights?

In general, the answer was no—not unless they had some sort of contract or agreement. Of course, one partner could always make out a will in favor of the other partner, or set up a trust, or make some other kind of plan. As one popular guidebook put it, if you are "not legally married," then "not planning is not an option."[96] But many people, alas, never do get around to planning; so many of us, after all, keep putting things off or just drift through life. If a partner dies and there is no plan, the surviving partner is, for the most part, out of luck. In New Hampshire, the statute that more or less created a kind of common law marriage could be helpful; but even this statute required the man and woman to "acknowledge" each other as husband and wife. If either one did not "acknowledge" the other—and this would seem to be the normal case—the other partner would have no inheritance rights.[97] This is true even in states that recognize common law marriage. South Carolina is one of those states. In a case decided in 2005, Page Callen filed an action for divorce against

Sean Callen; she claimed they had a common law marriage. They certainly had *something* together—two children were born. But Sean insisted they never considered themselves married. The relationship, he said, was at first "purely sexual"; later it was nothing but a child-sharing arrangement. A "lack of intent to be married," said the court, overrides any presumption "that arises from cohabitation and reputation."[98] In an earlier case (1990), a woman named Sandra Jennings claimed to be the common law wife of the actor William Hurt. Hurt admitted he was the father of her child but denied that there was a common law marriage. To "establish a common-law marriage in South Carolina," said the court, you have to show a "mutual agreement to create such a marriage"; marriage cannot "creep up" on either of the pair and "catch them unawares. One cannot be married unwittingly or accidentally."[99]

These were divorce-like cases; but they set out a principle that would apply equally in cases of inheritance. For these couples, Professor Lawrence Waggoner has proposed changing the intestacy laws, to give inheritance rights to committed partners who have lost their loved ones. The states have not gone along with this suggestion, by and large. At least so far. It is a fair bet that the current situation will not last. "Living in sin" is no longer much of a sin for millions of people, maybe even most people, in the United States. People feel that committed partners owe something to each other. The level of tolerance for gay couples is also much higher than it has been in the past. There is tremendous controversy over gay marriage; and when people have a chance to vote on this issue, they almost always vote no. But the tide seems to be turning; Massachusetts and California recognize gay marriages.[100] Millions of people who claim to be dead set against gay marriage feel much less strongly about civil union laws. And the same goes for inheritance rights. Mary Louise Fellows and her associates carried out a survey of opinion in Minnesota (the results were published in 1998). They sampled the general public and also couples in committed relations (both gay and heterosexual). They used various scenarios. All of the scenarios had this in common: one member of a committed couple (unmarried) dies, without a will. In every case, most people, in every group, thought the surviving partner should have inheritance rights. The general public was less generous than the partners in committed relationships—this is no surprise—but in no situation was there a majority of the sample who thought the surviving partner should get nothing.[101]

Minnesota is not, of course, one of our most conservative states. The old rule was stiff and unyielding: a domestic partnership—to use the current term—had no legal consequences. But this rule is rapidly eroding in some states. In Washington, the courts have brought back something that looks suspiciously like common law marriage, even though the courts insist that there is no such thing in the state. But the courts have applied principles of community property to "unmarried partners in committed intimate relationships." The partners have a right to "just and equitable" division of the property. The quoted words come from a case in which a man and woman who had lived together for about fifteen years died together in a car accident.[102] The Washington court, in another case, made it clear that these principles apply, not only to men and women who live together on a long-term basis, but also to gay couples in committed relationships.[103]

So far, Washington state seems to have gone further than other states. But the evolution of doctrine (and statute law) is genuine enough. What is evolving, however, is not the same as common law marriage, even though people often compare the new legal situation to that old set of doctrines. Common law marriage was supposed to be real marriage. The essence of the doctrine was reputation: whether the community considered that he and she were married. And at the heart of common law marriage was (theoretically) a real agreement to *be* married. The new rights for unmarried couples make no such assumption. To the contrary: these couples often agree quite specifically *not* to be married. And inheritance rights usually depend, not on informal understandings, but on quite formal arrangements. Statutes that give unmarried couples inheritance rights are often, basically, *registration* statutes. In Hawaii, a registered same-sex partner has the right to inherit if her partner dies without a will. In Oregon, same-sex couples have all the rights of married people under the "Oregon Family Fairness Act," signed into law in 2007. But these couples have to register as domestic partners. In Vermont, a same-sex couple can form a "civil union" in a ceremony performed by a judge, a justice of the peace, or a member of the clergy. The civil union is registered with the state, and the couple then has basically the same rights and duties as spouses in a traditional marriage.[104] Under California law, "domestic partners" enjoyed most of the same rights as "spouses," including inheritance rights. They had to formalize their relationship, however, by filing a Declaration of Domestic Partnership with the Secretary of State. "Domestic partners" were defined as "two adults who have chosen to share one another's lives in an intimate and committed relationship of mutual caring." They also had to live together (in a "common residence"). This statute, like the Vermont statute and some others, is meant for couples who are "members of the same sex." Persons "of opposite sexes" cannot "constitute a domestic partnership" in California unless one or both of them are "over the age of 62."[105]

California has now gone even further: by court decision, gay marriage is legal in California. (Whether this will survive a referendum is, at this writing, not yet known.) At one time, however, California had a domestic partnership law that did not include inheritance rights; these rights were added in 2003. Jeff Collman was a flight attendant on one of the planes that struck the World Trade Center on September 11, 2001. Collman lived in California with his duly registered domestic partner, Keith Bradkowski, a nurse and hospital administrator. Collman, unfortunately, had never made out a will. This meant that Bradkowski had no claim to the estate. He then lobbied, successfully, for change in the law, which gave domestic partners the right to inherit in intestacy.[106]

The statutes in these states only go so far, and most states have nothing on the subject. But it seems pretty clear that there is a trend, or at least the beginnings of a trend. Obviously, "domestic partners" are going to have to wait a long time before they get recognition in Mississippi or Utah. But other states are responding to changing times. In Massachusetts a gay couple can actually get married. In Maine, under a law of 2004, domestic partners do not have to be gay. The law applies to any "2 unmarried adults who are domiciled together under long-term arrangements that evidence a commitment to remain responsible indefinitely for each other's welfare."[107] In April 2007, Washington state legalized domestic partnerships; and New Hampshire joined the list of states that have legalized same-sex civil unions.

Note the insistence, almost everywhere, on formality: a marriage, a registration. Nobody wants to attach legal consequences to a one-night stand; and in an age when young people live together for a week, a month, a year, maybe more, without "committing" themselves, inheritance rights are going to be parceled out with caution, even in the most "advanced" jurisdictions. Conservatives wring their hands and worry about the decline of the West, and the decay of traditional values, and so on. But the "progressive" laws really *are* about traditional values: formality, permanence, commitment, and stable, solid, family life.

One reason common law marriage went into terminal decline is precisely because it left no formal footprints; and this, in today's world, created all sorts of problems. These problems would be just as severe if unregistered cohabiters had rights. Courts, at least sometimes, would be forced to paw through the fact-situation to find out exactly how committed he and she, or he and he, or she and she, had actually been. Take the case from Washington state in which Frank Vasquez claimed a share of the estate of Robert Schwerzler. Vasquez said he was involved "in a long-term, stable, cohabiting relationship" with Schwerzler. But Schwerzler's personal representative denied this, and even hinted darkly that the two had no sex life together. Yes (he said), the two men lived in the same apartment, but they "did not travel together on vacation"; and "each had his own bedroom." The appeal court sent the case back down and told the trial court to "weigh the evidence."[108]

In *Baschi* v. *New York*, decided in 1989, two men, Leslie Blanchard and Miguel Braschi, lived together in a rent-controlled apartment from 1975 on. In 1986, Blanchard died. The owner of the building tried to evict Braschi, claiming he was not "family" and had no right to stay. The highest court of New York disagreed. The court cited the "reality of family life"; protection against eviction should "not rest on fictitious legal distinctions or genetic history." The two men lived "interwoven" lives; they considered each other as "spouses." Braschi treated the apartment as his home; he listed the address on his driver's license and passport. He and Blanchard "shared all obligations," had joint checking accounts and joint credit cards. Thus these men "were much more than mere roommates"; they were family, and Braschi had a right to stay in his home.[109] Of course, under the law of New York as it then was, there was no such thing as civil union or gay marriage. What the court did, in other words, was to resurrect what seems like a form of common law marriage—though at that point it was presumably only for same-sex couples in stable relationships.

Who Is a Child?

"Child," like "spouse," is normally a clear-cut concept, but not always. Two situations in particular pose a question. Do illegitimate children have inheritance rights? And what about adopted children? For both of these categories, law (and custom) have changed enormously over the years.

The common law rule was that an illegitimate child was *filius nullius*—nobody's child. A bastard inherited nothing. Any property the child might have owned escheated to the crown in England upon his death.[110] It was as if the unfortunate child had no family at all. The first change was to recognize a child's right to inherit at least from the child's mother. The father was a more delicate issue. But if the father admitted he had fathered the child, and recognized his obligations, this altered the situation; a child could inherit from a father who admitted paternity. His rights even came under the exalted protection of the Constitution, according to the United States Supreme Court. In *Stanley* v. *Illinois* (1972), the father had never married the mother of his children; but he supported them, and when she died, he wanted custody. Illinois, however, considered them "wards of the state." No, said the Supreme Court, Stanley had a right to a hearing on whether he was a fit parent; and if he was, the children could not be taken away.[111]

The Stanley case stimulated a move to give unwed fathers more rights; but this was happening anyway. And in the late twentieth century the spread of "cohabitation" meant that huge numbers of children were technically illegitimate. It seemed to matter much less than it did at one time. In the old days, bastardy was a horrendous stigma. No longer, at least in urban areas. Children whose fathers acknowledge them (or are forced to do so) have the same inheritance rights as any other children.

Why was the law at one time so harsh toward bastards? The harsh rules buttressed the norms of traditional morality, including the strict (official) rules against sex outside of marriage. But many men (and some women) did have sex outside of marriage. Treating their children as children of nobody—in any event, as children without a father—protected the father's marriage and made it easier for him to keep these children a secret. It also protected the rights of middle-class and upper-class women and their legitimate children. And it did nothing to impair the "rights" of middle-class and upper-class men to sleep with prostitutes, servant girls, and whoever else they pleased.[112] The social stigma of illegitimacy fell heavily on the women who bore these children, and on the children themselves. The men were in many ways immune. In the United States too, there was a strong racial element in the rules. Slave owners who slept with slaves and produced children—a pretty large category—had no obligations toward those children; and the children had no demands on their fathers. They were, in fact, simply slaves like their mothers. There were rare instances in which white fathers recognized their black children, tried to free them, and even left them money; but these were the exception, not the rule.

Today, adopted children are mostly children whose parents, because they did not want them or could not care for them, gave them up for adoption. The main problem in the nineteenth century was not unwanted children, but orphaned children. In this period, thousands of women died in childbirth, and thousands of men were carried off by plagues. Adoption did not exist in the common law system. Massachusetts was the first state to pass a general adoption statute, in 1851.[113] But before then, state legislatures enacted a number of private laws which were, in effect if not in name, adoption statutes. In Mississippi, for example, in 1844, a statute changed the name of James Isaac Thornton Martin, the illegitimate son of David Killough; his new name was James T. Killough, and he was "legitimate and made capable to inherit of his said father, David Killough." Another statute changed the name of William James Normans to William James Melton and made him a "legal heir of John D. Melton, of Yalobusha County," with all the "rights and privileges as heir of the said John D. Melton, to which he would have been entitled if born in lawful wedlock."[114]

Some state statutes were somewhat more general. Mississippi, in 1846, gave local courts authority to change names, and also, "upon application of any person, to make legitimate any of their offspring, not born in wedlock." Courts could also, on petition, make "any other person the heir" of the petitioner.[115] This statute does not use the word "adoption"; but it is, in fact, an adoption statute. A Texas statute of 1850 was explicitly an adoption statute: anybody who wished to "adopt" and make that person an "heir" could do this by filing a statement in a local court.[116]

By the end of the century, adoption statutes were pretty much universal in the United States. What accounts for this development? The text of these statutes gives us one fairly clear answer. They are statutes about inheritance. Nobody needs an adoption statute to take in a child—an orphan, perhaps a relative—and raise that child, love it, cherish it, and treat it as your own. But then if the "adoptive" parent dies intestate, what becomes of the child? Does it have a claim to any of the family property? Although inheritance rights were probably the main point of the statutes, they were perhaps not the only one. And the United States needed this kind of law much more than England did.

In the United States, the average family in the North and Middle West owned a piece of land—a farm, a house in town, and perhaps some money. This was not the case in England, which, as I noted, made no provision for formal, legal adoption of children until much later.

The law of adoption, over the past century and a half, has been complex and sometimes quite controversial. Interracial adoption, and the right of adopted children to find and identify their "real" parents are only two of many sharply contested issues in adoption law. One trend, however, has been completely clear. With regard to inheritance, the law has steadily erased differences between genetic and adopted children. An adopted child is—the language here is that of a Colorado statute—"to all intents and purposes," the child of the adoptive parents once a court enters a decree. The adopted child "shall be entitled to all the rights and privileges . . . of a child born in lawful wedlock."[117] Adopted children are strangers to the bloodline; but they are very much part of the family of dependence and affection.[118]

CHAPTER 3

THE LAST WILL AND TESTAMENT

L AW AND CUSTOM allow people many ways to pass on their property. One of the simplest ways, of course, is to give most or all of it away while still alive. A rich father can make out checks to his children; or he can give them money in more complicated ways, for example, by setting up a trust. (In a later chapter, we will take a closer look at trusts.)

Most people, however, hold on to their money, or some of it. They pass on their property at death, and many of them do so through a document called a will. As we will see, the importance of the will has declined somewhat in recent times. But the will is still a very common, fundamental, and genuinely popular document.

THE FORMAL WRITTEN WILL

In modern colloquial English, a will is a document that disposes of the maker's property at death. No longer are there separate documents for real property and personal property; the two are combined and, while old-fashioned lawyers still pin on the label "Last Will and Testament," nowadays most of us simply call it a "will."

The ordinary will, the most common kind, and the kind that is recognized as valid in every state, is a highly formal document.[1] For one thing, it has to be in writing. In 1677, the (English) Statute of Frauds insisted that all dispositions of land at death had to be in writing, signed by the testator, and witnessed. Under the (English) Wills Act (1837),[2] these requirements applied to *all* gifts at death, whether personal property or real estate. The texts of these two statutes had important influences on the way American statutes were drafted.

The law takes very seriously the requirement that a will must be in writing. If a man gathers a roomful of friends and relatives, and announces clearly and distinctly that he wants his money to go half to his daughter and half to a home for abandoned cats and then drops dead on the spot, he has died intestate, and his expressed wishes make no difference. Oral wills ("nuncupative wills") were at one time valid;[3] but for two centuries or so, only under some highly restricted circumstances. In the middle of the nineteenth century, under New York law, an oral will was invalid "unless made by a soldier while in actual military service, or by a mariner, while at sea."[4] Most states no longer recognize such wills at all. They survive theoretically in a few states,, but are virtually useless. In Indiana, only a person "in imminent peril of death" can make an oral will; it is valid, however, only if the person actually dies, and only if he declares this will before two witnesses who write down what he said within thirty days and submit it to probate within six months of the testator's death. Even then, this will can only dispose of personal property up to $1,000 in value, although people on active duty "in time of war" can bequeath up to a total of $10,000.[5] My guess is that the total number of oral wills probated in Indiana, in any given year, is zero. I personally have never seen, in any probate file, the slightest trace of a nuncupative will.

How many witnesses are needed for ordinary wills? Holographic wills (handwritten wills) need none at all. These wills, in a bare majority of American states, are as valid as any other kind of will. (More on these wills later.) Wills that do not qualify as holographs need at least two witnesses in every state.[6] Some lawyers, out of caution, will throw in a third witness. This might spare the estate some trouble if one witness dies or moves to China or becomes demented. Witnesses were supposed to guarantee, through their testimony, that the will was executed properly and that all the legal details were buttoned up.[7] Every will has to have the testator's signature. And the testator has to *intend* the document to be his will. This is almost never a problem. After all, in the usual situation, the testator went to a lawyer for the specific purpose of asking the lawyer to draft him a will. The client tells the lawyer what he wants in his will, the lawyer draws up the document; the client signs it in front of witnesses, tells the witnesses (at the lawyer's prompting) that this is his will and asks them to witness it. As long as this little ceremony is carried out, nobody can question whether the document was a will and was meant to be a will, or that it was properly executed.

Nobody *has* to have a will; the state will be happy to distribute your property without one, using its intestacy laws. Still, it is a good idea for anybody with money to make out a will, unless one is absolutely sure the intestacy laws are good enough and that the right person will be appointed your personal representative. How many people actually do have wills? A telephone survey of 750 families, in five states (Alabama, California, Massachusetts, Ohio, and Texas), in 1977, found that 45% of the people interviewed had a will. Age was an important factor. Eighty-four percent of those over 65 had a will; 92% of those under 24 did not. Richer and more educated people tended to have a will; 60% of the people with advanced degrees had a will, but only 36.7% of people with less than a high school diploma. Surprisingly, 60% in Ohio had a will; but only 36% in Massachusetts.[8] This was a study of living people. There are also studies of dead people, through their probate files. In the San Bernardino study, for example, most of the estates were testate—342 out of 513, as opposed to 171 intestate, a ratio of two to one.[9] This is a much higher percentage of testacy than the survey just mentioned found. But this is only to be expected. Many people die without leaving an "estate"; they go gently to their graves without the benefit of the probate court. The various studies differ somewhat on this point; but every study found that less than half of the adults who died ended up with probated estates; and most studies show a third, a quarter, or even less.[10] The number of women who leave estates has increased more sharply than the number of men; but for both men and women, death without probate is the norm. When there is a probated estate, the deceased is much more likely than not to have a will. To be sure, not everybody who actually has a will ends up with a probate file. Sometimes a will cannot be found. If the estate is small, the family may not bother to file the will in court. Poor people usually die intestate, and their property rarely goes through probate.

The Issue of Intent

There are a few odd cases where there is some doubt whether the document presented as a will was actually intended to be such. In one of these cases, Butterfield, a sly dog, executed what looked like a will, in which he left money to Mary Fleming. But this was a "sham" (or so it was claimed). The will was meant as bait to persuade Mary to go to bed with Butterfield. (The case report does not say whether the trick worked or not, but the court did rule that she was *not* entitled to a share in his estate.)[11] Occasionally, courts confront the problem of the so-called conditional will. These are usually homemade documents, and almost always badly drafted. In a classic case, Caroline Holley said in her will, "I am going on a Journey and may not ever return. And if I do not, this is my last request."[12] Fortunately or unfortunately, she *did* return. Later on she died, without changing this will. The question was: did she really mean what she said—that is, did she want the will to lapse, if she came back hale and hearty from the trip? Courts do not like conditional wills; and they strain to find a way to ignore the conditions. Sometimes they do this by claiming that the so-called condition is not a condition at all but just a clumsy way of expressing the motive for making out the will. A question that arises in a few cases is whether some sort of handwritten scrap of paper, or a personal letter from A to B, can be classified as a (holographic) will. We will return to this point.

The will is supposed to contain the testator's last wishes—what he or she wants done with the property. The *intention*, the plan, is of paramount importance, though generally speaking only as that intention appears in the will itself. As I said, no matter how clearly a person *says* what he wants, it has no legal meaning outside the will. Also, if someone prepared and signed a will, but with one witness instead of two, the will would be a meaningless piece of paper. This was the case in *Smith* v. *Nelson*, an Arkansas case decided in 1957.[13] Harvey Nelson drew up a will, leaving his "personal property" to his "beloved wife Mary"; she was also to "have charge" of the real estate until she died. He signed this will, had it witnessed (by one witness), and deposited it in "the vault at the County Clerk's office." It was perfectly clear that he thought he had executed a valid will. He also drove the point home in two letters to his wife. In the second letter he wrote: "Honey you may wonder why I had my will fixed so you couldn't sell the houses. You are so big harted and good you would be talked into selling them," and then "you would be without an income." What he intended was completely obvious; but it was equally obvious to the Arkansas court that his intentions could not be carried out. A one-witness will was simply not valid.[14] And, on the other hand, if a person has a perfectly valid will but tells everybody in sight that she has changed her mind, that the last will does not say what she wants, this has no effect. She has to change the will or tear it up. Otherwise, it will govern what happens to her estate, even though we know this is not what she wanted.

Moreover, suppose the will was executed in good order but there is a mistake lurking in the text. There might be a really serious typo; or perhaps a paragraph was carelessly left out, or something was included that didn't belong there. Here too in theory nothing can be done. What the will actually says is paramount. Early cases were quite strict on this point. Recently, the courts and legislatures have begun to chip away at this particular notion; they have become, as we will see, a bit more willing to correct mistakes in wills.

This insistence on form may seem foolish or unjust. But it had a point, or at least, what some people *thought* was a point. The will, historically, was treated with enormous respect. It had a kind of magic to it. It was, after all, a fundamental document. Rights depended on it. Title to land might turn on what a will said or omitted. And the will was a document of record. Wills were filed, recorded, preserved. Spoken words are gone with the wind. Legal documents live on.

Tradition and Inflexibility

The law's insistence on formality was more effective than one might expect, because the will was also, in many ways, a popular as well as a formal document. The general idea, the ways of expressing the idea, even the language itself, seem deeply rooted in custom. In the early seventeenth century, among the first settlers in what is now the United States, and at a time when there were no lawyers to speak of practicing, colonial records show that people knew about wills, that executing a will was the custom, and that people roughly understood how a will should be framed. Early colonial wills have survived in great numbers—John Searles, in 1642 in western Massachusetts, for example, declared in his will that he was "very sicke in body." He then disposed of his property: to his brother-in-law William he left his "best coate" and a "cullored hatt" and forgave him part of a debt. The rest he divided equally between his wife and child.[15]

These wills often used standard clauses, and also vaguely poetic singsong phrases, clearly based on folk memories. Most legal documents have very little poetry about them. As literature, they are pretty close to absolute zero: consider the typical insurance policy or the impenetrable jungle of jargon in the Internal Revenue Code. And a lawyer's opinion letter, as a rule, tends to be written in leaden, cautious prose.

The typical will, too, has always been full of jargon. Yet its customary language was not just legal blather. And for all their technicality, wills were never as dry and pedantic as, say, the typical insurance policy. The will, after all, was an instrument of giving, of love, often, too, it was an instrument written in the shadow of death. Traditional wills were full of traditional, half-mystical phrases. These phrases often came in (redundant) groups of three: "I give, devise, and bequeath all the rest, residue, and remainder of my estate." ("I give all the rest of my estate" would have done just as well.) Old wills often began by invoking the mysteries of God and the painful reality of death: Here, for example, is the beginning of a will written in Maryland in 1652: "In the name of God amen—I William Jones . . . being sick in body but In perfect sence and form. . . . I give and bequeath my Soul unto God my Saviour and redemer and my body to the Earth from whence it Came."[16] And the very signing of a will has always been wrapped in ceremony. The witnesses gather around. There is a certain air of solemnity. Of course, in a lawyer's office, the ceremony can be brief, brisk, bland and businesslike. But the client is aware that something big is happening, that he or she is signing a document that means something awesome and significant.

The legal rules, in fact, insisted on ceremony. There had to be two witnesses. One witness, as we saw, definitely would not do. In one old case from 1895, Eliza Fish began making a death-bed will.[17] She was "exceedingly feeble" and had trouble even trying to sign the will; two doctors helped her out. One of the doctors then signed as a witness. But before the second doctor could put his name down, Eliza died. The second doctor then signed the will. To no avail. A will, said the court, "must be a valid, perfect instrument at the time of the death of the testator." When poor Eliza died, only one witness had signed—a "fatal" flaw.

The two witnesses also, under the codes, had to see the testator sign the will. Or, if he had already signed (a bad practice), he had to "acknowledge" his signature or tell the witnesses that this was his will, and this was his signature, or the like. The various probate codes had small technical differences on this point; and many wills failed because of some problem with signature or acknowledgment.[18] The witnesses were also supposed to be in each other's presence when the testator signed or acknowledged the will, although here too state laws showed some minor variations.

Many courts were quite sticky and insisted on strict, literal compliance with these rules. There have been, for example, dozens of cases about what it meant to be in the "presence of the testator." In a West Virginia case in 1998,[19] Homer Miller—disabled and in a wheelchair—went to his local bank to sign his will. He asked Debra Pauley, who worked for the bank, to act as a witness. She then took the will to two other bank employees to sign as witnesses. But these employees did not see Miller sign and did not see each other in the act of signing. The local statute required two witnesses who "shall subscribe the will in the presence of the testator and of each other." The court, somewhat reluctantly, held that the will was void—a worthless piece of paper. One judge dissented: the case, he said, was an instance of "slavishly worshiping form over substance"; the result of the case was "patently absurd . . . inconsistent with the underlying purposes of the statute."

But this was certainly not an exceptional result; and whether it was "inconsistent" with the aims of the wills statute is also open to question. The statute, historically, insisted on adherence to form. In another case, in Illinois, the testator was an elderly lady. She signed her will, after which her son Fred drove her to the house where the prospective witnesses lived. She stayed in the "rear seat of the sedan automobile which her son had parked in front of the . . . residence." Fred took the will inside, and the witnesses signed it at a table. There was an open window, and Fred argued that his mother could have seen the witnesses if she happened to be looking at the open window. But that was just not good enough. The witnesses, said the court, did not sign in her "presence"; the will was invalid.[20] In an Arkansas case in 1993, Nettie Frost asked her friend, Jewell Burns, to sign as a witness to her will. At that point, Nettie herself had not signed the will. Later she did and got a second witness. The will was held invalid.[21]

The modern trend is to relax some of these requirements, and courts today might well reach different results in some of these cases. There has been a definite movement away from "formalism." In some states today, witnesses do not have to be in each other's presence. And they can sign outside of the testator's presence—possibly even after the testator's death. These states would probably uphold poor old Mrs. Fish's will.

HOLOGRAPHIC WILLS

In a small majority of states another kind of will is recognized, the so-called holographic will. This is a much simpler document than the ordinary witnessed will. It has to be entirely handwritten by the testator; but if this is done, the law requires no further formalities.[22] In North Carolina such a will has to be found after the testator dies "among his valuable papers or effects," or in his safe-deposit box, or in possession of somebody to whom the testator entrusted it; but other states have no such requirements.[23]

The formal law has become more and more favorable to holographs. The rather slight evidence we have suggests that they are not used very much, however; and they are more likely to cause trouble than ordinary wills. Originally, the holographic will was recognized only in a band of western and southwestern states (and in Louisiana), where it was inherited from Spanish or Mexican law. Today North Dakota and New Jersey, among other states, also recognize such wills.[24] By the 1960's there were twenty-one states that accepted holographic wills, and by the early twenty-first century twenty-six states did so. This trend was engineered primarily by academics. Obviously, the general public played no role. The practicing bar has nothing to gain from holographs, and perhaps something to lose—holographs, after all, are homemade wills. Still, the holographic will is not much of a threat to the pocketbooks of lawyers and estate planners. People with money—and estate lawyers are interested mainly in people with money—usually consult an attorney before making out a will; and if the will has any complexity to it at all, nobody is going to use a holograph. Still, the spread of the holograph, legally speaking, is part of a more general trend away from formality in the law of wills.

There are quite a few reported cases about holographic wills. This is probably because they are home-made wills, often clumsy and ill-considered. How often are they used? A study of wills in San Bernardino County, California, for the year 1964 found that about 10% of the wills filed were holographic.[25] This suggests that the law is not a dead letter; but neither is the holograph particularly common.

Because nobody would bother writing a ten-page will in longhand, holographs are usually short and sweet. They are also usually, though not always, slapdash. In San Bernardino County in 1964, two of the holographs consisted of a couple of sentences on a napkin, written by elderly men.[26]

Holographs may be crude, but at least it is clear almost always that they are wills, intended to be wills, and nothing but wills. Most of them contain the magic words "Last Will." But there are quite a few cases about letters and memos where the magic words do not appear, and the courts have to wrestle with the question: is this a holographic will or is it not? Is it intended to be the "last will"? In one case, Mrs. E. J. White wrote: "To Whom It May Concern. If anything Should happen to me, I want all My Property & other thing & Bonds divided between Marvin, Arlene & my sisters. . . . I will finish this later." The last sentence was the problem—did this mean we were not supposed to take the document as a complete, final will? She lived seven more years and did nothing about "finishing"; but the court allowed the "will" into probate.[27]

In some cases, courts have been willing to construe ordinary letters as holographs. In 1921, Harry Kimmel wrote a letter to two of his sons. It began with some general advice: "you poot your Pork down in Pickle it is the true way to keep meet . . . & you will have good pork fore smoking." Then there was a weather report: "Plenty of snow & Verry cold"; only then did Kimmel say that his money, his "liberty lones" and "Post office stamps," plus his home, should go to the two sons he addressed in the letter. Kimmel died suddenly the same day. The Pennsylvania court construed the letter as a holographic will.[28] A Montana court was willing to stretch matters even further. Charles Kuralt, in a New York hospital, wrote a letter to Patricia Shannon, a woman with whom he had had, for some thirty years, what the court rather prissily called a "protracted personal relationship." (Kuralt's wife, Petie, had been kept completely in the dark.) The letter began, "Something is terribly wrong with me and they can't figure out what," despite "cat-scans and a variety of cardiograms. . . . I'll have the lawyer visit the hospital to be sure you inherit the rest of the place in MT. . . ." The reference was to property in Montana. No lawyer ever came, and Kuralt died; but the Montana Supreme Court decided the letter could be treated as a valid codicil (an amendment or addition) to Kuralt's regular will (which left virtually everything to his wife); the court reversed a decision that had rejected Shannon's case and ordered the matter to go to trial.[29]

This was not the only court that was willing to stretch a point. In a Texas case, the document was a greeting card, sent in the mail by Bill Hayes Daniels (a practicing lawyer, believe it or not). Was this a valid holographic will? The front of the card contained a poem, "The Ten Secrets of a Successful Relationship"; on the back were the words: "Last Will: I leave everything to Verneice Daniels. BHD." The court held that this was a valid will.[30] In *Button v. Button*, a California case from 1930,[31] Grace Button committed suicide, and a suicide note was found in the room where she died. The note was addressed to her exhusband ("Dear, dear Daddy") and talked about him and her two sons. "I am ruining our boys' lives.... When I am gone you can just breathe one long sigh of contentment. I'd like to be cremated. You can have the house on 26th ave. and all the things of value." The note or letter was over 700 words long; the "will" part was just the last two sentences quoted. Nonetheless, the court was willing to call the document a will, and the ex-husband inherited everything.[32]

Not all courts were so generous. Some were, for example, insistent on the rule that everything in the will had to be written by hand. In one classic case in 1920, Thorn, a resident of California, left his "country place Cragthorn" to the California Academy of Sciences; the balance of the estate was to be used to "improve or care for Cragthorn Park." The whole will was handwritten, except for the name "Cragthorn," which was inserted with a rubber stamp. The court held that the will was invalid.[33]

The more recent the case, the less likely that the court will be so fussy. This is another area where the formal law itself has bent quite a bit. Under California law today, Thorn's will would probably be valid. The current statute only requires "the signature and the material provisions" of the will to be "in the handwriting of the testator."[34] Most of the holograph statutes today have similar language.

In this age of computers, satellites, and trips into space, there does seem something a bit archaic about the will. It is, after all, a written document, requiring an actual signature (and, for the most part, the signature of witnesses). There has been talk about videotaped wills; but no state recognizes any such thing.[35] In Indiana a statute provides that a videotape may be "admissible as evidence" of the "proper execution of a will," the intentions of the testator, the "mental state or capacity of a testator," the "authenticity of a will," and other "matters" a court finds "relevant to the probate of a will."[36] But the will itself cannot be videotaped. Today, quite a few companies will make videos of the ceremony; one company advertises, for example, that a "carefully prepared videotape that records . . . the entire will's execution may prove indispensable should the will subsequently be contested."[37] And in a Texas case, where there was a question about what the will actually meant, dictaphone notes, made by the attorney who drafted the will, were allowed in evidence to explain the will and resolve an ambiguity.[38] What about an electronic will? One state, Nevada, has enacted a law that allows an electronic will. This is defined as a will "written, created and stored in an electronic record." It has to contain the date, and the "electronic signature of the testator"; it has to be "created and stored" so that there is only "one authoritative copy," which the testator controls; and it needs, too, at least one "authentication characteristic of the testator." This is defined to mean a "unique" trait, which can be measured and recognized; the examples mentioned are a "fingerprint, a retinal scan, voice recognition, facial recognition" or a "digitized signature."[39] This statute dates from 2001. There seems to be nothing in the literature to suggest whether anybody uses it.[40]

REVOCATION

A will is "ambulatory," as the phrase goes. It is a formal, legal document; but it has no bite, no validity, as long as the testator stays alive. He or she can change it, or get rid of it, without notice, and with very little fuss or bother. There are two main ways to revoke a will. The first is to make out a later will. Usually, the later will has a clause that specifically revokes all the earlier ones. This is standard: "I hereby revoke any and all wills heretofore made," or words to that effect. But even if these words are left out, if the later will disposes of everything the testator has to dispose of, then the earlier wills are as dead as if they had been specifically revoked.[41]

The second method of revoking a will is even simpler. You can revoke a will by killing it physically. A will is revoked, according to the California Probate Code, by being "burned, torn, canceled, obliterated or destroyed" (the language is typical), either by the testator himself or by somebody else in "the testator's presence and by the testator's direction."[42] The destruction, however, has to be deliberate: if the house burns down and the will burns with it, it has not been revoked, and if you can prove what was in the will, you can still have it probated.

A lost or destroyed will can, then, have a kind of life after death. Still, on the whole, the law places great emphasis, almost mystical emphasis, on the will itself, and its signatures. And on the original will. This is the important document—not a photocopy or the like. The will has a kind of magic. You can get rid of it only with another magic document, or by actually putting it physically to death. In an old Virginia case from 1934, Mrs. Kroll decided to change her will.[43] She was going to destroy it, but changed her mind; she decided to keep the old will as a kind of memorandum, to be used in drawing up a new will. The will was five pages long, fastened together with metal clasps. On the back of a cover sheet she signed a statement that said, "This will null and void and to be only held . . . as a memorandum for another will." The court held that the will was *not* revoked. A will is not "canceled" unless something is done that can "physically affect the written portion of the will, not merely . . . blank parts of the paper on which the will is written." Similarly, in an Ohio case Helen L. White's will left money to Jennifer Jones.[44] After Jennifer fell out of her favor Helen wrote, on the margin of the will, "This will is void. We have never heard or seen Jennifer Jones"; Jennifer did not come to "Jess' funeral so I do not leave her anything." But, said the court, this was not really a cancellation, since the writings on the margin did not touch the writings in the will. The will was valid, and Jennifer took the money after all.[45]

Destroying a will, then, was something like killing a vampire: the stake had to go through the vampire's heart; nothing less would do. Here too, many more modern statutes are less particular: in these states, canceling, burning, or tearing can revoke a will, "whether or not the burn, tear, or cancellation touched any of the words on the will."[46] This change in the law runs parallel to others I have already described or will be addressed later on. "Formalism" seems to be on the decline, and we will have to ask why.

Generally speaking, the law has stood firm on one crucial point. The law will not take into account the mere fact that a will is old, out-dated, and doesn't seem to fit the testator's present situation or conform to his later wishes. The message is plain: if your situation changes, then change your will. Otherwise, the old will stands. There has been one big exception to this rule. In many states a marriage automatically revoked a will. This was one change of situation that seemed significant enough to override the general principle.[47] In most states, however, this is no longer the case. For one thing, the rule seemed unnecessary.

Widows have rights. If a man makes out a will leaving everything to his mother, then marries, and dies a year later without changing his will, the statute law protects the grieving widow. She will get her statutory share. Why throw out the rest of the will?

On the other hand, under most probate codes today, divorce automatically revokes at least a part of a will. There is a similar rule in England.[48] Provisions in the will for the benefit of the ex-spouse are no longer valid.[49] This probably reflects what most people would want. There are some subsidiary problems. Does this rule also apply to will substitutes (revocable trusts and other arrangements of this sort)? If a teacher in Oklahoma named her husband as a beneficiary under the Oklahoma Teachers' Retirement System, does he still have those rights if the couple gets a divorce?[50] The Oklahoma court said yes in this situation; a Massachusetts court, on the other hand, said no to the ex-spouse in a case that involved a trust set up before love died between the two.[51] The issue even came up to the United States Supreme Court.[52] Washington state had a law that extended the rule of automatic revocation on divorce to will substitutes and pension plans ("nonprobate assets"). Under the statute, these were to be treated "as if the former spouse had failed to survive the decedent."[53] David Egelhoff had worked for the Boeing Company. Boeing provided him with a life insurance policy and a pension plan. His wife, Donna, was the beneficiary under both of these. In April 1994, David and Donna divorced. A couple of months later, David was killed in an automobile accident and died intestate. For whatever reason—probably ordinary procrastination—he had never taken Donna off the policy and the pension plan. Donna was his second wife, and David's children from his first marriage claimed the money under the Washington statute. But the Supreme Court held otherwise: the Employee Retirement Income Security Act (ERISA), a federal statute, "preempted" (shoved aside) the Washington law.[54]

MORTMAIN LAWS

In the nineteenth century, and into the twentieth, quite a few states had so-called mortmain statutes on their books. ("Mortmain" literally means "dead hand.") These were restrictions on gifts to charity by will. Under a typical mortmain statute, no gift to charity would be valid unless the will was made more than, say, thirty days before the testator actually died. Other statutes limited the amount the testator could leave to a charity—usually expressed as a percentage of the estate. Both types of statute usually applied only if the dead man had a wife or children surviving him. Some of the statutes combined both types. So, the Georgia statute, in the nineteenth and part of the twentieth century, provided that nobody who was survived by a wife, child, or grandchildren could leave more than one-third of the estate "to any charitable, religious, educational, or civil institution"; moreover, the will in question had to be "executed at least ninety days before the death of the testator"; otherwise the gift would be "void."[55]

In England, mortmain statutes were passed as early as the thirteenth century. These were powerful laws that, in essence, aimed to prevent land from passing permanently into the "dead hand" of corporate bodies—specifically the Catholic Church, which had amassed enormous amounts of land, depriving the king of some of his feudal dues. The mortmain statutes of the states seem, at best, only the palest reflection of these statutes. These nineteenth-century statutes, however, were still aimed at the Church, but with a different twist. The law expressed, in a number of ways, deep disapproval of religious bodies that amassed large tracts of land. Gifts by will to religious bodies were legally suspect. Indeed, the Maryland constitution of 1776 made this explicit: no one was to devise any land to support "any minister, public teacher, or preacher of the gospel . . . or any religious sect, order or denomination"; any "gift, sale, or devise of lands" of this sort was to be "void."[56]

The point of the mortmain laws was to express a policy against death-bed wills that left money to religion. As the end approached, dying people might be overcome with regrets for a sinful life, and could almost feel the heat of Hell on their tortured skin. Underlying the laws was the image—or fantasy—of the wicked priest preying on the dying man or woman, manipulating their fears of eternal damnation to squeeze out gifts for the church, and costing the family their inheritance.

But over time, this image faded, and the strong anti-Catholic bias that supported the statutes eroded. And, as we will see, "charity" in time no longer meant primarily religious bodies. The rise of the modern charitable foundation changed the image of testamentary gifts to charities. By 1970 there were only eleven mortmain statutes left.[57] Some state courts even went so far as to declare these laws unconstitutional—a sure sign that they had lost popularity, at least with judges. The Supreme Court of Pennsylvania, for example, struck down its statute in 1974.[58] This law invalidated any "bequest or devise for religious or charitable purposes" in a will, if the will had been executed less than thirty days before the testator died. The court thought this statute was "arbitrary" and unreasonable. Why invalidate a gift by someone "in the best of health at the time of the execution of his will," who "chances to die in an accident 29 days later," while accepting the "charitable bequests of another, aged and suffering from a terminal disease, who survives the execution of the will by 31 days"? In the court's view, such an "arbitrary" law violated the equal protection clause of the 14th Amendment.

Florida reacted the same way Pennsylvania did. Lorraine E. Romans died in 1986. She left her daughter, Lorraine Zrillic, nothing but "several sealed boxes of family antique dishes and figurines." Ms. Zrillic was cut off, her mother explained, because the mother had already spent a lot of money on the daughter's education; other money had been spent because of "her promiscuous type of life. My daughter . . . has not shown or indicated the slightest affection or gratitude." The rest of the estate was left to the Shriners Hospital for Crippled Children. The daughter brought an action under the mortmain statute, but the Florida court struck it down: mortmain statutes, the court said, were a remnant of feudal times whose purpose was "to restrict the church's ability to acquire property." But nowadays "charitable gifts, devises and trusts . . . are favored." The statute "offended property interests" protected both by the Florida and the federal constitutions.[59]

Very logical. But no nineteenth-century court would have followed this logic. In the Pennsylvania case that found mortmain statutes offensive, the testator had left the bulk of the estate to be shared by "The American Heart Association; The American Cancer Society Incorporated; The American Foundation for the Blind; Boys Town of Boys Town Nebraska; and Zem Zem Hospital for Crippled Children, of Erie, Pennsylvania."[60] It is hard to think of these gifts as a threat to the public interest. Even more than the courts, legislatures turned against these statutes. In New York, a mortmain statute passed in 1860 made gifts above the statutory limit (half the estate) vulnerable to attack.[61] In 1929 the statute was amended; from that point on, only the immediate family—a "surviving husband, wife, child, descendant or parent" had the right to attack the "validity of a devise or bequest."[62]

And, as it turned out it was quite easy to get around the statute, even if there *were* close relatives who had a right to contest the will. Suppose a testator in New York wanted to leave his whole estate to charity. All the lawyer had to do was add a few words to the will. The will could specify that in the event the gift to charity was overthrown, then the estate would go instead to Mary, the testator's next-door neighbor; or to a second cousin; or to anybody outside the immediate family. The result was, then, that *nobody* could challenge the will. Mary could not bring the challenge; she, after all, was not a member of the family, and the statute did not allow her to contest. But neither could disinherited children bring a challenge. This is because, if they won, the money would go to Mary, not to them. Hence, under standard law, they had no standing—no right to sue—because they had no possible way to gain from a lawsuit. The gift, in other words, was unassailable. Of course, the contingent gift to Mary was merely a subterfuge. The courts could have seen through this trick, if they wanted to. They did not. They winked at the device and accepted it.[63] In a New York case, Bertha Fitzgerald left nothing to her son and left her whole estate to the Archbishopric of New York. Her will provided that, in the event that somebody tried to contest the will "on the basis of an excessive distribution to charity," then the estate would go to the Archbishop "individually, and not in any representative, fiduciary or ecclesiastical capacity." This was good enough to cut off the rights of Bertha's son.[64] This kind of decision sent a clear signal: courts disliked these statutes.[65] By the 1990's, mortmain statutes were on the verge of extinction—in New York, as well as in other states. Only three of these laws were left in the United States. By the beginning of the twenty-first century, there were none at all.

Charitable gifts and trusts in general had once been extremely unpopular, and the legal system reflected this. The mortmain statutes were no anomaly. They were part of a web of legal rules that discouraged gifts to charity. What legislators had in mind when they enacted these laws was curbing the power of the Catholic Church, or established churches in general, as I pointed out. As charity evolved and became a matter not only of churches, but of gifts to hospitals for crippled children, libraries, universities, and public parks, the old restrictions eroded and charities became "favorites of the law" instead of pariahs. I discuss this in more detail in the chapter on charitable trusts and foundations.

MISTAKES IN A WILL

To err is human. This is true for lawyers as well as for ordinary people. Lots of wills have mistakes in them—spelling errors, grammatical errors, ambiguities, words or whole paragraphs left out, words or whole paragraphs put in by mistake, and so on. Lawyers who draft wills proofread them carefully, for the most part; but inevitably mistakes creep in, through carelessness or sheer ignorance.

Standard doctrine once insisted that courts had absolutely no right or power to correct a mistake in a will. If a will left money to Milly instead of Billy because somebody's finger slipped and nobody caught the mistake, then Milly would get the money (if there was a Milly). Wills were to be read literally. Courts refused to listen to testimony, or admit evidence, which contradicted what the will itself said. Even if the lawyer who drafted the will admitted the mistake, and beat his breast and cried out "mea culpa," the will would stand as written. Take the case of *Mahoney* v. *Grainger*, decided in 1933 in Massachusetts. Helen Sullivan, an unmarried schoolteacher, 64 years old, went to a lawyer to make out a will. She gave him some instructions about gifts of money to this and that person. What about the rest of the property? Oh, she said, "I've got about twenty-five first cousins . . . let them share it equally." The lawyer made out a will that left the balance of the estate to Helen's "heirs at law" living at the time of her death. It turned out that Helen had one aunt still alive. She was the closest relative and the sole "heir at law." She got the whole estate. The lawyer testified (sheepishly, I suppose) that this was not what Helen wanted. She intended the money for her cousins, not her aunt. He, the lawyer, had made a mistake in drafting the will. But the cousins were out of luck.[66] The court stuck to the so-called "plain meaning" rule: you read the text as it is. Outside ("extrinsic") evidence that something else was meant, that somebody made a mistake, was simply not relevant.

The approach was somewhat different when the mistake resulted in an ambiguity rather than in some other kind of error. Suppose the will is just not clear, or its words admit of two different meanings. In this case, the law does allow evidence to show which meaning the testator intended. Some courts, quoting from old sources, felt that the law should distinguish between *patent* and *latent* ambiguities. No evidence should be heard to cure a patent ambiguity; but to cure a latent ambiguity a court could take in evidence to try to discover what the testator really wanted.

A patent ambiguity was a mistake that was obvious on the face of the will. In an old English case (1791), a Mrs. Hewit left some of her pictures to "Lady"   ; that is, the word "Lady" appeared in the will; but after the word "Lady" there was nothing but a blank space. There was plenty to suggest that Mrs. Hewit meant a certain Lady Hort, but the Lord Chancellor refused to hear evidence to that effect; he said "he could not supply a blank by parol evidence," and the gift failed.[67]

Nowadays, the distinction is pretty unimportant; courts seem willing to look at outside evidence, whether the ambiguity is patent or latent. Cora L. Black, who lived in Santa Clara County, California, died in 1957. Her handwritten will left her "entire Estate for Educational purposes" to the "University of Southern California known as the U.C.L.A." Here anybody reading the will is bound to ask: which university did she mean, USC or UCLA?[68] This looks like a patent ambiguity, but the appeal court never used this label; instead, it ordered the trial court to take evidence to find out what Cora actually meant.

When the will *seems* clear until you try to carry out its terms, you have a latent ambiguity. In a Louisiana case in 1987,[69] Wilds Bacot, a gay man, was admitted to a hospital in New Orleans, seriously ill. On a piece of paper he wrote the words "I leave all to Danny." A little while later, he went into a coma and died. Bacot seemed to have a special fondness for people named Danny. No fewer than three lovers named Danny appeared to claim a share of the estate. This ambiguity was latent; the will made sense on the surface, and if there had been only one Danny in Bacot's life there would have been no ambiguity at all. The ambiguity surfaced only when the personal representative started looking for Danny. In a case of this type, the court is willing to hear evidence and clear up the ambiguity. Which Danny was the right one? As it turned out, the answer was fairly obvious. One of the Danny's was a current partner; he had lived with Bacot for nine years; the two men shared "household chores and duties" and "maintained joint bank accounts."

In a California case in 1968, Georgia Hembree wrote out a holographic will "on a small card." She left "everything" to "Chester H. Quinn & Roxy Russell."[70] This seems plain enough, and pretty unambiguous—that is, until you find out that, although Chester H. Quinn was a close friend, "Roxy Russell" was not a human being at all. Roxy Russell was an Airedale dog; it "died after having had a fox tail removed from its nose" and was buried in a pet cemetery. Roxy was replaced by another dog, "registered with the American Kennel Club as 'Russel's [sic] Royal Kick Roxy.' " The court described the situation as one of "latent ambiguity." Just reading the will would not tell you that Roxy Russell was a dog. But what did the testatrix have in mind? Did she want Chester to get all the money, on condition that he took care of Roxy? Or did she really, literally, want Roxy to get half the estate? Under California law (and the law of other states), money cannot be left to a dog. This reading of the will would mean that Ms. Hembree, despite her best efforts, had died intestate as to half her estate. Her closest relative, a niece, would get that half. This, in fact, is what the court decided.[71]

One more example: in a Texas case,[72] Otto Holtquist, a Swedish-American with poor eyesight, executed a will that left $1,000 to "Alma Ring," identified as a child of his sister Annie. This seems perfectly clear until one learns that Alma Ring was Otto's sister, not his niece. He did, however, have a nephew named Elmer, who was Annie's son. The court saw this as a latent ambiguity. How to resolve it? Since Otto's eyes were so bad, it seemed likely that the will was read to him. "Alma" and "Elmer" sound fairly similar, especially to "people of Swedish descent," who (said the court) "had difficulty in pronouncing the vowels 'E' and 'A' according to their English pronunciation." A good deal of evidence suggested strongly that Otto wanted the money to go to Elmer, not Alma. Alma had won at the trial court level, but the appeals court reversed.

Courts, then, often corrected mistakes, so long as they could be classified as "ambiguities," sloppy draftsmanship that left the meaning of the text unclear. As far as other kinds of mistake were concerned, the courts could be quite rigid and inflexible. This was even true in cases where the testator (or his lawyer, rather) made a simple mistake in an address or the legal description of a piece of property—leaving behind, for example, a house at 546 Elm Street, which the testator did not own (his house was at 645, instead). The mistake seems obvious, and easily correctable; but some courts in the nineteenth century refused to do so.

Why was the law, especially in that century, so strict in its attitude toward mistakes, and so stubborn in refusing to listen to persuasive evidence of what the testator really wanted? Theoretically, the intent of the testator was the guiding star for interpreting a will. Courts said this over and over again. But the intent was a guide only insofar as it was clearly expressed in the will itself. This rule makes sense, if you think of the will as an important *recorded* document—as evidence in itself, for all time, of who got the dead man's property, and on what terms. In particular, this was crucial for dispositions of land—and, if you go back far enough in history, land was the property that mattered most. If a will says, I leave my estate to Milly, and I meant Billy, a person who consulted the will in the court records should be able to rely on the fact that Milly, not Billy, inherited. A fair number of old rules can be explained on this basis. Note that a *patent* ambiguity, by definition, is obvious on the face of the will. Nobody can be deceived by it. It is there in plain sight. This gives at least some color to the old distinction between the patent and the latent.

Recall that intestacy rules were also hard and fast. The world of the nineteenth century was a world of poor and deficient record-keeping. Legal and social policy strongly favored a vigorous land market, and one that functioned smoothly. Clear, clean title to property was extremely important. Nothing was worse than a "cloud" on a title. Wills and deeds were sources of title and had to be as pure and unambiguous as possible.

Perhaps there was also some kind of mystic reverence for the "last will and testament." But even if so, this mystic reverence might have been more an effect than a cause. As we shall see, wills today are less important than they used to be; will substitutes are sprouting like mushrooms; and the will itself has less social and economic meaning. Mystic reverence, such as it was, is now history.

THE LATEST NEWS

It is important to understand why, in the past, courts took such a hard line toward mistake. If my explanation is correct, then it is no surprise that the old rules are taking a beating in our times. Something is definitely happening, at least at the level of doctrine. Tough old standards are eroding. People used to say that hard cases made bad law; they meant by this that it was better to stick to a good rule, even if it led to a bad result, than to give in to sympathy. In fact, hard cases make good law, if these hard cases show us what is wrong with old and obsolete rules.

But what makes a rule obsolete, rather than simply "old"? As I noted, the importance of the will is declining; it has lost much of its monopoly on transfers in contemplation of death. Also, in the days of title insurance and computerized records, nobody relies as much as they used to on the text of a will. Thus we would expect the rules about mistakes to have come under severe pressure.

This is precisely what has happened. Since the late nineteenth century, there has been a clear trend in the law toward relaxing the rules. More and more, courts seem willing to correct mistakes in wills. They do not often say out loud that they are doing this, but they seem quite willing to go some way, to use some subterfuge, to reach this result. They tend to twist the old rules, or even abandon them outright.

This is, I should emphasize, a clear tendency; but it is by no means universal. One can easily find old cases that seem modern and new cases that seem troglodytic. It is certainly true, though, that the trend is in one direction: toward allowing mistakes to be corrected. One neat way to do this is to relabel what seems to be a mistake, plain and simple, as an "ambiguity." The court can then resolve the ambiguity. The Supreme Court was willing to do this in a case as far back as 1886.[73] James Walker died and left to his "dearly beloved brother, Henry Walker, forever, lot numbered six, in square four hundred and three," in the city of Washington. What he actually owned was lot three, in square four hundred and six. It was clear that the dead man wanted to leave this property to his brother. He left property to all his other relatives; and he thought he had disposed of his whole estate. All this evidence, said the court, "raises a latent ambiguity." This was, incidentally, a bare five-to-four decision, and the dissent remarked, quite logically, that there was no ambiguity here at all—it was simply a mistake, and mistakes were not supposed to be corrected.

Another alternative is for the court to dismiss the mistake as a "misdescription" or ignore wrong "details" in a will. In a Wisconsin case, old Mrs. Gibbs left some money to "Robert J. Krause, now of 4708 North 46th Street, Milwaukee, Wisconsin." There was indeed a man named Robert J. Krause who lived at that exact address. But he did not seem to know Mrs. Gibbs at all. He was, however, a part-time taxi driver, and he wondered if Mrs. Gibbs was an old lady who once rode in his cab, to and from a hospital, and talked to him at length. In any event, the will plainly named him, and gave his correct address. Naturally, then, he wanted the money.

But why would Mrs. Gibbs leave money to a cab driver, even a friendly one? In the will, she left a whole series of gifts to people who had been employees of the Gibbses, in their business. Mr. and Mrs. Gibbs had given their lawyer a list of these employees. It included "Bob"; and "Bob" referred to one Robert W. Krause, a long-time employee of the late Mr. Gibbs. Clearly, the lawyer who drafted the will had made a mistake. He looked up "Robert Krause" in the phone book and put down the wrong Robert Krause. It's easy to guess why Mrs. Gibbs never caught the mistake. She probably had no idea what Krause's middle initial was or where he lived. The court admitted that the will was not *actually* ambiguous. But the majority of the judges argued that "details of identification," such as "middle initials, street addresses and the like," are "highly susceptible to mistake" and should "not be accorded such sanctity as to frustrate an otherwise clearly demonstrable intent." The cab driver lost his case. Still, it took a decision of the highest court of Wisconsin to reach this result; and it was a split decision at that.[74]

More recent courts have sometimes acted in an even bolder fashion. It would be hard to imagine, for example, a worse blooper than signing the wrong will. In the 1950's, Vasil and Hellen Pavlinko (who spoke little or no English) executed reciprocal wills, but Vasil signed Hellen's will and Hellen signed Vasil's. When Vasil died, the Pennsylvania court refused to probate Hellen's will, which he had signed.[75] (Incidentally, the wills were signed in a lawyer's office, and the lawyer was one of the witnesses. A careless lawyer, to put it mildly.) Exactly the same situation came up in New York a generation later. Harvey and Rose Snide, "intending to execute mutual wills at a common execution ceremony," signed each other's wills by mistake.[76] Harvey died, and Rose offered for probate the will he had signed (actually hers). But this court refused to be "formalistic." The wills were identical except that where one said Harvey it meant Rose, and vice versa. The will was admitted to probate.

In a New York case in 2002,[77] Eugenia Herceg's will left the "rest, residue and remainder" of her estate to—nobody. The "name of the intended beneficiary" was "missing." An earlier will had left this remainder to a nephew, Sergio Pastorino, or, if he were dead, to his wife, Columba. The lawyer who drafted the will testified (no doubt with a very red face) that he had made a mistake. Some "lines from the residuary clause were accidentally deleted." Ms. Herceg had given him instructions to make the same distribution as in the earlier will. The court felt it had the right to fix the will, so as to "achieve the dominant purpose of carrying out the intention of the testator." The residuary clause was "construed" to "insert the name of Columba Pastorino as the beneficiary" (Sergio was already dead). Some courts have been hesitant to go this far—in a case from the District of Columbia in 1990, the lawyer left out the name of the chief beneficiary, and in fact the will named nobody at all to take the bulk of the money. The lawyer "submitted an affidavit to the trial court" admitting his mistake, and also provided notes of his conversation with the testator. But the Court of Appeals refused to budge.[78]

No doubt typos and other mistakes are common enough in wills. Rarely do they make much of a difference; and as we know, only a tiny percentage of wills are ever challenged in court. The case law does show a strong trend toward relaxing the formalities—at least somewhat. This is in line with what most academics have been pushing for. John Langbein, in an often-cited article, begins by saying that the "law of wills is notorious for its harsh and relentless formalism." He argues that "substantial compliance" with the laws concerning wills should be enough.[79] A few courts have taken him seriously. In one New Jersey case, for example, the two witnesses never signed the will itself; instead they signed something else, the so-called self-proving affidavit. The court upheld the will.[80] In England, a statute of 1982 provided that a court has the power to "rectify" a will, if "satisfied" that the will "fails to carry out the testator's intentions" because of a "clerical error" or "failure to understand his instructions."[81] There are reported cases that have arisen under this law, so it is obviously not a dead letter;[82] but one doubts it is used very often. The Uniform Probate Code, drafted by legal scholars, contains a section on "harmless error" (§2-503). If the "proponent" of a "document or writing" can prove "by clear and convincing evidence" that the dead person "intended the document or writing to constitute . . . the decedent's will," the document can be treated as if it complied with the formalities. This, potentially at least, goes a lot further than the idea of "substantial compliance." A number of states have taken up this section and made it part of their law. Some other common law jurisdictions (Queensland, Australia, for example) also follow such a rule.[83] How far the courts will carry this idea remains an open question.[84]

Legal scholars, of course, have noticed what is going on; they are pretty universally in favor of it; they draft new codes and statutes; and they tend to think of all of this change as part of a broad revolt against formalism throughout the legal system. There may well be something to this notion. But at least in *this* field—succession—I hate to pin the source of change on legal theory, or on some vague and general shift in ideology. To be sure, modern courts seem, in many ways, and in many fields of law, less rule-bound, more willing to make exceptions, to look at a specific situation, than they were in the past. In the law of succession we see this plainly: in attitudes toward holographs, in rules about execution of wills, and in the law about mistakes. But a change in legal culture calls for a specific explanation; and a vague reference to some sort of ideological change is simply not enough. And we must remember that not every branch of law is less formalistic than it used to be. Courts reviewing death sentences, for example, may be *more* formalistic than they were in the past. In the law of succession, what drives the motor of anti-formalism is perhaps the gradual but very marked change in the importance, and the role, of the classical will. It now has formidable rivals: the so-called will substitutes. We will take a look at some of those devices in Chapter 5.

CHAPTER 4

BREAKING A WILL

Will Contests and Their Social Meaning

Every probate code contains clauses on procedures for "breaking a will," that is, contesting it. These procedures are more or less elaborate. But in fact, very few wills are ever contested. All the studies of probate estates agree on this point. In a sample of wills in 367 estates in Dane County, Wisconsin, between 1929 and 1944, there were only six will contests.[1] A study of 7,638 wills, filed for probate in Davidson County, Tennessee, between 1976 and 1984, found that less than 1 percent of these were contested—sixty-six in all.[2] In San Bernardino in 1964, out of 342 testate files, some attempt was made to contest the will in only seven instances.[3] And these "will contests" found in the files did not all go to trial. Some of them settled out of court; others were simply dismissed or withdrawn. In the Davidson County sample, twenty-four of the sixty-six were settled out of court; ten were dismissed or withdrawn by the plaintiffs themselves; the court discarded another four. Less than half of the contests actually went to trial.

Some of these dismissals and withdrawals might, of course, disguise an out-of-court settlement that leaves no record behind. It is possible, too, that more wills are contested—or at least *objected* to—than the studies suggest. Every year there are surely thousands of men and women who are disappointed with somebody's will. Every year there are probably thousands of wills that somebody *could* conceivably contest. But the vast majority of disappointed and disgruntled heirs and legatees will in the end shrug their shoulders and get on with their lives. The disgruntled heir who goes to a lawyer with his story is likely to be told that he has no case, either because he has no right to contest, or because, although he has a *right*, he would probably lose the case.

The main reason, no doubt, that will contests are rare is quite simple: most wills seem fair and just. A widow dies, survived by three children, and she leaves her money to the three, in equal shares. Her money goes to those whom the law calls the "natural objects of her bounty." Nobody has any reason to object; and nobody does.

For wills that *can* be contested, there are some huge hurdles. One is social. Even if daddy's will *was* unfair, bringing a lawsuit might cause bitterness and alienate the rest of the family. No doubt thousands of families do disintegrate because of anger and disappointment that pivots on inheritance. But probably most families survive. Cost is another hurdle. A will contest can be expensive; and the risks are high. A third hurdle is the law itself. It puts many obstacles in the path of those who might want to contest.

Many wills also try to protect themselves with no-contest clauses. These are standard clauses that threaten to disinherit anybody who contests the will, or leave one dollar to anybody who does so, or words to that effect. Of course, if you contest a will successfully, the no-contest clause dies along with the will. And if the will left you nothing, you have nothing to lose. The clause *can* be effective, on the other hand, if the will left you *something*, but (in your opinion) not enough. Contesting the will could cost you the something, and you would end up with nothing at all.[4]

To contest a will, too, you have to have "standing." You cannot contest unless you would gain personally if the will failed, in whole or in part. If your father disinherited you, and you are an "heir-at-law" (someone who would be entitled to a share if your father died without a will), then you have "standing" (a right) to contest. So too if you were supposed to inherit money under an earlier will. If I leave money to my friend Joe in my will, then revoke the will and make out a new one in which I give Joe nothing, Joe has standing to contest the second will. This is because, if Joe succeeds in knocking out the new will, the clause revoking the old will dies along with it and the old will springs back to life. Joe will then be entitled to the money I left him in that will.

No doubt rules about standing have prevented thousands of people from trying to contest a will. Take the estate of Maude Straisinger, who died in 1964 in San Bernardino County, California. In one will she left all her money to charity and explicitly cut off her heirs. A later will left everything to two friends. A letter in the file from Mrs. Ester Moster, Maude's niece, reflects a certain amount of bitter disappointment: her aunt, she said, had made all sorts of (vague) promises, and Ester felt she and her husband "have been deprived of what should be ours." There is no follow-up in the file. Had Mrs. Moster gone to a lawyer, he would surely have told her: you have no case. There was, perhaps, a slim chance of defeating the most recent will. But even if she won on this point, that would simply resurrect the first will, which also left Ester out. For whatever reason—and there were many good reasons—Ester Moster gave up.[5]

One might guess, then, that will contests usually involve the big estates—estates worth fighting over. The Davidson County study does not exactly bear this out: there is no simple linear relationship between the size of the estate and the likelihood of a will contest. In Davidson County, twenty-three of the sixty-six contests were over estates of less than $50,000; another sixteen were over estates worth between $50,000 and $100,000.[6] These were hardly small estates, considering the period; but the very largest estates did not in fact produce any contests. This might be, as the study's author suggests, because the wills in the larger estates were carefully drafted and executed. On the other hand, historically there have been some flamboyant and spectacular contests—epic battles over huge estates. I will mention a few of these later.

In rare cases too, as we have seen, some long-lost heir or would-be heir shows up and demands a share of the estate. The estate of Ernest J. Torregano, in California, is an interesting case in point.[7] Torregano was born in New Orleans in 1882 into a "fairly large Negro family." Socially, that is, they were "Negroes," but Torregano was light-skinned enough to pass for white. In any event, he married a black woman, and they had a daughter, Gladys. Torregano worked as a railroad porter, traveling between New Orleans and San Francisco. Later he settled down in San Francisco, and did pass for white. He studied law and passed the bar. In 1915 his mother visited him and told him an enormous lie: that his wife and daughter were dead. She went back to New Orleans and told another big lie to the wife and daughter: that Ernest was dead. Probably she wanted to help her son, who was living successfully in white society; a black family in New Orleans would certainly be no help to his career. Torregano remarried, but had no children. The new wife died before him. In Torregano's will, he recited that he was a widower. His will had a standard no-contest clause: he left one dollar to anybody who might contest his will, or "assert any claim to share my estate by virtue of relationship." In any event, somehow the news of his recent death reached his daughter in New Orleans, who came forward and claimed a share of the estate. The California Supreme Court, in 1960, held that she had a case; the no-contest clause was not meant to apply to a person in her position (so the Court said).

Ordinarily, of course, the contestant is not a missing or unknown heir, but a grumbling and disappointed one. A survey of estate litigators suggested that the most common type of contestant was children of the deceased—siblings who "go to war. They have no loyalty to each other or to their family."[8] The second most common source was "reconstituted families"—divorces and second marriages. In 1983, Seward Johnson, one of the heirs to the Johnson & Johnson pharmaceuticals fortune, left the bulk of his enormous estate to his third wife, Basia, a woman who was younger than his children from an earlier marriage. A huge will contest followed, which, as we will see, ended in a kind of split decision.[9] In the United States, family ties seem less strong than in many other countries. There are societies in which third cousins feel joined by a powerful bond; but in the United States in the twenty-first century, even brothers and sisters are often estranged from each other. The marriage bond is still a mighty force; but the divorce rate is also extremely high.[10] Contemporary will contests reflect this weakness in traditional family structure, and the complexities of the structures that replaced it.

Even if you have standing to contest, you must have a valid legal reason. That the will was unfair, mean, or unjust is simply not (formally) a reason. Another non-reason, for the most part, is that the will fails to reflect what the dead person actually wanted to do. This might be perfectly true: it might be obvious that he or she planned a new will and never got around to it. The courts on the whole refuse to listen to arguments about intention, or to receive any evidence of it, unless there was an actual will. The plots of countless mysteries and detective stories turn on this fact. Somebody killed the old lady because she was about to change her will. Or somebody pushed the mean old uncle's wheelchair down the stairs just before he signed a fateful codicil. What these stories reflect is a general awareness of a basic legal fact: it is one thing to change your mind, quite another to change your will. It is also difficult—though getting less so—to attack a will, or part of a will, on the grounds that somebody (often the lawyer) made a typographic error or a similar mistake.

FORGERY, FRAUD, AND OTHER CLAIMS AGAINST A WILL

On what basis, then, can you contest a will? You can say that it is not the dead man's will at all, that the will was a forgery. This is not a very common claim. There was, however, the lurid case of William Marsh Rice, who died at 84 in New York City, in 1900. Diarrhea, brought on by eating too many bananas, supposedly did him in. The more likely story is that Rice's young valet, Charlie Jones, killed him with chloroform. A lawyer, Albert Patrick, had allegedly engineered this plot after forging a will that left the lawyer much of the money.[11] And in Chicago, in a sensational trial in 1892, Dr. Henry Martyn Scudder, a minister of the gospel, was accused of forging a will for his mother-in-law and murdering her as well. Scudder died in a cell, an apparent suicide.[12]

Another notable case involved Howard Hughes, the eccentric billionaire who died in 1976. Hughes evidently had no immediate family, and nobody was able to find his will, if he had one.[13] Soon, however, a holographic will, supposedly signed by Hughes, appeared in Salt Lake City.[14] This, the so-called "Mormon will," left money to the Mormon Church, to the "Hughes Medical Institute of Miami," to various universities and charities, and to certain individuals, including one Melvin Dummar. Dummar, who was once a gas station attendant in Utah, told an odd story: one winter night, he picked up an old man in Nevada and gave him a ride into Las Vegas. The man told Melvin he was Howard Hughes. Two juries, one in Las Vegas and one in Los Angeles, decided the will was a forgery.[15] Was Dummar the forger? He denied it and managed to stay out of jail. But instead of inheriting millions, he had to become a humble fish salesman in Salt Lake City; later, he flipped hamburgers in Gabbs, Nevada.[16]

Who, then, would get Hughes's vast estate? After the Dummar debacle, a small army of men and women rushed in to claim the estate—more than five hundred in all, most of them claiming some sort of blood relationship with Hughes. Several women insisted they had married him secretly. Years of legal entanglement went by; since Hughes was now officially intestate, the question was: who were his closest living relatives? Most of the claimants ended up with nothing. Relatives who were second and third cousins lost out; as two authors put it, they were like "people with lottery tickets one number short of the winning number."[17] In the end, certain relatives—and certain lawyers—did reap a harvest from this estate.

Fraud is another basis for contesting a will. But this too is a rare claim, and rarely successful. The books and the cases talk about "fraud in the inducement," and "fraud in the execution." Fraud in the inducement means "willfully false statements of fact," which are "intended to deceive testator, which do deceive him, which induce him to make a will, and without which he would not have made such a will."[18]

An old Indiana case from 1896 is a good example of what sorts of things are at least *alleged* to be fraud in the inducement.[19] Godlove Orth was married twice. William was his son by the first marriage. He had two children with his second wife, Mary Ann. He left his estate to Mary Ann. But he also gave her a letter, in which he told her, "act justly towards yourself and towards all my children." And, he went on, when she died, "what is left give to all the children alike." But Mary Ann left everything to *her* two children, and nothing to William. William died soon after Mary Ann. His heirs, naturally, were angry and disappointed; and they raised a number of claims, including a claim of fraud. They argued that Mary Ann had tricked Godlove. She talked him into leaving her everything, in exchange for a promise that she would take care of William in her own will. She broke her promise; and this, they claimed, amounted to fraud in the inducement. But courts are very reluctant to accept this kind of argument; and these disappointed heirs lost the case.

Lies about the will itself—the document—which induce the testator to "execute an instrument of whose nature or contents he is ignorant," constitute fraud in the execution.[20] In one case from 1893, the "will" was executed by a woman who was 94 years old, desperately ill, under the influence of sedatives, and "so debilitated that she could neither read nor write."[21] This so-called will left everything to her nephew, who drew it up and got her to sign it. Unlike older wills, it left nothing to her husband and brother. The judge was convinced that the old lady had no idea she was signing a will; she thought she was putting her signature on a paper about her burial wishes. Hence, in his judgment a "fraud" had been "perpetrated" and the will should be denied probate.

The cases on "fraud" often involve old, feeble people. Some of them seem really to be cases of undue influence, or lack of competency—issues I discuss later in this chapter. In any event, there are no more than a handful of fraud cases on the books; and even fewer were successful. We have no information about litigation that never gets past the trial court level; but the cases are obviously exceedingly rare. No study of probate files ever mentions fraud as an issue of any particular importance.

A disappointed heir can also contest a will by claiming it was not properly executed. The statutes set out requirements for a valid will, and they have to be followed. In fact, very few wills have fatal flaws. There are, however, plenty of decisions on technicalities: whether the witnesses and the testator are in each other's "presence," whether the signature was in the right place, whether the will was properly signed, and so on. Enough decisions, in short, to provide editors of casebooks with plenty of material to fill their pages. Still, such cases represent a tiny minority of contested wills, itself a tiny minority of wills filed in court. In fact, over 99% of all wills *are* properly executed. This is almost always true when a lawyer is involved. Complying with the statutes is not rocket science. If you follow a few simple rules when the client comes in to sign his will, there is almost no chance of making a mistake. Any lawyer, unless he is utterly incompetent, can guarantee, with close to 100% assurance, that a document she prepared, and which was signed and witnessed in the office, was properly done. Besides, as today's courts become more indulgent, it is getting harder to break a will by showing some minor flaw in execution.

Where does that leave our disappointed heir? What grounds can he possibly have? Imagine the scene in the lawyer's office. The disinherited son is hurt, frustrated, angry. What, nothing was left to me? That has to be wrong! There must be something I can do. Fraud, forgery, bad execution—none of these will work. Is nothing left? Yes, the lawyer could say to him. Two grounds are left. These are, by far, the most common grounds for attacking a will: lack of capacity, and undue influence. Very often, the contestant throws both of these into his claim. In the Davidson County study, there were sixty-six will contests; undue influence was alleged in forty-nine of them, lack of capacity in forty-eight. In twenty-nine cases, *both* were advanced as grounds of contest.[22]

Lack of Capacity

"Lack of capacity" means either that you are too young to make out a will or are, to put it bluntly, too deranged or demented to do so. Too young is almost never grounds for a contest. The statutes typically say that you have to be an adult to execute a will. In Georgia, for some reason, a person is mature enough to make out a will before he or she is mature enough to marry or drive a car. Under the statute, anybody who is 14 or older can become a testator.[23] But you either are or are not underage—the test is biology, not maturity, or even legal emancipation. Not many young people are in the habit of making out a will.

Insanity or dementia is another question. Most testators are elderly, many are in wretched health, and all of them are human. It is so easy to claim the testator was delusional, suffered from senile dementia, or was otherwise out of her mind; incapable, therefore, of making a valid will. There are literally hundreds of reported cases on testamentary capacity. Thousands more, judging by newspaper accounts, may lie hidden in the files. The reported cases, on the whole, tell pathetic and demeaning stories about old people. Dr. A. H. Marshall died in Missouri in 1968; he left an estate of half a million dollars, almost all of which he wanted to go to a list of charities. His daughter contested the will. A thousand pages of transcript detailed Dr. Marshall's oddities: he thought he talked directly to God; sometimes, when he talked about these conversations, "his face would get red, his eyes would bug out . . . he would slobber and shout"; he once came to visit a friend at a factory, dressed in "nothing but his nightgown and his house shoes . . . he was talking about a rash on his body and opened his housecoat and exposed his private parts to the female secretary." The trial court denied probate; and the appeal court affirmed.[24] Edgar E. Duryea was "known in New York as a man of probity, a millionaire manufacturer, a shrewd and conservative businessman"; but he was "hardly more than cold in the grave" when the "family skeleton came tumbling out of its closet" in the New York Surrogate's Court in 1900, and "his own daughters pilloried [him] in open court as an imbecile and a habitual drunkard for years."[25] In the contest over the will of Mrs. Florence Pratt, a rich heiress of the Singer Sewing Machine fortune, in 1934, Mrs. Pratt's sister claimed she was "of unsound mind" when she drew up her will. Mrs. Pratt left money to some relatives and to a motley crew of others, including a saleswoman in a Paris corset shop and "another Parisian corsetière"; but she excluded the sister. Part of the evidence (according to the sister's lawyer) was this: a doctor told her that her husband, Henry Pratt "was not to be given a tub bath when he had been seriously ill"; but "she had placed her husband under a shower and turned on hot water, causing him to scream for help."[26]

People today are living longer than in the past; and alas, many of them lose touch with reality as the years go by. Some suffer from Alzheimer's; others suffer from more flamboyant delusions. In July 2007, the *Times* of London reported the sad case of Branislav Kostic, a "pharmaceutical mogul," who left his entire estate (of some £10 million) to the Conservative Party. Kostic, his son claimed, believed he was the victim of a "devilish organisation" with "three monster ladies," that a vice ring was trying to poison him, and that only Margaret Thatcher and her party could save the world from a dark international conspiracy.[27]

Many of these cases make depressing reading, but not only because the testator seems so pathetic and deranged. If Kostic's son was telling the truth, old Kostic had truly gone off the tracks. But the cases are not always so clear-cut. The stories they tell are often stories less of incapacity than of the disgusting greed of some family members who contest the will. Disappointed heirs dredge up whatever evidence they can about human frailty and the ravages of age. Alas, the ravages of age are real enough. And is there anybody, old or young, totally lacking in quirks and peculiarities? Probably not. Thus, no will is really 100% secure; any will can be attacked on the grounds that the testator lacked capacity. Of course, if, like Dr. Marshall, you publish an article in a newspaper that says, "I am that prophet that Moses and all the other prophets have spoken about. I am the Messiah," it can hardly come as a surprise that disappointed heirs might claim you were crazy.

A few bizarre cases also turn on the concept of "insane delusion." The idea here is that the testator, though not totally out of his mind, has one mad idea, an idea completely irrational; this delusion has taken over his brain, in such a way as to affect his last will and testament. There are two common types of "delusion." One, according to Thomas Reed, might be called "They're Out to Get Me"; these are "cases in which the testator believes that someone in his family is out to do him or her harm"; the other type consists of "Crank" cases, where the testator "holds eccentric, bizarre or strange religious, scientific or political views."[28] Dorothy Killen, of Arizona, fell into the first category. She thought that two of her nephews and a niece "lived in her attic . . . and sprinkled chemicals and parasites down on her, put her to sleep and then pulled a tooth out and cut her arms and hands with glass"; also that they "were in the Mafia and were trying to kill her so they could take her property." She cut these relatives off, leaving them $1 each; but they successfully contested the will.[29] In other cases, the argument is that the testator, against all reason, believed his wife was cheating on him, or his children were stealing from him, or the like. Frank Honigman, who died in 1956, was obsessed with the idea his wife was blatantly and luridly unfaithful, that she was "hiding male callers in the cellar . . . in various closets, and under the bed," that she was "hauling men from the street up to her . . . bedroom by use of bed sheets," and so on. Honigman left his wife a life interest in some of his property, and gave all the rest to brothers and sisters. The wife, Florence, contested the will; a jury in the court of the Surrogate of Queens County, New York, decided that Frank Honigman lacked a "sound and disposing mind and memory." The will was thrown out, and the Court of Appeals of New York upheld this decision.[30]

Dorothy Killen's will and Frank Honigman's both failed; but many (most?) claims of insane delusion do not achieve their goal. My impression is that appellate courts have been cool or hostile toward these claims. At least this is what the reported cases suggest. When the probate court denies probate on the grounds of insane delusion, the appeal courts usually reverse. And when the probate court allows probate, the appellate court affirms. In an old Indiana case, *Addington v. Wilson* (1854), the testator, Francis Stephen, had an unhappy marriage, which nonetheless produced five children.[31] The wife was dead, and he had quarreled with some of his children. There was evidence Francis thought his wife was a witch, and "at her death, she had left her witch-sticks to her children," which is why they treated him badly. Both trial and appellate court thought the real reason for the disinheritance was "harsh, undutiful conduct" by the daughters. The appeal court added this deep thought: "From the visits of the angels to Lot . . . down to this time when the spirits, like Poe's stately midnight raven, come gently rapping, rapping at the chamber doors of modern mediums," many people have "believed in spiritual existences, some being good and some evil." Believing in witches, then, was not such an odd idea—at any rate, not odd enough to overturn a will. In another case, a man left his estate to the Society for the Prevention of Cruelty to Animals. The testator believed that the souls of people, when they die, cross over into animals; but this belief in "the transmigration of souls, or the doctrine of metempsychosis," was not enough to overturn his will.[32]

Any will is vulnerable, as I said. But how vulnerable? As just suggested, not very. Newspapers are eager to print bizarre or intriguing stories about will contests, especially if the dead person was rich or famous. But such accounts can be misleading. When all is said and done, it is easy to claim the testator lacked capacity, and hard to convince a judge or jury that this is true. The courts have to draw a line between people who are somewhat eccentric and those who, at least in the eyes of contemporaries, would be considered downright insane. And of course conventional standards of the times determine what is considered insanity or depravity.[33] The courts repeat certain stock doctrines endlessly. But in truth, the cases turn on their particular facts. Contests usually fail; still, results are not always predictable. There are cases where the testator seems senile, or a lunatic, or hopelessly drunk and befuddled, or even an inmate of a mental institution; and yet the will passes muster. Courts routinely state that a person does not need much in the way of brain cells to make out a will. The "test" for testamentary capacity is not the same as the "test" for the capacity to enter into a contract, or to function very well at all (financially speaking). Some cases seem to stretch this point to the limit. The court can always say that the testator made out the will during a "lucid moment." In a Georgia case, the testator, Burton Anderson, had been declared "both insane and incompetent" by the Veterans Administration. The witnesses claimed he was "perfectly sane," which was surely not true. The court pointed out that it was "well-settled law that a lunatic during a lucid interval may make a will. . . . The weak have the same rights as the strongminded to dispose of their property."[34] Courts have upheld, at times, wills of hopeless alcoholics, drug users, and people who seemed really weird. In a Pennsylvania case in 1882, the court considered the validity of David Dougal's will. Dougal died at the age of 101; before making out the will, he had had a "paralytic stroke . . . his mind and memory were very much enfeebled"; he was blind, "very filthy and even obscene in his habits," and spent most of his time sleeping. The will survived.[35]

On the other hand, in other cases the will fails, even though the testator seems nothing worse than odd or a bit eccentric. In a Wisconsin case, from 1920, John Shanks had committed suicide. He had been married more than fifty years. In his declining years, he "became the victim of the insane delusion that his wife was criminally intimate with a neighbor." Shanks was adjudged insane and sent to a state asylum, but later "adjudged sane" and released. In his will he admits that he had a "violent temper and a jealous disposition." He admits, too, that he had "wrongfully accused" his wife of "infidelity. . . . I am sorry I made those statements. . . . I have no feeling of enmity or jealousy against my good wife." He left her a life interest in his homestead and some money; but the balance went to nephews and nieces. The trial court threw out the will as the product of an insane delusion, and the Supreme Court of Wisconsin agreed. A "sane man" would have left everything to his wife, who needed the money.[36]

Undue Influence

The rather strange notion of undue influence is often paired in the cases with testamentary capacity. Undue influence has been defined as "the exercise of acts or conduct by one person toward another person" with the result that "the mind of the latter is subjugated to the will of the person seeking to control it."[37] This conjures up an image of some kind of Svengali, mesmerizing a person who then makes out a will in some sort of hypnotic trance. Or the image of some poor, weak creature kept in slavery to a dominant personality. The cases, however, and there are literally hundreds of them, tell a more mundane story. They are typically about very old people, weak in mind and body. Disappointed relatives attack the will, claiming that somebody (a housekeeper, a relative, a neighbor, a trophy wife, a girlfriend, or a gay lover) took advantage of Grandma or Grandpa and inveigled him or her into leaving money to the undue influencer. Many of the cases are about "unnatural" wills (wills that disinherit close relatives); undue influence is "presumed," too, if the alleged Svengali stood in a "confidential relationship" to the deceased. So, if a person suddenly cuts off his relatives and leaves almost everything to his doctor, lawyer, priest, guardian, or the like, the will may be in trouble. The influence, of course, has to be "undue." If an old man executes a will leaving all his money to his housekeeper, who is in the room hectoring and badgering him, that situation will seem exceedingly suspicious to a court. But if it's his wife in the room hectoring and badgering, and he leaves her everything, this is much less likely to be considered "undue" influence. It is influence of course, but not "undue." As an old treatise put it, there is no "presumption of undue influence," even though the wife "procured" the will "by her solicitation and importunity," even though she was the sole beneficiary, cut out children of a former marriage, and even if the husband might be "of yielding disposition and disposed to follow the guidance of his wife."[38]

There are exceptions, to be sure. This general statement, about wives and their influence, does not hold quite so true for second wives, especially if the will disinherits the children from a former marriage. One notable example of this situation was the epic contest over the will of Seward Johnson, mentioned earlier. Johnson, a fairly wretched specimen of humanity, was heir to a vast fortune (which he, personally, had done absolutely nothing to accumulate). His main contribution to humanity was to father six children. When he was already elderly, his roving eye fell upon a young, pretty woman, Basia Piasecka, an immigrant from Poland, who worked in his house as a maid. She became his mistress, and then his wife. Johnson was then in his late seventies. She was more than forty years younger than her husband. They lived together for about twelve years, more or less happily; then he died and in his will left a gigantic fortune to Basia Johnson. The children contested the will, although Seward Johnson had set up trust funds for them years earlier. They claimed that Basia had exercised "undue influence" over Johnson. A nasty and lurid trial followed, in which absolutely everybody, including the judge, came out looking bad. Ultimately, the parties reached a settlement. But most of the money stayed with Basia Johnson.[39]

Sometimes it is the widow who complains of undue influence. Billie Jean Hamm tried to set aside her husband's will, which left most of his estate to nursing homes and other charities in Custer, South Dakota, where they lived. Billie Jean was not exactly your ordinary grieving widow. She married Robert Hamm when he was 72 and she was less than half his age. She was, in fact, a prostitute; and after the wedding, at one point she took off "for other climes with his car and a portion of his money." Moreover, at the time the will was executed, Billie Jean was facing a murder charge—she was accused of having a hand in the killing of Robert's son, who had been murdered on his ranch. It was not much of a surprise that her claim did not get very far.[40]

Stepchildren do not hesitate to sue a stepmother; but there have even been instances where children accused their own mother of "undue influence."[41]

Much more common are cases where the battle is between brothers and sisters. An "unnatural" will may be dangerous, but so is a lopsided will, leaving more money to one child than to another. Thomas J. Reed, in an article published in 1981, analyzed sixty-three reported cases of undue influence in Indiana.[42] Thirteen were "David and Bathsheba" cases, similar to Basia Johnson's; in these, children of a dead or discarded wife accused the new wife of getting her doddering husband to leave the money to her and not to the kids. No fewer than twenty-six were "Esau and Jacob" cases—that is, squabbles between the testator's children—brother against brother, or sister against sister, or the like. In nine more, the "undue influencer" was the testator's relative—a brother or sister, or a niece or nephew. Nine cases were "Uriah Heep" cases, cases involving "importuning professional persons"—chiefly doctors or lawyers. Finally, six were "Mary Worth" cases—where the "undue influencer" was a "non-professional friend of the family who intervened as helper and counselor to the testator" and ended up with a big chunk of the estate.

At one time, a number of cases of undue influence reflected the fantasy of the evil priest. In 1890 the children of John Sparks, a "wealthy Perth Amboy man," contested his will. He left his residuary estate to Father Connolly, of the local Catholic Church; Father Connolly had drawn up the will and named himself executor. This, it was alleged, constituted undue influence.[43] Newspaper accounts describe contests of wills leaving money to unpopular churches—Christian Science, for example. The treatises still *say* that gifts to priests and ministers raise a suspicion of undue influence. But the old animus against the wicked priest seems almost extinct. My impression is that, despite a few recent examples, cases of undue influence involving the clergy have become quite rare.[44]

Claims of undue influence, as I said, often go hand in hand with claims of lack of capacity. They show the same tendency to dredge up evidence of weird and pathetic behavior. A good example is *Olsen* v. *Corporation of New Melleray*, an Iowa case decided in 1953.[45] Old man Feeney was unmarried. He left most of his estate to the Society for the Propagation of the Faith, and little or nothing to two nieces and a nephew. They contested the will, claiming the society had exercised undue influence through some of its agents. Part of their case consisted in showing Feeney's "weak mental condition," which made him more vulnerable to this kind of "influence." One niece testified that he failed to recognize her when she visited; that he was "cross and irritable"; that he "dressed for church by removing one dirty shirt and putting on another; that he had a silly grin on his face"; and that his "living conditions were deplorable, dirty and unkempt." At a funeral he was "spitting on the floor." A neighbor farmer added more delectable details: "his eyes . . . had a starey look to them." He refused to eat "anything that wasn't cooked. Water he drank had to be out of the barrel, not out of the fresh water spout"; he "wiped off the nose of hogs before ringing them." An appellate court held that there was enough evidence to go to the jury on the issue of undue influence, and the will failed.

WILL CONTESTS IN SOCIAL CONTEXT

As we have seen, there are some limits to freedom of testation written into the statute books or developed in case law. Perhaps only men or women who die unmarried or widowed, with an estate of some respectable size, really do have total freedom of testation. Even that person has to be careful if he or she is old and sick, if the will is "unnatural," or if it favors one child over another. Lopsided wills can lead to bitter family quarrels. Of course, brothers and sisters, in this society, are quite capable of hating each other fervently for all sorts of reasons. But a skewed will can make a bad situation worse. Doctrines like undue influence open the door a crack for disgruntled heirs, especially when the testator is old and feeble.

The layman often imagines that the world of the law consists of clear, binding, and unambiguous rules. In fact, the legal system is riddled with loopholes and leeways of all sorts, some explicit, some implicit. Undue influence is only one of many devices that give courts (and juries) a little bit of wiggle room. The good news is flexibility; the bad news is that the doctrines are applied sporadically, and somewhat irrationally. Whether a court actually finds undue influence depends on the facts of each case—plus social norms and the court's own prejudices and opinions. The cases thus are very dependent on time and place.

For example, a hotly contested case of "undue influence" in the first half of the nineteenth century involved the will of one William Farr of South Carolina. The case went up to the Court of Appeals of South Carolina no fewer than three times over a five-year period.[46] Farr had "lived for many years in a state of illicit intercourse with a mulatto woman, his own slave, who assumed the position of a wife." The slave, Fan, gave birth to a son, Henry, "who was acknowledged by the testator as his son."[47] Farr left his entire estate to W. P. Thompson and appointed him executor, but with the understanding that Thompson would use the assets on behalf of Fan and Henry. The heirs-at-law battled on and on, claiming that Fan had exercised undue influence on Farr. They persuaded a jury to throw out the will; but in the end, they lost the case on appeal.

Farr's will did prevail, then, but only after a monumental struggle. At all stages, the evidence of undue influence was thin to the point of vanishing. What gave the heirs-at-law their chance was behavior that would hardly raise an eyebrow today. But this behavior was, after all, deeply offensive to genteel society in South Carolina during the age of slavery. Leaving money to a slave mistress was risky business in the antebellum South. As recently as the 1960s it was also risky business to leave the bulk of an estate to a mistress, of any color, or even worse, to a gay partner. In a Colorado case from 1935, Samuel Braden, a childless widower, 60 years old, left the bulk of his estate to Mrs. Lamborn, his mistress, rather than to his sister and his nephew. The will failed on the grounds of undue influence. The appeals court felt that "unlawful intimacy" raised a "presumption" of undue influence.[48] In a 1964 New York case, *Matter of Kaufman*, Robert D. Kaufmann left the bulk of his estate, not to his brother and other relatives, but to Walter A. Weiss, his housemate and probably his lover.[49] This was a case (said the court) of undue influence, "insidious, subtle and impalpable . . . which subverts the . . . will of the testator." The will was denied probate. By 1996, however, times had changed. In a Texas case, Jack Knickerbocker made out a will for the benefit of Carl May, described rather prissily in the case as Knickerbocker's "lifemate" of some thirty years. This will withstood attack.[50]

The same general point can be made about lack of capacity. What is considered obviously crazy in one period may not seem so abnormal in another. As we said, lack of capacity is probably the single most common grounds for attacking a will. It is impossible to tie all the cases into a single neat package, or even a few neat packages. What is clear is that this concept, too, opens the door—at least slightly—to attacks on wills that are "unnatural" or lopsided. In Georgia, the testator has the right to leave his "entire estate to strangers, to the exclusion of his spouse and children"; but up until 1998, the statute added that, if he did so, the "will should be closely scrutinized" and probate should be refused "upon the slightest evidence of aberration of intellect, collusion, fraud, undue influence or unfair dealing."[51]

This language goes a lot further than the cases tend to go; but it does say openly what some of the case law implies. Mental condition is not always easy to assess. To be sure, some cases are fairly clear. There are people who are obviously crazy, or so ravaged by senile dementia that they cannot possibly make a valid will. Millions of people, on the other hand, are (or seem to be) perfectly in command of themselves and not the least bit crazy. How one judges the people in the middle is another story. Courts are clearly influenced by whether the will is "unnatural," and also by their attitudes and prejudices. Consider the case of Louisa Strittmater, whose will was litigated in New Jersey in 1947.[52] Her doctor—a female general practitioner—testified that she "suffered from paranoia of the Bleuler type of split personality." Louisa was unmarried. She did volunteer work for the National Women's Party and left her money to the party. In 1938 she wrote that her father "was a corrupt, vicious and unintelligent savage, a typical specimen of the majority of his sex. Blast his wormstinking carcass"; she also described her mother as a "Moronic she-devil." A master at the trial court level referred to her "morbid aversion to men," and described her as a woman who carried her "feminism to a neurotic extreme." She did exhibit some peculiar behavior—she killed a pet kitten—but according to testimony, she was "entirely reasonable and normal" in her dealings with her bank and her lawyer. Probate of her will was denied. The court talked about her "paranoic condition," and her "insane delusions" about men. Louisa was, no doubt, hardly the picture of mental health; but her unpopular opinions must have played a role in the decision. Would this case come out the same way today? Somehow I doubt it.

We can, in other words, find cases where we think the court is straining: it is stretching a point so as to throw out a will on the grounds of incapacity. Yet there are many cases where the opposite can be said. As I mentioned, courts have upheld wills, even though the testator had hallucinations, behaved very erratically, or had even been formally declared incompetent. In a California case in 1936, Lorenzo D. Wright had died at the age of 69. Wright had been "engaged in driving a garbage wagon in the city of Venice." He owned two pieces of real estate, one of which he left to a woman friend, and the other to his daughter and granddaughter. They nonetheless contested the will. A notary had drawn up the will. The notary, and both witnesses, said they thought Wright was "of unsound mind." A Mrs. Brem testified that she too thought he "was not right." Once he gave her a fish soaked in kerosene. Her husband added that Wright "often chased the children out of his yard and turned the hose on them." A cousin voiced the view that Wright was "unsound in mind." Sometimes he ran out of the house "only partly dressed"; he "picked up paper flowers from the garbage cans, and waste, and pinned them on rose bushes." The trial court denied probate. But the appeal court reversed—rather angrily, one feels. "Testamentary capacity cannot be destroyed by showing a few isolated acts, foibles, idiosyncrasies," unless they "directly bear upon and have influenced the testamentary act." The testimony in the case was "trivial"; and the will should have been sustained.[53]

What seems clear is that there are chinks in the armor of the law of succession. Doctrine appears smooth and orderly, but underneath the surface, there were always unwritten rules and hidden leeways. The wills of people who violated social norms were at risk. There were, generally speaking, no *rules* against leaving money to a mistress, or cutting off one's children and giving the money to a friend or to charity; but most people did what society expected them to. Judges (and juries, when they were involved) could "find" facts in such a way as to reach the result they wanted; or stretch a point here and there. "Unnatural" wills were more liable to be overturned than "natural" wills. A ragbag of doctrines and presumptions tilted the scales against "unnatural" wills. Not that there was any consistency (as far as we can tell). Wills that violated social norms were certainly vulnerable; but the word "vulnerable" is not a synonym for "doomed."

How different, then, is the law in the early twenty-first century? It is different in two ways: first, the norms have changed. What once looked extremely risky (a white man leaves money to a black woman; a gay man leaves money to his partner) is much less risky today. And the *formal* law too has changed. The leeways, more and more, have come out of the closet. Besides, here too the decline of the will has left a mark; it is no longer the crown jewel of succession. For this reason, among others, its doctrines have lost their smooth finish. More and more, they are pockmarked with all manner of exceptions.

CHAPTER 5

WILL SUBSTITUTES

EVERY YEAR, thousands and thousands of wills are probated. To be sure, many people die without leaving any money behind; and many others die without a will. In Ward and Beuscher's study of Wisconsin deaths and probates, from 1929 to 1944, only 42% of the people who died had probate estates. And of those who did, only 47% had made out a will.[1] Since then, the percentage of testate estates has gone up. In San Bernardino, California, in 1964, about two-thirds of the estates were testate, one-third intestate.[2] In Bucks County, Pennsylvania, in 1979, 59% of the deaths produced an estate and 36% of the decedents left a will; there was a will in a majority of the estates that actually went through probate.[3]

For many people, then, the will was and is a significant document. But even though more people who die have wills, the actual significance of wills has been going down. And this is true even though the country is incomparably richer than it was, say, 150 years ago; there is more wealth, and there are more wealthy people. The will once had a virtual monopoly over gifts at death. This is no longer the case. The rise of will substitutes has, in turn, affected the law of wills itself. This is probably a key reason why the law of wills has become less formal and formalistic. After all, now one can draw up a document that looks like a will, sounds like a will, and acts like a will, but isn't a will. This document will not need witnesses, a ceremony, and the whole hocus-pocus surrounding the ordinary will. If so, then it is natural to ask if there is any point in insisting so rigidly on all the formalities and the hocus-pocus. We have seen the power of this argument already in discussing the growing tendency to correct mistakes in wills.

Of course, realistically, there have always been will substitutes. You can, after all, simply give your money away when you get older. Or, if you are a farmer, you can give one of yours sons your land in exchange for a promise to take care of you in your old age. Arrangements of this kind were well known in the past. A "contract" of this sort is, to be sure, not a will; it is essentially a promise to make a will; and whether it was binding was always an issue. Hendrik Hartog has discovered "hundreds, perhaps thousands" of cases, between the middle of the nineteenth and the middle of the twentieth century in which family members claimed property on the basis of an oral promise. The promise, it was alleged, was conditional: if you work for the old man or take care of the old woman, and give up other opportunities, the testator will make it worth your while. Many of those who filed claims based on such promises won their cases.[4]

TRUSTS

The trust—or to be more precise, a certain kind of trust—is one of the most important of the will substitutes. A trust is a legal arrangement in which certain assets—land, money, stocks and bonds—are put in the hands of a trustee, who manages the assets and has control over them, but who exercises his powers on behalf of one or more beneficiaries.

The trust has quite ancient roots in England and goes back to the Middle Ages. It is one of the more distinctive features of English law, and of common law systems in general. There is no exact equivalent in civil law countries. Historically, the rise of the trust depended on one very odd feature of English law: the existence of courts of chancery, courts that administered what came to be called *equity*. From the Middle Ages on, in England, two quite separate court systems coexisted, more or less side by side. In one system, the ordinary court system, the judges administered the rules of the common law. But in the chancery courts, the courts of equity, the judges ("chancellors") followed entirely different rules. Procedures in equity, too, were completely different from common law procedures. Equity procedure resembled the procedure in continental Europe. There was, for example, no jury in courts of equity. Equity was (in theory at least) more "equitable" than the common law—fairer, more flexible, more sensible. It began as a way to grant relief to litigants who were unfairly impaled on the horns of some rigid and inflexible legal rule. Equity developed its own, rather competitive rules; these, in the course of time, became as rigid and hidebound as the rules of the common law. It is equity, not the common law, that Charles Dickens flays so mercilessly in *Bleak House* as a labyrinth of red tape and delays—a far cry from the original idea that equity would moderate the rigor and formality of the common law.

Trust law was an invention of the courts of equity. Suppose I transfer property to a trustee, with the understanding that the trustee will manage the property on behalf of my young daughter. The trustee is, on paper, the actual owner of the property. If the property consisted of stock, the trustee would collect the dividends and vote the shares, like any other owner. The trustee has "legal title." As far as the common law is concerned, the trustee is the actual owner. But courts of equity, which could look beneath the surface, recognized clearly that the "legal title" masked a deeper reality: the trustee holds the title, to be sure, but not for its own benefit. The trustee has the duty to manage the property for the benefit of my daughter, or whoever the beneficiary might be. The beneficiary, then, has rights, and the trustee must respect those rights. Indeed, those rights are in many regards superior to the rights of the trustee. The beneficiary has what is called the "equitable title."[5] Although the trustee takes care of the trust property, manages the trust, and controls it, he does this in the name of the beneficiary, and in the interests of the beneficiary. And the beneficiary has the right to go to court and force the trustee to do his duty. That duty, of course, is spelled out first and foremost in the document that creates the trust. The trustee is, then, in a sense acting also in the interests of the settlor, that is, the person who set up the trust in the first place. The text of the trust document is the trustee's bible; but there are also elaborate rules of law about trust management that the trustee is required to obey.

Historically, beneficiaries could not enforce their rights in ordinary common law courts. These courts were blind to everything but the "legal title." The beneficiary would have to knock on the door of the chancery court, the court of equity, which *did* recognize those rights. The separation between "law" and "equity" was stubbornly maintained in old England. If you went in the wrong courtroom door, you were simply out of luck. This was also true in many American colonies and states. But during the nineteenth century, except in one or two states, the courts of law and the courts of equity were merged into a single system. The beneficiary can go to any court to assert his rights. There is no separate chancery court. History still matters, however. Since there were no juries in chancery court, cases on trusts never went to a jury. There is a constitutional right to trial by jury; but that does not apply to cases that were part of the realm of equity. Beneficiaries can sue trustees, of course; but not before a jury. Even today, trust cases do not go before a jury.[6]

The trust is an ancient device, but it has changed a lot over the years. It has adapted itself to modern life. It survived the passage of centuries because, like another ancient and surviving device, the mortgage, it fills a modern need. Laypeople, perhaps vaguely aware of the doctrine of precedent, often think that the law is in love with its past, and that much of the law is obsolete, hoary, and crusted with barnacles. But the exact reverse is true. Law is totally unsentimental. It has no nostalgia, no reverence for the past. It prunes away ruthlessly whatever is useless or unpopular. The trust, however, *is* useful; enormously so. Consequently, it survived. It is probably more common today than it has ever been.

In theory, a trust does not have to be in writing; but in practice, it almost always is. When a person wants to create a trust, he or she will almost certainly go to a lawyer, who will draft the trust. It can be a formidable document. It spells out the powers of the trustees, the terms of the trust, when it is to begin and end, who gets the money, how long the trust will last, and so on. To this extent, trusts are highly formal; but they do not need witnesses, and they do not need any particular ceremony, which a will of course requires.

Trusts are flexible and malleable and can be used for all sorts of purposes. One very ordinary type of trust might have terms something like this: the settlor, a rich woman, wants to provide for her two grown children, her son John, and her daughter Susan. But she feels they are not particularly good at managing money. She executes a trust agreement, which her lawyer drafted, and transfers stocks and bonds to a trustee. This might be a family member or a bank, whatever the settlor wishes (or her lawyer recommends). The trustee will hold title to the assets. Outsiders will deal with the trustee with regard to anything that has to do with the assets. But the trustee is not like an ordinary owner. The trustee must follow, religiously, the terms of the trust, and also the (rather strict) rules of law. This trust is divided into two parts, one for John and one for Susan. The trustee will pay over all the income in Susan's half to Susan, as long as she lives; John will get the income from his part. The trust tells the trustee to make payments every three months and also gives John and Susan each the right to ask for a share of the principal, say 5%, each year. It might also authorize the trustee to "invade" the trust—dip into the principal—if there is some emergency in the life of Susan or John.

When Susan dies, our hypothetical trust provides that her trust comes to an end. The trustee will now give the assets in her part of the trust to her children. If she has no children, the money goes to whomever the settlor has designated: John or his children, charity, or another relative, for example. There are similar provisions with regard to John's part of the trust. When the second of the two children dies, the trust is now finally at an end; and after the trustee pays out the last of the assets, the trustee's work is done.

This is a common pattern. But there are all sorts of other possible patterns. The trustee usually is required to distribute the income on a regular basis; but the settlor, if she wishes, can create a *discretionary* trust. That is, she can allow the trustee to decide whether to pay out the income or accumulate it, either totally at the trustee's discretion or according to some standard. The settlor can also insist on certain investment policies. The settlor, in short, is pretty free to craft the trust to suit her needs or wants.

Many trusts are *irrevocable*. Once the trust is set up and the assets transferred, it is a completed gift. The settlor cannot change her mind. She cannot get the money back. It no longer belongs to her. Since dead people have no minds to change, trusts set up in a will are by definition irrevocable. But living settlors have a choice. They can make their trusts revocable or irrevocable, as they see fit.[7] And vast numbers of trusts are, in fact, revocable trusts. Many elderly people put some or all of their assets in "living trusts," reserving the right to change their mind about any of the provisions of the trust, or to get rid of the whole thing altogether and take the money back. Such provisions are not the least bit unusual. Yet notice that the revocable trust, functionally speaking, is very much like a will. A will is said to be "ambulatory"—that is, it can be changed or revised at any time. As long as the testator is alive (and sane), he can change his heirs, shift his estate from this one to that one, and make new arrangements as he pleases. But a revocable trust is "ambulatory" too: the settlor can get rid of it for any reason, or for no reason at all.

Now suppose one further term: instead of paying the trust's money to the children, the settlor tells the bank to pay *her* (the settlor) all the income of the trust, until she dies; and only *then* to give the income money to the children. In this case—and this too is perfectly common—it is hard to see much difference between this "living trust" and an actual will. We have here what amounts to an almost perfect will substitute. But if it is functionally the same as a will, why is it *not* a will? Why isn't it subject to the same rules that wills are? The short answer is, that it isn't a will because the courts say so. This was not always the case: a century ago, some courts thought that arrangements of this sort *were* wills, and that as wills, or attempted wills, they would be plainly invalid.[8] After all, wills need witnesses and have other requirements in order to be valid. Trusts almost never have these trappings. So when the courts say no, this is not a will, this means that the trust can act just like a will, but without the formalities of a will. The living trust, then, is a will substitute, and a crucial one.

But what is the point of setting up a trust of this sort? Why not just make out a will? A living trust has two primary virtues. First, it avoids the cost and delays of the probate process. When the settlor dies, trust assets do not get funneled through the probate court. Technically, they are not part of the estate. The settlor in legal theory has already given these assets away—to the trustee. The trustee will simply go on running the trust, smoothly, without interruption. All trusts set up during the settlor's lifetime have this virtue, whether or not the settlor keeps the right to revoke or change them. The beauty of the revocable trust is that it really acts as a will, without the headaches of probate. Second, this trust—like other trusts—can also be used to get rid of the chore of managing your assets, if you are lucky enough to have assets worth managing. Getting a professional to manage them is, for many people, another advantage of having a trust. Of course, it comes at a price. Banks and trust companies do not take on this work out of the goodness of their hearts. They are happy to help, but for a fee.

Does the living trust save on taxes? Not really. As far as probate law is concerned, a woman who puts her assets in a living trust has given them away.

She saves money on probate fees and costs. But taxes are another story. The federal government is more cynical and hard-nosed about trusts than trust law is. If you have the power to change your mind, to revoke the trust, or to alter the terms of the trust, then (says the federal government) you have really given nothing away, at least for tax purposes. The assets in a living trust are still subject to federal death taxes. Still, the advantages of living trusts are sturdy enough to encourage thousands of people to execute them.

To be honest, many people have no idea *why* they are doing this; or they have an idea, but the idea is wrong. Norman Dacey's book *How to Avoid Probate*, published in 1965, was a huge success. It became, according to Dacey, "the number 1 best-seller" in the country, beating out *Human Sexual Response*, which was merely number two.[9] Dacey's book was a bitter attack on probate and probate lawyers, embroidered with horror stories about the costs and delays of the probate process. Probate, according to Dacey, was a "corrupt" system that acted as a "form of private taxation levied by the legal profession upon the rest of the population."[10] Lawyers battened off the estates of the dead, sometimes leaving the heirs with next to nothing. What he recommended was a detour around the probate process, chiefly through the use of living trusts.

Dacey's book was controversial; many lawyers and jurists attacked its facts and its premises. But there is no doubt that it stimulated the business of living trusts. Nowadays, elderly, wealthy people flock to seminars and workshops to hear about estate planning; and the speaker usually praises the virtues of these trusts to the skies. The trusts are "touted as money-saving vehicles."[11] Many folks in the audience will buy into the idea. They will then hire a lawyer to provide them with these marvelous devices that will save them so much money. But do these trusts really save money? They do; but not as much as some of their customers think. The customers are often confused about the difference between probate costs (which are not enormous) and succession taxes. They imagine somehow that probate costs will eat up the estate, an exaggerated notion. For sizable estates, death taxes (as of this writing) are far more substantial than probate costs.[12] Yet living trusts have no impact whatsoever on death taxes.[13]

It is hard to get current figures, but the use of living trusts is certainly growing. John Price compared inheritance tax returns in Washington state for the period 1967–72 with probate files. Estates that filed tax returns, but did not go through probate, had obviously used will substitutes. The number of these increased in the period from 28.04% to 37.80%.[14] They may be more common in some states than in others. Washington is a community property state, and this probably makes a difference. In California, at the present time, one lawyer, whose practice is almost entirely estate planning, told me that he recommends living trusts to all his clients; most of them follow his advice. His estate-planning firm, therefore, handles very few "estates." It deals in trusts. His clients, to be sure, are fairly rich.

Because the trust is a flourishing institution, there is a huge body of law about trusts. Much of it has to do with the powers and duties of trustees. The trustee is a "fiduciary," subject to fairly strict rules about what can and cannot be done, and what should and should not be done. The beneficiaries, after all, may be minors, very elderly people, or those most shadowy and helpless people of all—unborn and contingent beneficiaries. The rules are supposed to make sure the trustee plays the game honestly, selflessly, and in the interests of the beneficiaries. Of course, "selflessly" has to be taken with a grain of salt. There are plenty of selfless trustees—family members or friends. But others are lawyers or accountants. And then there are banks and trust companies. Individual trustees will often waive the right to collect a fee; but the banks and trust companies most certainly will not. They are in the game, as we said, for the money.

TOTTEN TRUSTS

Another will substitute, of a more homely type, is the so-called Totten trust. This is simply a form of bank account. John Smith can, for example, open a bank account, put in some money, and label the bank account "John Smith in trust for Mary Smith." John keeps control over the account as long as he lives, can put money in and take money out, can close the account, and can change the name of the beneficiary; but when he dies, the "beneficiary" takes the balance in the account. This is called a Totten trust, after the leading case in New York in 1904, *Matter of Totten*.[15] The argument against the "trust" was the same as the argument against revocable trusts: that the Totten trust was really a will. Like a will, it was ambulatory. Nobody had any rights until the account holder died. Up to the moment of death (or dementia), the account holder could throw out beneficiaries and put new ones in, eliminate the account, and so on. Indeed, the Totten trust has been called a "poor man's will." The person who sets up a Totten trust can do whatever he wants with it, although this probably takes a trip to the bank and whatever formalities the bank asks for. Notice, however, that these are not the formalities the law asks for in a will.

All this supports the argument that the "beneficiary" has no rights; the money, when the account holder dies, should go into the estate, rather than to the "beneficiary." This is quite a good argument. But it was not a winning argument. The New York court upheld and accepted the Totten trust. One could have also argued that the Totten trust was a genuine trust, and one that gave firm rights to the "beneficiary," so that even if the account holder changed his mind and closed out the account, the money should go to the "beneficiary." That too was a losing argument. Most American courts have gone along with the original decision, and the Totten trust is today a going concern.[16] Sometimes courts refer to the Totten trust as a "tentative trust," which is as good a name for it as any.

Obviously, the Totten trust is a will substitute, and a rather cheap and easy one. But it is nonetheless a formal device. It is backed by powerful interests—the banks. It has a solid basis in commercial practice. And the courts have been more and more willing to accept will substitutes if they seem formal enough, trustworthy enough, and useful enough. The Totten trust works for people who do not have the time or the money or the inclination to set up a living trust. It is certainly a useful device for the middle class.

There are other, somewhat similar arrangements—for example, P.O.D. (payable on death) accounts. A person sets up a bank account, and the bank agrees to pay anything left over on the death of the depositor to some person or institution she names. In the meantime, the depositor can do anything she likes with the account—put money in, take it out, change the terms. In Kansas, Lena Hogan set up four of these accounts, including an account with the First Federal Savings and Loan Association of Dodge City, Kansas, payable on her death to the "Pentecostal Holiness Conference Board (for Missionary work)." In 1974, in *Truax* v. *Southwestern College*,[17] the Supreme Court of Kansas refused to honor these terms. It said that the accounts were "testamentary in character" (that is, they were too much like a will). The laws of Kansas laid down rules for making out a will, and opening this kind of bank account simply did not qualify. What is interesting is what happened next. The Kansas legislature quickly enacted a statute that undid the *Truax* case. A P.O.D. account was not to be deemed "testamentary"; on the death of the depositor, the balance in the account was to go to the beneficiary, and not into the estate.[18] Later on, in 1987, the Kansas Supreme Court interpreted the statute to validate Totten trusts in the state of Kansas.[19]

There are other types of will substitutes, and there is a strong legal tendency to validate them. In a 1955 case, *Farkas* v. *Williams*,[20] Farkas bought stock sold by a company called Investors Mutual, Inc. When he bought the stock, Farkas signed "declarations of trust." He kept the right to the income as long as he lived. He had the right to name a "beneficiary," and to change beneficiaries, whenever he wanted to. If he named a beneficiary and the person died before Farkas did, then the "trust" would lapse. All of this, of course, makes the "declaration of trust" look suspiciously like a will. Indeed, that was the issue in the case. Farkas had bought some stock as "trustee for Richard J. Williams." But was this "trust" really a will? If it was, then of course it was invalid, because it lacked witnesses and so on. Williams would get nothing. The court had to admit that Farkas had retained enormous power over this trust. What rights did Williams actually have? Not many. If I make out a will, naming Mary as a beneficiary, Mary has nothing more than a hope, since I can tear up the will at any minute. It is hard to see that Williams had anything greater. But the court disagreed. The court felt that Farkas had created a real, honest-to-God trust. True, he could undo it at any minute; but while it lasted, Farkas had to act as a trustee, not as an owner. And, the court added, one "historic" purpose of the law of wills was to avoid "fraud." Here that was not an issue; Farkas had "manifested his intention in a solemn and formal manner," and that was enough.

Ways of disposing of property that are *functionally* the same as wills are particularly common between married people. The community property system, in a way, acts as a kind of will substitute. In a state that recognizes community property, the income and property that comes in during the marriage belongs equally to the two spouses. And this is so even in the old-time traditional family with (let us say) an employed husband and a hard-working but unpaid wife. If the husband dies first, half of the property avoids probate, because it already belongs to the widow. It is also extremely common for husbands and wives, or domestic partners, to hold property in joint tenancy, even in states without community property. In legal theory, crazy as it might sound to a layperson, each joint tenant has complete ownership—100% ownership—of anything held in joint tenancy. This seems as absurd as the square root of –1; but, like the square root of –1, it is a useful absurdity. What the doctrine means, practically speaking, is that either "joint tenant" of a bank account has the right to withdraw the whole amount; and the bank is not entitled to say: wait a minute, only half of this is yours. It also means that when you die, the whole bank account now belongs to your joint tenant. There is no need to go through the probate process. After all, the joint tenant already owns it all. This strange idea can be (and is) extremely convenient. A husband and wife who own everything in joint tenancy, and who want the whole estate to go to the survivor, arguably do not need a will. When one of them dies, everything passes automatically to the other.[21]

Both wills and will substitutes are devices for transferring property at death. Seen in this light, many life insurance policies can also act as a kind of will substitute. Also the biggest asset for many people is some kind of pension fund or annuity. This is their main hope of leaving something behind for children or other relatives. Designating who or what is the beneficiary acts as an important kind of will substitute.

In short, in the twentieth century, will substitutes grew like mushrooms. The courts accepted them—sometimes sooner, sometimes later. So did the legislatures. This evolution, then, looks like another instance of the erosion of formalism. It is important, though, not to confuse a theoretical or philosophical movement with the practical affairs of life. There are solid practical reasons—and political reasons—for this erosion of formalism. After all, recall what happened when the Kansas court had the audacity to hand down a decision—on perfectly logical and "legal" grounds—that annoyed and embarrassed banks and possibly cost them some business. The legislature quickly changed the law. No doubt the banks had made their wishes known, loud and clear, in the halls of the legislature.

CHAPTER 6

DYNASTIC AND CARETAKER TRUSTS

Social change, of course, molds trusts and the law of trusts, just as it molds every aspect of the law. The rise of the family of affection and dependence leaves its mark, as one might expect, on trust practices. At one time, it was common for men to leave property to their wives for their lifetime only, by setting up a trust, or through a so-called legal life estate (basically, leaving the property to the wife, but only for as long as she lived). Many men no doubt felt their wives had no talent for managing property. It was also a way of making sure that the widow would not have any say about the ultimate disposition of the estate.[1] It was also common to give the wife an estate that would last only as long as she was a widow. In other words, if she married again, her interest would come to an end. These provisions, in short, reflected an ethos rather similar to the ethos of dower, which, before the middle of the nineteenth century, gave the wife a kind of life estate in real property. Life estates for widows were common in wills in colonial Virginia, for example.[2] In Bucks County, Pennsylvania, nearly two-thirds of the testators, in the 1790's, "made the major part or all of the wife's legacy roomspace and provisions for life or, more often, for widowhood."[3] In Essex County, New Jersey, in the nineteenth century, men also left quite a few gifts to wives during their widowhood.[4] In 1897 a testator in Salt Lake City, Utah, gave his most recent wife $10 plus the "privalege of living on the Homestead," support for life, and also the "privalege of keeping two (2) cows and other Domestic animals"; but all this was to be revoked, including the cows, if she remarried.[5]

The trust during widowhood became rarer during the course of the nineteenth century,[6] and was almost totally obsolete in the twentieth century, which is not surprising. A 1964 study of San Bernardino, California, for example, found no trace of such trusts. In Cuyahoga County, Ohio, in 1970, there were only two examples: a 73-year-old man left to his third wife a life interest in his real estate, with "full and unrestricted use . . . so long as she remains my widow." The second example, surprisingly, came from the estate of a woman, who left real property to her second husband, but only as long as he remained a widower.[7]

On the other hand, so-called marital deduction trusts are quite common today. These are, essentially, trusts for the benefit of a surviving spouse. Under the federal estate tax, property left to a surviving spouse pays no tax. If the property is left to the widow (or widower) in trust, the situation is much more complicated. This too can be tax-free—but the trust has to follow certain rules rather closely. In one form, the wife must get all the income; and she must have the absolute right to decide, through a will or some other document, what will become of the estate after she dies.[8]

UNLIVING TRUSTS

Not all trusts are living trusts by any means. Settlors every year set up a vast number of irrevocable trusts. Once the machinery is set in motion, there is no stopping it. The settlor has no power to monitor or control the trust in any way. A great many rich people transfer property into such trusts while they are still alive. A great many more leave some or all of their estate in the form of a testamentary trust (that is, a trust embodied in a will). These are, necessarily, irrevocable trusts; the donor, after all, is dead when the trust springs to life. And living trusts, too, turn to stone and concrete when the settlors die.

Irrevocable trusts have important tax consequences. If you give away, permanently, in trust or otherwise, a million dollars in shares of some company, you will no longer pay a tax on the company's dividends. Somebody else will enjoy the income. And the assets you transfer will not be part of your taxable estate when you die. You may, however, have to pay a gift tax on property put in trust, above a certain minimum. At one time, gift tax rates were lower than estate tax rates. The rates are now equal, but if a wealthy person makes large gifts during his lifetime, there will still be a tax saving when he dies.[9]

There is a huge body of law about trusts, and treatises on the law of trusts can run to many volumes. Trusts come in all shapes and sizes. The settlor is generally quite free to set up a trust that suits the settlor's purposes, and can insert almost any sort of provision he or she likes (within certain limits). Most of the rules, therefore, are default rules—rules that apply only when the trust document does not cover the subject. Although trusts are extremely varied, we can identify, analytically, two broad categories. I call one type the *caretaker* trust and the other type the *dynastic* trust.[10] A caretaker trust is exactly what its name implies. Suppose I have two children, ages 3 and 5, and I want to provide for them if I die unexpectedly while they are still children. It is not a good idea to leave them money outright. Because they are minors, some sort of guardian would have to be appointed—my spouse, if I have one, or somebody else—but in any case, a guardianship will involve red tape and expense. I can avoid a guardianship if I set up a trust for them in my will, naming a relative or a bank or a friend or some combination of these as trustees; the trustees will manage the money and spend it as I direct in the will. This arrangement is much more flexible than a guardianship. I can specify, too, how long the trust should last. The kids will be adults, legally speaking, at age 18; but if I am skeptical of exactly how "adult" they might be at 18, I can have the trust last until they turn 21, or 25, or whatever I wish. A settlor can also set up a caretaker trust for someone who is disabled, or incompetent, or who (the donor feels) would just squander the money if it were given to him outright.

The second type is the *dynastic* trust. Here the donor's motive—or one of his motives—is to perpetuate and control the estate as long as possible. If you leave money outright to your children as soon as you die, they can do whatever they want with the money. They could, for example, sink all of it into a Broadway play and lose every penny; or they could go to Las Vegas and spend your hard-earned money at the blackjack table. Or they could lavish the money on their friends, or give it to charities you might not approve of. But if you set up a trust, and tell the trustee to give the children nothing but the income from the trust as long as they live, without power to invade the principal, then you can, in effect, keep your estate alive, and out of harm's way, as long as they live—and longer. Perhaps you might specify, too, that the trust will continue during the life of your grandchildren. Or even past this point. You are creating, or trying to create, a kind of dynasty. How long can you keep it going? A complicated rule, the so-called rule against perpetuities, sets the outer limits. The details are quite involuted; but practically speaking, the rule cuts off dynastic trusts at something just short of a century. Many states, as we will see, have tinkered with or eliminated this rule. Some have removed all limits on dynastic trusts. I deal with this issue in a later chapter.

Formally, the law does not distinguish between the two different types of trust. A trust is a trust is a trust. But the two types have very different needs. Caretaker trusts are usually short-term. They are often managed by amateurs (family members or friends). Most do not suffer very much if the trustee makes conservative investments, but if the trustee is reckless and foolish they can suffer a lot. Suppose I set up a trust in my will for the benefit of my 10-year-old son, Bobby. I name as trustee Bobby's Uncle Harry. He is to use the money for Bobby's benefit; and when Bobby celebrates his twenty-first birthday, Harry is supposed to turn over the money to Bobby. This trust will not last very long—eleven years to be exact. The best investment strategy is caution—especially since Harry is, say, a schoolteacher with very little savvy about stocks, bonds, and markets. Early cases and statutes, accordingly, gave Harry very little power to decide on investments. Shares in corporations were out. No gambling on the stock market. Government bonds would probably be best. This would have seemed especially wise in the nineteenth century, with no Securities and Exchange Commission, no deposit insurance, and a wild and wooly stock market, full of traps for the innocent and the unwary.

Dynastic trusts, by way of contrast, are usually managed by professionals (today these are mostly banks and trust companies). They last much longer than caretaker trusts, so they need to have much more flexible investment policies. The general rule for dynastic trusts has been the "prudent investor rule." This was one of the law's ubiquitous non-rule rules. In a state with the prudent investor rule (or standard), there were no hard and fast norms about what to invest in. Anything "prudent" was fit for investment. A lottery ticket would not qualify. Good solid stocks and bonds, on the other hand, definitely would.

The prudent investor rule is actually quite old. It can be traced to a Massachusetts case, *Harvard College* v. *Amory*, decided in 1830.[11] John M'Lean died in 1823, leaving an estate of a quarter million dollars—a large fortune in those days. He left part of his estate in trust for his wife for life, after which it was to go to Harvard College and the Massachusetts General Hospital. The trustees invested estate funds in corporate stocks, and Harvard objected. These stocks, Harvard argued, were unsafe. The court agreed that stocks had risks, but risk was an inevitable feature of investment. "Do what you will, the capital is at hazard." So long as trustees acted the way "men of prudence, discretion and intelligence" acted with respect to their *own* money, "not in regard to speculation, but in regard to the permanent disposition of their funds," and if they took risk into account, while acting prudently, then they were not violating their duties as trustees.

That this rule emerged in Massachusetts is probably no accident. Boston was the home of the first *professional* trustees. These were men from good families who managed the wealth of other members of the elite, and did this as a business. Indeed, M'Lean's trustees were Jonathan and Francis Amory, members of an old Massachusetts family. The "rule" is of course pretty vague. But it is not meaningless. It appeals to the standards of "men of prudence," that is, businessmen from the upper circles of Boston society. These were cautious but sophisticated men. The trusts that professional trustees managed were also, on the whole, relatively long-term trusts. For them, as opposed to Uncle Harry, a more flexible rule made sense.

Interestingly, although some states followed the lead of Massachusetts, many others rejected the prudent investor rule. They insisted, instead, on a more conservative, more cautious standard for investment.[12] Government bonds were a safe harbor. So were gilt-edged first mortgages on real estate. Anything else was suspect.[13] Liquidity was an important factor. Some states eventually enacted "legal lists"—catalogs of investments from which a trustee could and should choose. A trustee who invested exclusively in what was on the list was safe; he could not be accused of mismanaging investments.

The philosophy of the legal lists was appropriate for caretaker trusts; and the philosophy of Harvard College was the right one for dynastic trusts—at least in the nineteenth century. But the world of trust management did not stand still. The rise of the professional trustee—not private individuals, as in Boston, but trust companies—was an important new development. Banks and trust companies managed more and more trusts. They also tended to insist that the actual trust document should give them a great deal of latitude and discretion in investment. History also came to show the dangers of inflation; fixed-income securities, like government bonds, eroded in value over time. And the legal lists were not as safe as they were supposed to be. The depression of the 1930's tore through the legal lists like a tornado. "Safe" investments like railroad bonds (which were on many of the lists) sank like lead weights in this period. As a result, the "prudent investor" standard began to look better and better. After 1940, the long boom period, too, made fussy and conservative investment rules look less satisfactory. State after state got on board and adopted the prudent investor standard as the norm. Sometimes they enacted laws that quoted the very words of the Harvard College case.[14] This development seemed, in a way, like the triumph of the dynastic trust. Or perhaps, a recognition that Uncle Harry no longer mattered. Even short-term trusts could use good management; and good management is flexible management. The current trend, as we will see, goes even further than the prudent investor rule.

SPENDTHRIFT TRUST DOCTRINE

Legally speaking, over the past century and a half, the dynastic trust has won victory after victory. The rules have been reshaped in all sorts of ways that suit the interests of this kind of trust. The triumph of the prudent investor rule is probably a good example. Another is the so-called spendthrift trust doctrine.

This is a doctrine that seems, on the surface, rather odd. Consider a fairly typical sort of trust. A rich woman transfers a sizable chunk of money and stocks into a trust. The chief beneficiary is her only son, Rodney. The trustee, a bank, is supposed to pay Rodney all of the income from the trust, in quarterly installments, as long as he lives. When he dies, the trust will end, and Rodney's children will inherit.

Rodney, then, has a nice thing going for the rest of his life. Suppose the trust yields, more or less, $100,000 a year. And suppose Rodney is 48 years old. One might suppose that Rodney, if he wanted to, could cash in on this lifetime right to income. Some financial institution would certainly be willing to pay him a lump sum in exchange for his right to an income stream, year in and year out. Actuarially, it is easy to figure out what Rodney's interest is worth. It depends on his life expectancy. Of course, anybody who bought his interest would buy it at a discount; but that's not the point. Rodney could use his interest in the trust to get immediate cash. He could also give his interest away, if he felt like it, to his girlfriend, or his children, or some charity, or whomever he wished. But there's a hitch: his mother (or her lawyer) added language to the trust document saying, in effect, no, Rodney, you cannot do this. You cannot sell or give away your rights. And the language also says, quite definitely, that Rodney's interest in the trust cannot be used to pay off his creditors. The trustee must pay the income to Rodney and to nobody else. Suppose that Rodney, for example, had run up big gambling debts or business debts. The creditors cannot collect their money directly from the trust. They cannot force the trustee to pay the income over to them. Of course, once the trustees make a quarterly payment and the money is in Rodney's hands, creditors can go after this money. But they would have to do this for each individual payment. And this might not be so easy. Rodney might be in Brazil, for example, or Timbuktu. No creditor can get a court order, binding on the trustee, requiring the trustee to pay the money over to them, rather than to Rodney.

That situation, this immunity, is exactly what the settlor wants. She puts in these provisions—which we call the spendthrift clause—because she wants her plan to be safe from creditors and girlfriends and everybody else, including Rodney himself. But should she have her way? The most logical answer is that she shouldn't. The common law strongly disfavors "restraints on alienation." Roughly what this means is this: if you own something, if you have a valuable asset, you should be able to sell it or give it away. The right to receive trust income for life *is* a valuable asset. Why should *this* asset be treated differently? Why can't Rodney handle it in the same way that he handles his other assets (if he has any)? And if Rodney really is a spendthrift, and is head over heels in debt, why should he be protected? Shouldn't the creditors be able to reach this valuable asset, Rodney's right to an income from the trust? Yet in *Broadway Bank* v. *Adams*, a Massachusetts case of 1882,[15] the court flatly endorsed, and enforced, the spendthrift clause.

Moreover, this was no isolated decision. It was widely followed by many other courts. It became the standard rule and standard practice. The spendthrift clause appears routinely in wills and trusts. There is some variation, to be sure, among the states; not all of them accept the spendthrift trust in its purest form. And even states that embrace the rule admit some exceptions—for example, in

California, child support payments trump the spendthrift clause.[16] Federal tax liens also override the spendthrift trust, which should come as no surprise. In a few states, if the trust consists of land, the spendthrift trust protects only as much of the income as the beneficiary needs for his support and education.[17] There are other statutory wrinkles in other states. In short, the legal situation is rather complicated. But very few states reject the spendthrift trust outright.

The spendthrift trust doctrine was, in its early days, somewhat controversial. The courts seemed to love it, but some legal scholars were shocked. John Chipman Gray, writing in 1895, smelled the evil influence of "paternalism," which was the "essence alike of spendthrift trusts and of socialism," a rather strange way to describe a legal device useful only for rich people.[18] The doctrine protected beneficiaries from creditors; but it also hurt them, because it took away the valuable right to use their assets as they saw fit. The real winner was the settlor, whose estate plan was protected, from both inside and outside impairment. The dead hand of the settlor controlled from beyond the grave. And this was especially important for settlors of dynastic trusts.[19]

The settlor can outfox a beneficiary's creditors in other ways too. One common device is a *discretionary trust*. Suppose the settlor gives the trustee absolute discretion to pay or not pay income to a particular beneficiary. That beneficiary, let us say, is head over heels in debt. Paying out the money would frustrate the settlor's plan; and the trustee will probably decide not to pay. Can the creditors force the trustee to pay out the money (which they would then grab)? The simple answer is no.

A good illustration is a recent, and bizarre, California case, *Young* v. *McCoy*.[20] Lucile McCoy had two sons, Steven and Richard. At Lucile's house, Steven and Richard quarreled—pretty badly it seems, because Steven tried to murder his brother, Richard. Richard survived, and Steven was sentenced to life in prison. Lucile had a trust for Steven, whose "primary purpose" was Steven's "needs and comfort," taking into account what he required for his "support, health, maintenance, and education." But these payments were at the trustee's discretion. Richard sued his brother and won a judgment of over a million dollars. He tried to get the money out of the trust, but the trustee refused and the court upheld the trustee's decision. The state of California was taking care of Steven's needs, and the trustee was perfectly justified in refusing to pay over money that would only end up in Richard's pocket.[21]

TERMINATION OF TRUSTS

Another interesting doctrine deals with the right of beneficiaries to force a trust to end (or "terminate"). When and how can beneficiaries force this on trustees, and get them to distribute the money to the beneficiaries, ahead of time? In what regards can beneficiaries gain the right to change the terms of the trust? A doctrine, traceable to the late nineteenth century, essentially denies these rights to beneficiaries. The doctrine is associated with another Massachusetts case, *Claflin* v. *Claflin* (1889).[22] Here the testator, in his will, set up a trust for his son, Adelbert. The trustee, under the will, was to give Adelbert $10,000 at age 21, another $10,000 at age 25; and the rest of the fund at age 30. Adelbert, who had reached 21 (but not 30) at the time the case was decided, asked the trustee to close out the trust and give him the money right away. After all, there were no other beneficiaries, and Adelbert thought the money was simply his. The trustee refused, and the court backed up the trustee. Adelbert's trust would come to an end when the dead hand said it would end, and not a second sooner.

The *Claflin* doctrine is another example of the triumph of the dead hand. The doctrine, like the spendthrift trust doctrine, is particularly useful for dynastic trusts. The Claflin trust was not itself a dynastic trust; and since it had no spendthrift clause, Adelbert, presumably, could sell or give away his interest. Yet these facts made no impression on the court. The net effect of the Claflin doctrine is to make almost all trusts, in effect, indestructible. The doctrine is usually put this way: a trustee can end a trust ahead of time, and distribute the assets, only if two conditions are met: first, all beneficiaries agree; and second, the "purpose" of the trust has been fulfilled. Very few trusts—certainly no dynastic trust—could possibly meet these conditions. It is even hard, most of the time, to get adult beneficiaries to agree. Minors are a special problem. Moreover, most long-term trusts have unborn or contingent beneficiaries; and obviously, getting the unborn and the contingent to consent to anything is beyond human power.

The second condition seems easier, but in fact it is not. Few trusts ever say anything explicit about their "purpose." What the Claflin doctrine seems to mean is that the structure *is* the purpose. If the dead testator had a plan, and put it in writing, and if he specified that the trust would last until a specific event happened, then that was what he wanted, that was the purpose of the trust. In *Estate of Brown*, a Vermont case from 1987,[23] Andrew Brown, in his will, created a trust, to be used to pay for the education of the children of his nephew, Woolson Brown. Afterwards, the income was to be used "for the care, maintenance and welfare of my nephew . . . and his wife Rosemary . . . so that they may live in the style and manner to which they are accustomed" for the rest of their lives. Woolson and Rosemary, after their children were educated, asked to have the trust terminated. It was supposed to be used to "maintain their lifestyle," and (they said) the only way to accomplish this goal, was to end the trust and give them the money. But the court refused to go along. Ending the trust would defeat Brown's "intention to assure a life-long income to Woolson and Rosemary Brown." Of course, the court had nothing to base this conclusion on—nothing except the words and the structure of the trust. For the court, the structure *was* the purpose. The settlor's wishes prevail beyond the grave.[24]

In short, the law, in the late nineteenth century and well into the twentieth century, evolved in such a way as to favor the dynastic trust—rules that put the dead hand very firmly in control. There were limits, of course. The dead hand ruled, but not forever. The so-called rule against perpetuities, which I deal with in the following chapter, represented one of the most important limits. And the firm rules have begun to soften in recent years.

Still, how do we explain the rules and doctrines just discussed—and the apparent triumph of the dead hand?

In the first place, today's dead hand is not the dead hand of two centuries ago. It is, for one thing, much more liquid. Assets are not "tied up" any more. Nobody can argue that long-term trusts monopolize anything or clog the drainpipes of society. Trusts in contemporary times do not consist primarily of land or other assets that are fixed and frozen in place. Trustees, particularly under the prudent investor rule, follow fluid and liberal investment policies. The *structure* of the trust may be sacred; but the portfolio shifts and alters with changing times.

Also, the rules surely reflect attitudes toward wealth and wealthy people. By the late nineteenth century, a new American aristocracy of wealth had emerged—bankers, industrialists, captains of industry. Judges were, by and large, men who sympathized with society's elites. The doctrines catered to the needs and wishes of rich dynasts. These were men who were beginning to endow universities and create huge charitable foundations. They were often—not always—benefactors of society. The law reflected the conservative views of these men. It supported the wishes of founders and owners of great fortune.

CHANGING TIMES

In recent times, however, the rules that supported dynastic trusts have shown definite signs of wear and tear. There has been, for example, some decay in the Claflin doctrine.[25] A number of statutes now open the door somewhat. A statute in Missouri, for example, allows a court to deviate from the investment terms of a trust when this might be "expedient." It also modifies Claflin. If all "adult beneficiaries who are not disabled consent," a court can change the terms of a trust, and even terminate it, provided the court "finds" that the change "will benefit the disabled, minor, unborn and unascertained beneficiaries."[26] How a court figures out what will benefit "unborn and unascertained" people is not spelled out. I suspect the subtext of the statute is that the court is entitled to ignore these shadowy people.[27]

Even in the high and palmy days of the Claflin doctrine, courts distinguished between changing the substance of the trust and tinkering with its administrative provisions. The Missouri statute, as we saw, allows change in the investment policy. Under modern statutes, influenced by the Uniform Trust Code, courts can "reform" trusts to fit "the settlor's intention" if there is "clear and convincing evidence" that "both the settlor's intent and the terms of the trust were affected by a mistake of fact or law."[28] Another provision gives the court authority to make changes that will rescue the trust from bad tax consequences.[29] Despite these provisions, courts are still generally quite skittish about terminating trusts, and they still tend to think that the structure of a trust *is* the purpose. After all, the settlor decided to put the money in trust, rather than give it to beneficiaries right away. Postponing distribution until somebody dies or something else happens is one crucial purpose of the trust.[30] Courts are especially reluctant to terminate spendthrift trusts ahead of time.[31] They have the same attitude toward "support" trusts, trusts that order the trustees to pay money to support certain beneficiaries, but give the trustee discretion to decide how much.[32]

Still, although nobody can predict the future, it seems likely that the Claflin doctrine will continue to decay. The dynastic trust has achieved, in recent years, one of its greatest triumphs: restrictions on how long it can last are rapidly eroding. Paradoxically, however, this development increases the pressure and the felt need for more flexibility, for a power somewhere (in the courts, presumably) to modify trusts that last a very long time, or perhaps forever. There already is such a power for charitable trusts, which I deal with in a later chapter. It is interesting to note that the Canadian province of Manitoba, which abolished the rule against perpetuities—in effect allowing trusts to last forever—simultaneously enacted a statute that gave courts power to modify trusts on behalf of unborn and contingent beneficiaries.[33]

English law has been less hospitable to dynastic trusts than American law. For example, the spendthrift trust doctrine has no real counterpart in England. This seems at first blush paradoxical. After all, England was the very motherland of dynasties, a country dominated by the nobility and the landed gentry. As late as the nineteenth century, the "heir" (for the landed gentry at least) meant the oldest son. Titles of nobility followed this pattern as a matter of course: the oldest son of an earl or a duke became the earl or the duke when his father died. But by custom he often inherited the estate—the land—as well as the title. From the novels of Trollope to *Brideshead Revisited*, this fact influenced the plot of countless English novels.

There were no titles of nobility in the United States, and nothing very much like the landed gentry (except, perhaps, plantation owners in the antebellum South). Why, then, should the United States, not England, smile so benignly on the dynastic trust?

The paradox may not be such a paradox at all. Social change in England, from the nineteenth century on, was often aimed at getting rid of the awesome power of the landed gentry. It was England, not the United States, where a major political party at least claimed to be a socialist party. In England, but not in the United States, death taxes were at one point almost confiscatory. Many old families in England now squeeze themselves into apartments in some nook or cranny of their great house, while tourists pay admission to roam the rest of the estate and drink tea. The class system still exists, but it is definitely embattled; and it has been embattled (though powerful) for more than a century. Americans, on the other hand, have always insisted they had no class system at all. And American dynasties are not old, noble families, but the descendants of men who made their money in business. To be "in trade" was not a disgrace; it was one of the highest callings a man could have. The dynastic trust triumphed in the United States in the late nineteenth century, when big business became really big. The great landed fortunes of England were in the decline; the great business fortunes of the United States were on the rise.

In recent years, there are signs that England and the United States are converging. The English still do not recognize spendthrift trusts, but it is easy to set up something quite similar in England. Creditors cannot reach purely discretionary trusts. If you set up a trust and give the trustee discretion to pay or not pay, in any given year, to beneficiary X, then the creditors of beneficiary X cannot reach his interest. This is because X *has* no interest. He has only hopes and expectations. In England too, so-called protective trusts are common. In a protective trust, the settlor can provide that beneficiary X gets all the income; but if X tries to give the money away, or creditors swoop down on X, or X goes bankrupt, then the trust converts automatically to a discretionary trust. A statute of 1925 expressly authorized such protective trusts.[34]

TRUST INVESTMENT

For many years, only Massachusetts and a few other states followed the prudent investor rule. The others clung to more restrictive rules. In the twentieth century, however, state after state adopted the prudent investor rule. Toward the end of the century, however, the prudent investor rule, in its classical form, came under attack—not because it was too flexible and bold, but for the opposite reason. Many scholars in the legal academy, and in the world of banks and trust companies, thought the prudent investor rule was too constraining. They were eager to substitute a rule based on "portfolio theory." The basic idea is simple: courts should not judge "prudence" by looking at each individual investment. They should look at the whole portfolio. A good trustee will invest in a variety of stocks and bonds. Some of these might be riskier than the old rule would allow. But if the portfolio as a whole is "prudent," then the trustee has done its job and should not be open to criticism (or to lawsuits).[35] The argument makes a lot of sense for professional managers. It makes no sense for Uncle Harry and for many caretaker trusts.[36] The commentators, on the whole, do not seem to care very much about Uncle Harry.

Portfolio theory seems to be winning the day. The Uniform Prudent Investor Act was drafted and promulgated in 1994. Its language clearly adopted a form of portfolio theory. Section 2 (b) of the statute provided that a trustee's investment decisions "must be evaluated not in isolation but in the context of the trust portfolio as a whole and as a part of an overall investment strategy." Many state legislatures have adopted this act, or something along these lines.[37]

One might imagine that, for most trusts, and certainly those that are professionally managed, all this is much ado about nothing. Professionals draft the trusts, and they button it up from top to bottom with clauses that try to protect the trustee from ungrateful or cranky beneficiaries. The professionals stuff into the document phrases like "in the trustee's sole discretion"; and they try to make life as safe as possible for trustees, and to grant them pretty much immunity. To a large degree, they have succeeded. Yet the new investment rules apparently *do* make a difference. A survey of sixty-one banking institutions in Iowa suggests as much. Most of them (85%) said they used the "risk-return analysis suggested by modern portfolio theory." Seventy-five percent felt the rule in Iowa did not prevent them from "taking advantage of investment opportunities" they would "otherwise pursue in portfolios of personal trusts." Seventy-two percent held common stocks that do not pay regular dividends. The bankers were hardly wild speculators, however. They still felt that conservative investment policies were the best thing for trusts. The new rules had led to some changes in policy, but these were not exactly radical or revolutionary.[38]

Is it fair to say that the net result of the legal rules discussed in this chapter is to favor long-term trusts? Is it fair to say that the rules give more and more power to the dead hand, allowing rich people to control their fortunes long after their death? Superficially, the answer seems to be yes. And this is something of a long-term trend and a change of course. Leaders in the early republic did not like long-term trusts, if they liked trusts at all. The late nineteenth century went in a different direction. The spendthrift trust doctrine, the Claflin doctrine, the doctrines that favor charitable trusts and foundations, the evolution of investment rules: all of these suggest the triumph of the dynastic trust. The only significant rule that *limited* the dynastic trust was the rule against perpetuities. As we will see, this rule, the chief constraint on these trusts, is decaying at a rapid rate, and may soon be extinct. But things are not always what they seem. The situation, it will appear, is somewhat more complex.

CHAPTER 7

CONTROL BY THE DEAD AND ITS LIMITS

The Rise and Fall of the Rule against Perpetuities

Our legal system allows the dead to control the living, at least up to a point. The right to make out a will guarantees this. A person with property, money, and assets can cast a long shadow. You can (within limits) leave your money to anyone you please. And you can do more: you can add conditions. Often this is done by creating a trust. In a trust, you can, for example, stipulate that your children will only get the income from your property. You can keep them from getting their hands on the fortune itself, the capital that is producing this income; and you can specify that the trust will last as long as they live—or even longer. You can control the estate for years, decades, and even more, long after you are dead and buried.

But how long? Forever? No, not forever—at least this has been true in most states, and for at least two centuries. Under the law, there comes a point where the dead hand has to relax its grip. A very curious and complicated doctrine, known as the rule against perpetuities, acted in most states as a crucial factor limiting how long trusts could last. The details of this rule are notoriously involute. The rule tortured generations of law students (and a fair number of estate lawyers). It is not hard to state the rule in a single sentence. Explaining what it means, and how it works, is another matter.

PERPETUITIES LAW: THE BASICS

The rule against perpetuities tries to answer one basic question: how long can a testator, or the creator of a trust, tie up an estate, or a gift in trust? Here "tying up" refers to *contingent* interests. If I leave money in trust for my daughter for life and, after her death, to those of her children who are alive when she dies, the interests of her children are contingent. After all, it is tragic but hardly unknown for a child to die before its mother. To get my money, though, her children have to live longer than their mother. Until the mother dies, we do not know which children will inherit. Hence their interests are "contingent." An interest is "contingent," then, if it turns on something that may or may not happen—in this case, living longer than a child's mother.

Now suppose I leave money in trust for my daughter as long as she lives, then to *her* children as long as they live, then to *their* children as long as they live; and when the last great-grandchild dies, I provide that the money should be distributed to those of my descendants who happen to be alive at the time. If I follow this plan, it will be quite a long time before we know where the money is ultimately going to land (or, in legal terms, when it will "vest" and in whom). How long can I postpone this "vesting"? That is the job of the rule against perpetuities.

One might imagine a fairly simple rule that fixed a definite time limit. This rule might say to the testator: you can postpone vesting for fifty, or seventy-five, or one hundred years. Some states, in the twentieth century, did exactly this.[1] But the classic rule against perpetuities, as it was formulated in the nineteenth century, and as it flourished for more than century, was never this simple. In fact, as we said, it was notoriously complex.

The rule could be summed up in one simple, lapidary formula. Any interest in property created by will or trust had to vest, if at all, no more than "twenty-one years after some life in being at the creation of the interest."[2]

But what does this mean? Suppose I die and my will leaves all my property in trust, with the income to go to my daughter, Mary, and after her death in equal shares to *her* children—my grandchildren—until the youngest grandchild reaches the age of 21. At that point, according to my will, the trust will come to an end and the money will go to my descendants then living. Let us say that my daughter, Mary, is alive at my death: she is therefore a "life in being."

Her children may or may not be alive at my death—she might be a young woman and have children after I die—but in any event, all of her children will be born while she is alive, so that even if she dies giving birth to her youngest child, and this sad event happens after I die, that child will reach the age of 21 within twenty-one years of a "life in being," that is, within twenty-one years of the death of my daughter Mary. But suppose I try to have the trust last until the last *grandchild* dies. Grandchildren might be born after my death. Any such grandchild would not qualify as a "life in being" at the time I died. This grandchild could, conceivably, outlive all the measuring lives by more than twenty-one years. The trust would thus violate the rule against perpetuities. In that case it would be totally invalid.

One of the factors that made the rule so devilish and so technical was the sub-rule that the rule was violated if there was even the slightest *possibility* that the rule might be violated. The rule was inexorable. It applied even if, in real life, violation of the rule would be very, very unlikely to occur. Take the case of the unborn grandchildren. Suppose there is, in fact, another grandchild, born after I die. And suppose this is the tenth grandchild. What are the chances that some horrendous disaster will sweep away the other nine, so that only this grandchild, the one born too late, would survive? Fairly slim, yet this slim chance is enough to kill the trust.

And in some cases the violation is not just unlikely; it is downright impossible. This, for example, is the notorious case of the "fertile octogenarian."[3] I leave money in trust, in my will, to my sister, who is 90 years old. The trust is to pay the income to her as long as she lives. When she dies, the trustee is to pay the income in equal shares to her children; and when the last of her children dies, then the trust will end, and the trust will be distributed among her grandchildren.

The classic case law was pretty much unanimous: my will was no good. I had violated the rule against perpetuities. But how could that be? The rule was violated because there was a chance that my sister, the 90-year-old woman, might give birth to a baby, after I died. This baby could not be a "life in being." If the baby were the only survivor of my sister—some plague carries off all her other children, and *their* children—then the trust will end when this baby dies, and this could be much later than twenty-one years after the relevant "lives in being."

Your natural reaction is to say: this is completely ridiculous. Women of 90 do not have babies. My 90-year-old sister is not going to give birth. All of her children are "lives in being," and to say that there is a problem here is simply absurd. Absurd it may be; but that was the law. Unquestionably, the trust in this case violated the rule against perpetuities. And this was no more absurd than the case of the "unborn widow."[4] A man, in his will, leaves his estate in trust, for the benefit of his son, a grown man. The income is to go to the son for as long as he lives, then to his widow for as long as she lives, and then to his direct descendants who are alive when she dies. This too is bad. Why? Because the son's wife might die, and he might marry a woman who wasn't even born at the time the testator died. In that case, she would not be a "life in being." Of course, assuming the son is in his thirties or forties when the testator dies, the chances he would marry a woman so much younger than he is seems extremely unlikely—close to impossible. But there it is.[5]

These are only two examples of the hidden traps and quirks that made the rule seem so strange and irrational. And maddening. A rule that imagined old ladies having babies, and conjuring up the image of the unborn widow, seemed to deserve the famous line of Mr. Bumble in Charles Dickens's *Oliver Twist*: "If the law supposes that . . . the law is a ass—a idiot."[6] But we have to be cautious before we label a rule of law nonsensical—especially one that was so powerful in its day, which lasted well over a century and a half, and which still has considerable vitality. The underlying policy did, of course, always make sense. The rule has a kind of medieval, feudal ring to it; but in fact there is nothing medieval about it. Quite the contrary. Feudalism did not see anything wrong in land dynasties. Land dynasties were at the very core of the social structure. Estates were handed down from father to eldest son under arrangements that could very well be, in form, perpetual.

The rule against perpetuities, rather, is a rule that fits a rising capitalist economy. It assumes a situation in which land is, or can become, a commodity, something that is bought and sold and traded on the market. Legal institutions that interfere with this market are disfavored. Long-term trusts of land kept property off the market, under the control of the dead hand of some former owner. The rule, then, acted as a kind of compromise: it was a way to respect the dead hand's wishes, but only up to a point.

But if so, then why not a simple rule: seventy-five years, or eighty years, or whatever. Partly because the rule was a judge-made rule, not something laid down by an act of Parliament. It evolved slowly over the years. No court would have had the nerve to enact a simple, quantitative rule: that would seem far too legislative.[7] Like many human institutions, then, the course of its development was messy. By about 1800 it had more or less reached its modern form. The only quantitative term in the rule was twenty-one years—which was also the age of majority, a number, in other words, that already had some legal significance. The thrust of the rule—the restriction to "lives in being" plus twenty-one years—meant, as I said, that one could "tie up" an estate for about seventy-five years quite easily; perhaps even for ninety or a hundred years—but no more. This is arbitrary, of course, but it does represent a kind of rough judgment: the dead hand can control, but not for more than a century.

That is certainly a defensible idea: a kind of compromise. But what about the ridiculous sub-rules? How could one possibly defend the fertile octogenarian, or the unborn widow? Yet here, as almost always, we should hesitate before dismissing these rules as nothing but craziness. These sub-rules may seem absurd; but notice that they have one virtue—an almost mathematical precision. In other words, a good lawyer, a person who actually understands the rule, can tell whether a will or trust violates the rule just by reading the text. This good lawyer does not need to know anything about the actual situation to come to this conclusion.[8]

But in order for this to be true, we have to have rules like the fertile octogenarian. If I leave property to my sister for life, then to her children for life, and then ultimately to her grandchildren living at the death of the last child, does this violate the rule? The answer may depend on whether my sister can or cannot have more children. That in turn might depend on how old she was. But the will or trust does not give this information to the reader. In order for the rule to operate mechanically, then, we have to have a bright-line rule, something hard and fast. Two such rules are possible: we can assume, conclusively, that all women can bear children; or assume, conclusively, that none of them can. The first assumption is better than the second. But that gives us the fertile octogenarian.

The peculiar shape of the rule, then, makes it possible for somebody—a lawyer, say—to know with complete certainty whether or not a will violates the rule. To do this, the rule has to be firm and unbending. John Chipman

Gray, in his 1886 treatise on the rule, put it this way: "In no part of the law is the reasoning so mathematical in its character; none has so small a human element." And: a "degree of dogmatism, therefore, may be permitted here which would be unbecoming in other branches of the law."[9]

But why is it useful for the law to be so "mathematical"? What is special about the rule against perpetuities? Imagine a period with poor records. Imagine that in some instances the document itself (the will, the trust) is the best, perhaps the only, evidence to go on in deciding who had the better title to some piece of property. This made some sense in, say, the early nineteenth century; or at least people could reasonably think so. It goes without saying that this makes very little sense today. Also, the rule arose at a time when landed wealth was still king and personal property (money, stocks and bonds) was secondary. The rule expressed a policy against tying up assets—chiefly land—for long periods of time, and keeping them off the market. But today the rule is *only* about trusts.[10] And the assets of most trusts are stocks, bonds, and other securities. The trustee can and does buy and sell and trade; normally, then, no assets are actually tied up for any length of time at all.

The rule, consequently, has eroded. In the first place, nobody needs the mathematical certainty any longer. Changes appeared, aimed at getting rid of the sub-rules that made lawyers nervous and seemed, in the worst cases, absurd. The Uniform Statutory Rule Against Perpetuities, which is in effect in quite a number of states, adopted the so-called "wait and see" approach. This statute begins, essentially, with a statement of the common law rule. But then it goes on to say that an interest does not violate the rule if the "interest either vests or terminates within ninety (90) years after the interest's creation."[11] This does the trick of getting rid of the technical traps; but of course the "mathematical certainty" is gone. In at least an occasional rare case, one would have to wait the full ninety years to know whether the trust was good or not. It might be sensible, then, to replace the rule (as some states did) with a simple time limit.

Many states got rid of the weird sub-rules explicitly. In Illinois, for example, "any person who has attained the age of 65 years shall be deemed incapable of having a child" (although this is hardly true of men).[12] Some jurisdictions have combined the two approaches: they have adopted a "wait and see" policy; and have also moved to get rid of the worst of the technical traps.[13] In England, the Perpetuities and Accumulation Act, originally passed in 1964, fixed the period at no more than eighty years, and other sections of the statute got rid of the fertile octogenarian and other quirks of the classic law.[14] Some courts have simply gone ahead and "construed" or interpreted trust provisions in such a way as to avoid holding that the rule was violated; they thus have been able to prevent destruction of an otherwise sensible estate plan.[15] In any event, lawyers who draft wills for clients, and who know their business, can include a clause that says explicitly that all trust interests must vest at the end of the perpetuities period, whatever else the will might say.

So far, so good. These reforms and practices have ended the rule's "reign of terror," once and for all. But note that the reforms accepted the basic idea that underlay the rule: the idea that the dead hand must crawl back into its grave, and end its dominion, at some reasonable point. The reforms simply aimed at a cleaner and more efficient operation. Yet in recent years, a growing number of states have flat-out abolished the rule, or have modified it so drastically that it might as well not exist. Delaware got rid of the rule altogether for trusts of personal property; if real property is left in trust (and not to be sold, presumably), the trust has 110 years to keep the land, and after that, it has to be sold and the proceeds distributed.[16] In some states, statutes ended the rule; but retained a rule against suspension of alienation. In other words, so long as the trustee can sell any asset in the trust—the usual case—there is no limit on how long the trust can last. In those states that have abolished the rule against perpetuities, at least in its orthodox form, it is possible, then, to set up a trust that lasts forever. There are at least twenty such states.[17] In Rhode Island, a statute passed in 1999 states baldly that the "common law rule against perpetuities shall no longer be in force and/or of any effect in this state."[18] In Washington state, the perpetuities period was extended to 150 years.[19] In Wyoming, the common law rule against perpetuities does not apply to any recent trust if it officially disclaimed the rule, and if the trust is to "terminate no later than one thousand (1,000) years after the trust's creation."[20] In some states—New Hampshire, for example—the rule does not apply to any trust that "contains a provision which expressly exempts the instrument from the application of the rule against perpetuities."[21]

What brought about this dramatic change? Basically, banks and trust companies lobbied for the change. A tax on generation-skipping transfers (GST) entered the law in 1986 (I mention this tax again in the chapter on succession taxes). The parts of the Internal Revenue Code that deal with the GST are incredibly involute—mind-boggling, one might say. But the general idea is to tax transfers of wealth that skip a generation. So, if I leave my estate to my daughter for life, and then to her children after she dies, the GST will tax the transfer when she dies. Without the GST, there would be no tax at that point.[22] But two million dollars of each transfer is exempt. Hence, if I can set up a trust that lasts many, many generations, the two million dollar gifts can escape tax for as long as the trust itself might last.

But how long is that? Only as long as the rule against perpetuities allows. However, if the state abolishes the rule, then a rich man can set up a very long-term trust and take full advantage of this tax loophole. Bankers and trust companies saw this opening and brought their considerable influence to bear on state legislatures, which were happy to oblige.[23] The people who run estate-planning seminars were also happy to help people create these "dynasty trusts," and law firms in the abolition states bragged about the local laws, and about their skill in drafting "megatrusts" or "dynasty trusts." One firm in Nevada announces on its website that the firm can set up a "megatrust" for any multi-millionaire who wants one, under the law of *any* of the states that permit it. "You DO NOT need to reside in one of these states."[24] The various legislative changes had stunning results. Business flowed into the states that made the first moves. Two scholars estimated that, up to the end of 2003, the "movement to abolish the Rule Against Perpetuities" had affected the situs of $100 billion in reported trust assets—roughly 10% of the total amount of assets reported, in 2003, to banking authorities.[25] The big gainers, of course, were the pioneers. But later states probably felt the need to abolish the rule in order to prevent a hemorrhage of their funds to the pioneer states.

Many of these states took other steps to seduce trusts into their domain. The so-called spendthrift trust doctrine (described in an earlier chapter) allows a donor to set up a trust that is insulated from the claims of any creditor, and which the beneficiaries themselves cannot pervert by selling or giving away their interests. There was one big exception to this rule: you were not allowed to set up such a trust for your own benefit. Creditors could reach the settlor's interest in the trust, no matter what words he had put in the document. But since the late 1990's, some eight or so American states have removed this limitation; they have permitted so-called asset protection trusts. Here too the "driving force behind these legislative initiatives is clear enough. States are vying for trust business."[26] Delaware is one of the states that made this change; and the legislature was "quite candid (even brazen) about its intentions," which were "to maintain Delaware's role as the most favored domestic jurisdiction for the establishment of trusts."[27]

In short, the motive behind this movement seems obvious. States are scrambling for trust money. The chief executive of a South Dakota company that administers trust funds claims the state is "so intent on building its trust business that state government officials have greeted out-of-state trust clients at the airport."[28] Weakening or abolishing the rule against perpetuities and enacting asset protection laws is a way to suck money into the state. The campaign is testimony to the power of banks and trust companies. But the campaign could not be successful without a bigger, broader change in the culture. Joel Dobris put it succinctly: "We like rich folks these days. Socialism is out of fashion. We identify with the rich. We revere the capitalist and the entrepreneur. . . . We love lifestyles of the rich and famous. . . . [W]e tend to value rich winners."[29] As we will see, there is plenty of other evidence to support this idea. The blatant—and very successful—attack on "death taxes" is another example, which I will consider in a later chapter.

The question is, if we do in fact "like rich folks these days," why is this so? This was not always the case. Franklin D. Roosevelt used to talk about "malefactors of great wealth." Nobody uses this language today—certainly no political figure. At one time, apparently, it was easier to hate rich people—old John D. Rockefeller and others of his type, or the "robber barons." But of course there still are malefactors of great wealth—the men who ran Enron, for example. Some of them went to jail; but, unless I am mistaken, the public outcry over this and similar scandals was fairly muted.

One thought, commonly heard, is that people imagine *they* might be rich some day—for example, by winning the lottery. This, then, colors their attitudes. But lotteries have been around for centuries. There must be other, more powerful factors. Perhaps one clue is in the new *image* of the rich. The "lifestyles of the rich and famous" are the lifestyles of basketball players, rock stars, and other celebrities; these are, at any rate, the most visible of these "lifestyles." Celebrities are, on the whole, people who seem just like us in most regards, and are terribly familiar; of course, they can shoot a basket or strum a guitar much better than other people we know.[30] Even the few businesspeople who are in the public eye—Bill Gates and Donald Trump, for example—are also celebrities. In any event, they lack the sinister air of John D. Rockefeller or J. P. Morgan, who seemed like crafty and malevolent men, too powerful for the good of the country. Nor do the rich today seem like idle parasites living on inherited wealth. Other rich and famous people—the Queen of England, the late Princess Diana, or for that matter the Pope—are also celebrities, which means that, underneath the glamour or the glitter or the holiness, one senses an ordinary human being, a person we can admire or even worship, while at the same time, and in some deep sense, *relating* to them. There were no photographs of Queen Victoria in a babushka; she was remote from the English public. There were no photographs of the Dalai Lamas at all, until the current one.

This cultural change, I think, is extremely significant. But there is also an important institutional factor. Trust law, and the law of succession, were historically judge-made law. They reflected ideology and culture, of course; but legislatures played only a limited role. For the most part, legislators did not care very much what happened.[31] Ideology and culture have shifted; but the new changes in the laws often come from the chambers of the state capitals. And why? Legal scholars played a role; but more important, I believe, was the influence, power, and lobbying of banks and trust companies. The rise of this particular interest group is the second, and perhaps decisive, historical change.

In the second half of the nineteenth century, the new professional trustees, the trust companies (or banks with trust departments), became, for the first time, significant players in the game of trust management. The history of these companies is complex; and many of them at first had rather limited investment powers, for example.[32] But their powers grew and grew; and in the twentieth century they largely took over the business of trust management from private individuals, certainly with regard to larger and dynastic trusts.[33] And by the end of the twentieth century their influence on trust law was felt in decisive ways.

The rule against perpetuities, then, may be on its last legs. Still, is this good or bad for society? And does it make any difference? The province of Manitoba, in Canada, abolished the rule in 1983.[34] A report of a Law Reform Commission in the province had recommended this move. The commission, in preparing its report, made an effort to find out what lawyers thought of the rule. Very little, it seems. To begin with, they were quite ignorant about its exact requirements. They also "regarded the rule as an irrelevance and a fossil." And they doubted whether people with estates really wanted to stretch out their control more than two or so generations.[35] Probably most lawyers today feel the same way. But what about the settlors, the men and women who create the trusts?

The abolition of the rule against perpetuities raises two separate questions. The first is, how many people actually *want* to set up long-term or perpetual trusts? In abolition states, how many people are creating such trusts? It is hard to tell. Only quite rich people would have any use for perpetual trusts. But in a country of 300 million people, even though the poor and the middle-class vastly outnumber the mega-rich, there are still enough of these people to make a difference. Dukeminier and Krier, in an article published in 2003, quote a New York City lawyer who "guesses, based on his own experience, that the number of perpetual trusts created nationwide now runs into the thousands per year"; his own firm "probably does 100 or more annually."[36]

The second question is: assuming some people want to set up these trusts, is this a danger to the polity? Is there some chance that, say, a billionaire will set up a gigantic trust, for his family, that lasts forever, getting bigger and bigger like a snowball rolling downhill? Here too the danger is probably exaggerated. Most of the mega-rich prefer to create foundations; they pour most of their wealth into these institutions. This strikes them, apparently, as a better way to gain a kind of immortality than passing their money on to remote descendants. Bill Gates has done exactly this. Also, if our billionaire has children, and the children have children, the trust will certainly grow; but it will fragment more and more among many direct descendants.

Even without perpetual trusts, the very rich have a tendency to *stay* rich. No doubt some rich families fizzle out; the descendants squander the money and end up with little or nothing. Yet the Vanderbilts and the Astors and the Duponts seem on the whole to be doing quite well, without perpetual trusts. There is a general increase in the national wealth, and the very rich profit from it more than anybody else. Money makes money. Rich people have many chances to make profitable investments. They can afford the best investment advisers, the best accountants, the best lawyers. They also tend to marry each other. Inequalities in wealth are rampant in the United States. I doubt that perpetual trusts will make things much worse, or worse at all.

Forever is a long time. Nobody alive today really knows what will happen to perpetual trusts, after a century or two goes by. It is a good guess that if these trusts proliferate, some sort of legal control will be demanded. I have not seen any analysis of what is actually *in* these perpetual trusts. They may have special provisions that allow the trustee or a group of beneficiaries to put an end to the trust.[37] For their actual impact on society, or on the economy, we will have to wait.

ACCUMULATING TRUSTS

The snowball danger is not terribly real for ordinary trusts, which pay out all of their income every year. Naturally, the principal can get bigger and bigger, as the economy grows. But the real danger would come from an accumulating trust—a trust that does not pay out all of its income, but hoards it, adding some or all of it to principal. Such a trust could indeed become monstrously large—theoretically, it could in time suck into its maw all of the assets of the country, or even the world. Obviously, this is not likely to happen. But for how long can you set up a trust that just accumulates income?

The issue came up in a famous English case, *Thelluson* v. *Woodford*, decided in 1805.[38] Peter Thellusson, who died in 1797, had made a lot of money during his lifetime. He left behind a long and complicated will, with many specific gifts of money and other property for his wife, children, and other relatives. But he also created a trust, consisting of land in England (yielding some £4,500 a year), some real estate in the West Indies, and personal property estimated to be worth more than £600,000—a gigantic fortune. The income from the trust was to be accumulated during the lives of those of his children, grandchildren, and even great-grandchildren, who were alive at the time of his death. The money was then to be divided among those of his descendants living on the date when that last survivor died. At that time, the estate would be truly immense—at least this was a possibility.

In court, those who attacked the will argued that the arrangement was immoral, destructive; the thought of such a huge fortune growing, growing, growing, like some sort of horrific primal ooze, struck fear into their hearts. Or at least they raised horrific images as a way of attacking the scheme. Nonetheless, the highest court of England upheld the trust. The net result was to tie accumulations to the rule against perpetuities. An accumulating trust was acceptable, so long as it did not last past the orthodox period: lives in being plus twenty-one years, or in practice, something short of a century. In fact, this seemed much too long to Parliament, which, in the so-called Thelluson Act in 1800 cut the time down considerably.[39] In the United States, however, many statutes gave the question the same handy answer as the House of Lords: let a trust accumulate as long as the period of the rule against perpetuities.

But this raises a question: what happens when a state gets rid of the rule against perpetuities? In one of these states, a person can, after all, set up a trust that lasts forever. Can a perpetual trust also act as an accumulating trust?[40] One way to solve the problem is simply to get rid of the rule against accumulations. Delaware, for example, which abolished the rule against perpetuities, also discarded the rule against accumulations.[41] But in many states, the question remains open. In theory, a perpetual and accumulating trust could eventually suck up all the assets on earth.

How important is the issue of the accumulating trust? Probably not very. The perpetual trust itself is more problematic; but only if there come to be too many of them, and they turn out to have bad side effects. This is not very likely. Old Peter Thellusson set up a pure accumulating trust: that is, the income *had* to be accumulated. Canny lawyers drafting perpetual trusts do not do this. Instead they give trustees the *discretion* to accumulate. This is a very different kind of animal. The idea is not to set up some kind of monster trust, growing like the proverbial snowball rolling downhill. The idea is, rather, to make the trust more flexible. The trustee will accumulate income at times; but at other times, pay out most of the income. And in any event it seems unlikely that any of these trusts will actually grow to some huge, unshapely mass. The trusts, after all, will be subject to taxation. Trusts have to pay income tax on any income that they accumulate instead of paying it out to beneficiaries.[42] There will also be fees and commissions for trustees and other agents. All of these factors will impose a "drag on trust fund performance."[43]

The rule against perpetuities does not apply to charitable trusts. These trusts have always been forever. Normally, they are supposed to spend their income for charitable purposes. It would be most unusual to give them the power to accumulate. Two eccentric testators in Pennsylvania, however, were intrigued by the idea of snowballing a small amount into an enormous fortune by letting the trust accumulate for centuries. The first of these, one Frank James, in the

1960's left the residue of his estate in trust for the "Right Worshipful Grand Lodge of Free and Accepted Masons of Pennsylvania," for the benefit of "the Masonic Homes at Elizabethtown, Pennsylvania."[44] The Worshipful Grand Lodge would get half of the income, the rest to be accumulated for 220 years. Then the Grand Lodge would get 75%; and finally, after 400 years, the trust would end, and the principal would be turned over to the Grand Lodge. James left $41,000; the idea was that this modest sum would turn into millions of dollars, even assuming a low rate of return; and if you assumed a higher rate, billions of dollars. The court found this scheme "unreasonable and void . . . unnecessary, charitably purposeless and contrary to public policy."

The other eccentric testator, Jonathan Holdeen of Pennsylvania, was a man who hated the very idea of taxes. He thought he had hit upon just the plan to get rid of taxes in Pennsylvania. In the 1970's he set up trusts that were supposed to pay some income to the Unitarian Universalist Association; the rest was to be accumulated for periods "ranging in duration from 500 to 1000 years." Eventually the income could be used as an "endowment" that would "pay all governmental expenses." But this scheme too came to grief in the courts. Accumulations for charity, according to the trial court judge, had to be "reasonable"; this scheme, however, like the scheme in the James estate (which was prominently cited) was "unreasonable, contrary to public policy," and consequently "void." The Supreme Court of Pennsylvania agreed. The opinion never made clear exactly what was "unreasonable" about the scheme, but the plan clearly startled and frightened these judges.[45]

Another unconventional testator, Charles Walker of Texas, in his will called for the executor to sell a tract of land "for cash" and to put the money "in safe and secure tax-free U.S. government bonds or insured tax-free municipal bonds." This would constitute a trust fund, which would accumulate (he thought) until it could "provide a million dollar trust fund for every American 18 years or older." He thought this would take 346 years. This plan too came to grief in the appeal court, which decided this was not a valid charitable trust at all. Simply handing out money indiscriminately was not charity. They sent the case back to the trial court, to see if it could be salvaged under Texas perpetuities law.[46]

In one Missouri case in 1977, a court did accept a trust that called for perpetual accumulation.[47] Corry T. Meeker set up a trust for the Shriners' Hospital for Crippled Children in St. Louis, Missouri. The hospital would get 75% of the income; the rest would be accumulated and added to the principal. The will that set up this trust said nothing about how long this accumulation would go on. Presumably forever. Was this provision void? The court refused to say it was. But this was because, by law, courts of equity could modify the trust when "continued accumulation of income no longer furthers the purpose of the trust or is in detriment to the public interest." That had not yet happened; and so they gave the trust a reprieve. In any event, for charitable trusts, at the present time, the issue of accumulation is almost purely theoretical. Modern tax law does not allow charitable trusts and foundations to accumulate at will. The rules require them to pay out a certain percentage each year of the market value of their assets.[48] Giant foundations, with the power to suck into their maws a big share of the country's wealth, simply cannot exist.

CHAPTER 8

CHARITABLE GIFTS AND FOUNDATIONS

Charitable trusts and foundations are a striking feature of modern American society, and the role played by the great foundations is particularly salient.[1] These trusts and foundations, created either by will or by gifts made during the lifetimes of the rich, give away, year after year, a great deal of money—in 2005, 68,000 foundations made grants on the order of $33.6 billion.[2] This is serious money. Of course, the American economy amounts to trillions of dollars; compared to that, $33.6 billion is not that impressive. Yet universities, the arts, some religious organizations, and some forms of research would have difficulty carrying on without the money they get from trusts and foundations. This chapter concerns these long-term trusts and foundations.

Americans, to be sure, make gifts to charities all the time. They do it mostly during their lifetimes; and they can also leave money to charity at death, in their wills. In fact, however, most people leave nothing to charity; their money goes at death to members of their families. Billionaires may be different; but the percentage of ordinary people, even ordinary rich people, who leave money to charity is quite small. This is a consistent finding of all of the studies of testamentary behavior. An old study of wills in New York County from 1880 to 1885 found that only 8.4% of the wills made any provision for charity; and in about half of them the gifts "amounted to only a small percentage of the total estate involved." Moreover, this was not a random sample of estates, but a study of the estates of "prominent" people.[3] Gifts to charity were found to be equally rare in a study of estates in Providence, Rhode Island, in the 1980's.[4] Olin Browder's study of wills in England and in Washtenaw County, Michigan, for 1963, found only thirty wills out of 187 that contained charitable gifts; this is a higher percentage than in most studies; but in four of the wills, the charitable gift was "substitutional"—that is, it went into effect only if the main heir died.[5] In Essex County, New Jersey, there was only one gift to charity in 1850, out of sixty-eight wills; in 1875, six gifts out of sixty were charitable (one was a bequest for Masses; and one was only contingent); in 1900 there were two charitable gifts in 150 wills.[6] In a 1975 study of King County, Washington, four out of fifty-nine decedents who left wills (6.78%) made substantial gifts to charity.[7] A study of Alameda County, California, in the late nineteenth and early twentieth centuries found that only 8% of the wills included charitable bequests.[8] In San Bernardino County, California, in the 1960's, the proportion was just about the same—7.9% of the wills made any provision at all for charity, and some of these were contingent gifts, which most likely never took place. About 60% of the gifts were to churches and other religious organizations.[9]

The situation, however, is quite different with the rich and the super-rich. It is standard today to expect the super-rich to set up a foundation and pour much or most of their money into it. For many years, the Ford Foundation was the largest of the charitable foundations. When Dwight Macdonald wrote about it in the 1950's in a witty series of articles in *The New Yorker*, it was "by far the biggest wholesaler" in this field, and dwarfed all its rivals. Macdonald called it a "large body of money completely surrounded by people who want some."[10] The Ford Foundation is still a very large and powerful foundation: it was worth more than $12 billion in 2006, and was spending more than half a billion dollars a year. But Ford has been overtaken by the Gates Foundation and now occupies a distant second place. As of the end of 2004, the Bill and Melinda Gates Foundation had assets worth over $28 billion, more than twice the size of Ford. At that time, too, there were no fewer than forty-nine foundations with more than $1 billion in assets; and more than 100 that had at least half a billion.[11] The Gates Foundation got even larger when Warren

Buffett, the second richest man in America, decided in 2006 to hand most of his enormous fortune over to the Gates Foundation.[12] This was a most unusual act of self-abnegation. Usually, the very rich, no matter how generous, want foundations to carry their names; and they want to see their names plastered all over the buildings their money makes possible.

The total number of foundations and charitable trusts runs into many thousands. The Internal Revenue Service received "information returns" from 31,171 "domestic private foundations" in 1985; by 2002 the total had reached 73,255. And this number surely understates the actual total. They range from very small funds to giant foundations with billions of dollars in assets.

The small funds are sometimes dedicated to quite narrow and specific purposes. The Conrad Cantzen Shoe Fund, created in 1928, was established for the benefit of Actors Equity Association, but chiefly to buy shoes for "needy actors of the theatrical profession." As the donor put it, "Many times I have been on my uppers," and "the thinner the soles of my shoes were the less courage I had to face the manager in looking for a job."[13] At the opposite end of the spectrum, the big, famous foundations tend to have rather sweeping mandates. The Ford Foundation, which has sumptuous offices in New York City, lists as its goals to "strengthen democratic values," to "reduce poverty and injustice," to "promote international cooperation," and to "advance human achievement." This allows the foundation to do just about anything. The Russell Sage Foundation, which began life in 1907, was supposed to apply its income "to the improvement of social and living conditions in the United States of America." The largest foundations can make quite a big splash. The Gates Foundation has been working on international health problems, among other matters—giving away millions of dollars to such institutions as the Swiss Tropical Institute and the World Health Organization, as well as money to fight AIDS and to advance global health. The MacArthur Foundation is famous for its "genius awards," grants of "unrestricted fellowships to talented individuals who have shown extraordinary originality and dedication in their creative pursuits and a marked capacity for self-direction."[14]

No foundation, no matter how rich, can afford to do everything it might like to do. Some concentrate on medical research or on education. Some smaller foundations are even more specialized. The Robert Schalkenbach Foundation was organized in 1925 to "promote public awareness of the social philosophy and economic reforms advocated by Henry George (1839–1897), including the *'single tax on land values.'*"[15] But generally speaking, foundations have broad mandates; and the larger the foundation, the more likely that this is so.

Charities, courts often say, are favorites of the law. There is plenty of evidence that they are indeed favored by courts, and by law in general. To begin with, American courts (today, at least), take a very broad view of what constitutes charity. There are limits, of course—in one old case, the testator left money to keep his "family monument and burial place" in repair, forever; and also to pay for a "military band" to march to the cemetery on the anniversary of his death, and on holidays, "and then and there perform a funeral march and . . . other appropriate music." This was disallowed.[16] The marching band would probably still not make it today; but perpetual care of graves is specifically authorized by statute. It is not quite true that almost anything goes, so long as the trust is even arguably for the public benefit; but compared to English law, American law is quite open-minded. The playwright George Bernard Shaw left money in trust to reform English spelling; he had devised his own phonetic alphabet, which he obviously hoped would carry the day. An English court, however, felt this was not a proper charitable purpose.[17] English spelling remains as chaotic as ever.

Other ways in which the law favors charities are much more significant. Charities, for example, do not pay an income tax on their earnings. Any money left to charity, including money left to a charitable foundation, escapes estate and gift taxes entirely. This is in line with American culture, and Americans more or less take this for granted. An American billionaire who leaves all his money to a foundation avoids succession taxes. This, of course, deprives the government of money it otherwise would have collected. Compared to (say) the contributions of government in most European countries, the role of governments in the United States in support of symphony orchestras, art museums, ballet companies, and the like is pinched and grudging. The United States, too, has many rich and flourishing private universities—again in contrast to Europe and Latin America. Arts and higher education, then, have come to depend on gifts from rich people—a situation that has its pluses and its minuses, but is deeply embedded in our way of life.

Other rules that apply generally to trusts are relaxed for charitable trusts and foundations. A perpetual trust is still impossible in many states, by virtue of the rule against perpetuities. In all states, however, a perpetual *charitable* trust is perfectly legal. And perpetual charitable trusts are, in fact, the norm. A few charitable trusts or foundations have had "sunset" provisions—they were set up with a definite, short life, told to spend all their money, and then go out of business. But the vast majority of trusts have no time limit at all; and some are more than a century old. Benjamin Franklin set up a trust under a codicil to his will, which he meant to last at least two hundred years. The codicil gave money to Boston and to Philadelphia, to be "let out . . . upon interest, at five per cent. per annum," to "young married artificers, under the age of twenty-five years, as have served an apprenticeship in the said town." Franklin was clearly looking ahead: the terms of the trust were such that the principal was bound to grow. After a hundred years, Philadelphia was to use some of the extra money to bring water from Wissahickon Creek by pipes into the town.[18]

Normal trusts, too, must have definite, identifiable beneficiaries—people who in theory could enforce the trust. If you cannot find such a beneficiary, the trust (it is said) is invalid. In fact, normal trusts always have such beneficiaries; otherwise, why would anybody bother to create a trust in the first place? In a few instances somebody has set up a trust for the children of X, who is unmarried and has no children; in these cases, there is a serious question whether the trust is valid.[19] The courts have also struggled with the problem of testators who set up trusts for the benefit of pets—cats, dogs, horses. Obviously, the "beneficiaries" of these trusts can hardly go to court and enforce them (one could say the same thing about a trust for the benefit of a baby). The courts are willing to uphold these "honorary" trusts, if the trustee in turn is willing to do his duty by the particular cats, dogs, or horses.[20] In some states, New York, for example, statutes specifically authorize enforceable trusts for animals. In one case, the "income and principal beneficiaries" of a trust were five chimpanzees. The beneficiaries lived at the "Chimpanzee and Human Communication Institute" and were "widely known for their proficiency with American Sign Language."[21] When Leona Helmsley, the real estate mogul (and "queen of mean") died in 2007 at the age of 87, she left $12 million in trust, to be used (apparently) for the benefit of her beloved dog, Trouble.[22]

In any event, with regard to charitable trusts, the *normal* situation is the opposite: normally, there is no definite beneficiary. Or, to be more precise, for most charitable trusts, you cannot point to anybody who can claim, legally speaking, to be a beneficiary with the right to sue the trustee. So, you can set up a charitable trust "for alleviating the sufferings of the poor," or "to preserve wetlands," or to "encourage the arts"; yet no specific individual can claim to be a beneficiary and enforce the trust in a court. The fact that I am poor and suffering, and the trust is for the benefit of the poor and suffering, is not enough. This raises the question, who *can* enforce the trust? Who can make sure that the trustees do their duty? There are devices for monitoring charitable trusts; I will deal with these later.

THE HISTORY OF CHARITABLE TRUST LAW

The history of charitable trusts is not a smooth story of continuous grace and favor. Charities, in fact, were not always favorites of the law. Indeed, in many ways, they were strongly disfavored. And, in the early years of the republic, there was considerable doubt whether they were legally acceptable at all.

In 1819 this issue—whether charitable trusts were valid—came before the United States Supreme Court. Silas Hart, a resident of Virginia, in his will made a gift to the "Baptist Association that . . . meets at Philadelphia"; the gifts consisted of "a perpetual fund for the education of youths of the Baptist denomination, who shall appear promising for the ministry."[23] Hall died in 1795. The will had been executed in 1790.

A key act of Parliament, passed during the waning days of Queen Elizabeth I, the Statute of Charitable Uses, had dealt with the enforcement of charitable gifts and trusts.[24] But in 1792 the legislature of Virginia, in the heady days of early independence, passed a law that, in effect, nullified the force of all English statutes enacted before the American Revolution. This included the Statute of Charitable Uses. What, then, was the status of Hart's gift?

John Marshall's opinion begins by declaring the gift void, on what we would consider rather technical grounds. The Baptist Association had not yet been incorporated at the time Hall died; it got itself a charter, but only later. Under the law at the time, an unincorporated association was not capable of inheriting property by will. This made the gift invalid, unless something special about its charitable nature saved it. Marshall then embarked on a long historical excursus about the Statute of Charitable Uses, and whether there was some power in the courts, independent of this statute, to enforce charitable gifts. The ultimate answer was no, and Hall's gift failed.

The charitable trust came to the attention of the Supreme Court again in 1844, in *Vidal v. Girard's Executors*.[25] This was a landmark decision on a number of legal issues. The facts of the case are also extremely interesting. Stephen Girard had been born in France, emigrated to the United States, and settled in Philadelphia, where he died in 1831. He was a widower and had no children. He was also enormously rich—worth perhaps $7 million, which probably made him the equivalent of one of today's billionaires.

His will left his vast estate to be used to build a "permanent college, with suitable out-buildings, sufficiently spacious for the residence and accommodation of at least three hundred scholars." The college was to be located on land that Girard owned. The estate would pay the teachers and supply the college "with decent and suitable furniture as well as books and all things needful" to carry his "general design" into effect. That "general design" was extremely specific. The college building was to be "at least one hundred and ten feet east and west, and one hundred and sixty feet north and south. . . . It shall be three stories in height, each story at least fifteen feet high in the clear from the floor to the cornice." The building was to be "fire-proof inside and outside." No wood was to be used "except for doors, windows, and shutters." The residents were to be "poor white male orphans, between the ages of six and ten years," with preference given to orphans born in Philadelphia; next in line were orphans from other parts of Pennsylvania, then orphans from New York City, then orphans from New Orleans ("being the first port on the said continent at which I first traded"). The food was to be "plain but wholesome"; the clothing "plain but decent apparel, (no distinctive dress ever to be worn)." There was to be "suitable and rational exercise and recreation." The curriculum was minutely specified. They could learn French and Spanish ("I do not forbid, but I do not recommend the Greek and Latin languages"). The students were to remain until "between fourteen and eighteen years of age," and then were to be "bound out by the mayor, aldermen, and citizens of Philadelphia . . . to suitable occupations." Moreover, "no ecclesiastic, missionary, or minister of any sect whatsoever, shall ever hold or exercise any station or duty whatever in the same college"; or even be "admitted for any purpose, or as a visitor, within the premises." This was to keep the "tender minds of the orphans . . . free from the excitement which clashing doctrines and sectarian controversy are so apt to produce."

Girard's will had many other provisions; and it was to produce, in the course of history, a long line of litigated cases. (At the time, for example, nobody seemed to care that only *white* orphans were eligible; but this became an issue during the civil rights era.[26]) The will itself is enormously interesting from a psychological standpoint. Girard, and some other rich men and women later on, was looking for a kind of immortality; and his device for achieving this goal was through setting up a permanent and perpetual charity, in this case a school. Girard's aims were, however, in a kind of tension. The urge to set up something that would last forever tends to clash with an urge to specify, in minute detail, exactly how this something was to operate. In both regards, his charitable trust was an extreme example of the dead hand at work.

The will was attacked by Girard's relatives—nieces and nephews who saw a vast fortune slipping from their grasp. They made a number of arguments. They claimed that the city of Philadelphia had no power to take property in trust. They claimed, too, that charitable trusts were not authorized under the laws of Pennsylvania. And they also insisted that the peculiar restrictions on members of the clergy were "derogatory and hostile to the Christian religion," and therefore "void, as being against the common law and public policy of Pennsylvania."[27] The Supreme Court, however, in an opinion written by Joseph Story, upheld the trust. Story decided that Philadelphia did have power to accept property in trust, and that charitable trusts were perfectly valid in Pennsylvania. As for the alleged hostility to Christianity, Story brushed that aside. Just because no "ecclesiastics" were to teach at the school did not mean that Christianity itself was not to be taught; lay people could teach it, too.

This case, of course, depended on Pennsylvania law. The states differed in their attitude toward charitable trusts, and in their doctrines on the subject. In short, the legal situation in the first part of the nineteenth century was quite confused. The law in New York state was particularly interesting and complex. Courts, in part because of the way the legislature had tried to reform the laws of property, seemed to wobble back and forth on the question whether a will could leave money to a charitable trust at all. It is hard to generalize; but, at the very least, the charitable trust in New York was under a cloud.[28]

Samuel Tilden (1814–86) was a prominent Democratic politician, a one-time governor of New York, presidential candidate in 1876 (the famous contested election which ultimately sent Rutherford B. Hayes to the White House), and, despite never getting to be president, he was a very rich man. Like Girard, Tilden was childless; he was survived by a sister and several nieces and nephews. His will left the bulk of his fortune in trust for the purpose of establishing and supporting a "free library" in New York City. Tilden was aware that New York law made his scheme difficult, and he thought he had a way around the legal difficulties. He left his money to trustees, directing them to "obtain, as speedily as possible," an act of the legislature incorporating the trust. This was done, and the Tilden trust was incorporated in New York in 1887. But to no avail. Some of Tilden's relatives filed suit to set the trust aside, arguing that the trust was invalid under New York law. In 1891 the New York Court of Appeals, the highest court in the state, agreed, and the relatives won their case.[29] The trust was not a total loss, however. One of the relatives, Laura Hazard, had given up her claim and settled for a payment just shy of a million dollars. The other relatives also in the end reached an agreement with the trust. The trust ended up with substantial assets. Ultimately, then, New York City got its library.

Nevertheless, the failure of the Tilden trust was a traumatic event. James Barr Ames, of the Harvard Law School, published an essay on the subject. He began the article with this remark: "Melancholy the spectacle must always be, when covetous relatives seek to convert to their own use the fortune which a testator has plainly devoted to a great public benefaction."[30] New York was by this time one of only a handful of states where the trust would have failed. Its law, which (according to the courts) did not permit the formation of charitable trusts, was (said Ames) an "unmixed evil," which robbed the "community at large for the benefit of unscrupulous relatives."[31] The New York legislature obviously felt the same way; in 1893 it changed the law to get rid of the objections to charitable trusts.[32]

The New York case was already an anomaly. Another nineteenth-century will—it reminds one of the will of Stephen Girard—had quite a different legal fate from Tilden's will. John Crerar died in Chicago in 1889. He was very rich, had never married, and had no relatives closer than cousins. He left money to various charities, including a gift of $100,000 to be used to erect "a colossal statue of Abraham Lincoln." He also directed that the residue of his estate should go toward building and endowing a "free public library," to be called the John Crerar Library, in the south part of Chicago. The building was to be "tasteful, substantial, and fire-proof"; the books and periodicals were to be "selected with a view to create and sustain a healthy moral and Christian sentiment in the community." All "nastiness and immorality" were to be excluded; specifically, he banned from the library "dirty French novels and all skeptical trash and works of questionable moral tone." Rather, the "atmosphere" was to be "that of Christian refinement."[33] Relatives attacked the will, but the Illinois courts upheld it. The "fixed policy of the law," said the Illinois Supreme Court, is to "uphold charitable bequests"; it would be wrong to defeat "this magnificent bequest" for the "endowment of a free public library in a great city."[34]

What lies behind the changes that took place in the law of charitable trusts and foundations in the nineteenth century? Crucial was the change in the image of the charitable foundation or trust. Memories of the dead hand of the church tarnished that image in the earliest years of the republic. Land passing into the clutches of the church, to be held there forever, kept off the market, hoarded, monopolized: this was the picture, a supremely negative one. It was the image that underlay the mortmain statutes as well. As we saw, James Barr Ames, writing after the failure of the Tilden trust, said the decision was one that hurt the community as a whole. Why did he think so? Perhaps because the new image reflected the new American millionaires, men and women of enormous wealth, and their occasional decisions to give some or all of their money to advance the public good; the law, Ames thought (and no doubt most other people would agree) ought to encourage these men to do so.

The great gifts that created these foundations, in the Gilded Age, were gifts by American plutocrats. They went not to the church; nor were they held narrowly for some sectarian purpose. Rather they were gifts to and for the public benefit. Two historians of philanthropy, Barry Karl and Stanley Katz, have a slightly different take on this development. They make a distinction between charity and philanthropy, between "palliative charity, and scientific research into the root causes of social ills."[35] They connect the rise of the great foundations to "philanthropy"; and to the idea of progress. Many people believed that such age-old problems as poverty and disease could be attacked, and perhaps conquered, through science, technology, and careful investigation. This was one of the aims of the new foundations.

The United States also had, as they put it, a "tradition of local and private initiative."[36] Unlike European countries, this was a land of fragmented government, a land in which power was widely dispersed for most of our history, like a glass shattered into a thousand little pieces. This was a structural fact, and also a cultural one. The country was born as a union of more or less independent states, and there was a deep strand of suspicion of central power and national government. Americans in the nineteenth century did not "accept the idea of a national social order," but, as Karl and Katz argue, this was not because they objected to "the fact of social control"; they objected only to "its location in the central government." A group of rich elites began to realize that "local charitable support and local reform" might not be adequate to the country's problems. The result was the "creation of the modern foundation and its legitimation as a national system of social reform—a privately supported system operating in lieu of a governmental system."[37] They argue, in other words, that law and society in this country tend to favor institutions that can be labeled "private" over those that could be labeled "public." Encouraging private charity and private foundations thus seems very appropriate—in line with an individualistic, market-oriented system. One might add that foundations and charitable trusts can also do some things that government simply cannot do under our constitutional system. Giving money to churches and religious organizations is one obvious example.

And the great foundations do not, today, suffer from the problem of Girard's will or McKee's: their charters never get down to grubby details. The Rockefeller Foundation, for example, began life with a charter granted by the legislature of New York in 1913. Its purpose was to promote "the well-being of mankind throughout the world."[38] It is hard to be more general than that.

Sheer benevolence is not the only reason why the very rich set up charitable trusts and foundations. The tax motive is also powerful. Money left to charity, as we mentioned, avoids estate tax. The creation of the Ford Foundation, for example, owed a lot to this fact. The Ford Motor Company was privately held and controlled by the Ford family. By the 1920's, the tax was as high as 40% on estates that were greater than $10 million. When members of the family died, the family would be forced to sell stock to raise money for the taxes; this would weaken or eliminate their tight control over their company.[39]

The family hit on the following scheme. They divided the shares of the company into two classes. Ninety-five percent of the shares were class A stock, which had no vote. The rest were class B, and they had the vote. The family created the Ford Foundation in 1936, and Henry and Edsel Ford, in their wills, left all their class A stock to the foundation; the class B stock went to the family. Taxes on the voting stock would be paid from the nonvoting stock.[40] Since the foundation would inherit 95% of the stock in the company, the estate tax would not be large, and the family would be able to pay it without selling shares in the corporation. The foundation would own most of the company, but the family would retain its absolute control of the company's affairs.

Eventually the Ford Motor Company became a public corporation; its stock came to be widely held by ordinary people and institutions; and the foundation also diversified its assets enormously. Control of the foundation passed out of the hands of the family into the hands of managers, many of them from the academy. This has become the pattern for all of the foundations that have lasted any length of time. The founders die; the families disperse; and the foundations become, in the end, independent and free-floating entities. Wealthy dynasts must be aware of this fact, but they continue to give their money freely to foundations. At least the foundations perpetuate their names, and for a while at least, their massive influence. In the end, this particular dead hand has to loosen its grip; but that may be years, decades, even centuries away.

And the law continues to smile on foundations. Gifts to them continue to be tax-free. They benefit, too, from the general favor the law grants to dynastic trusts, as we saw in an earlier chapter. This is not to say that charitable trusts and foundations, especially the very big ones, have been free from politics and controversy. During the McCarthy period in the 1950's, when the country—or large parts of it—was obsessed with communism and saw Communists under every bush, Congress saw fit to investigate what it thought were the sinister doings of these great foundations, particularly the Ford Foundation. The Reece Committee, in 1954, was the brainchild of U.S. Representative Brazilla Carroll Reece. This great statesman thought he saw in the Ford Foundation a "diabolical conspiracy" to turn the United States into a socialist or communist country.[41] In an article in *American Mercury*, Reece wrote, "Tax-exempt philanthropic foundations clearly have become one principal source of Communist influence, infiltration, and subversion in the United States." According to Reece, Moscow had given "direct orders to American Communists to penetrate our philanthropic foundations."[42] The Reece Committee issued a report full of wild and ridiculous charges. Fortunately, nothing much came of it.

Even then, in the palmy days of McCarthyism, such charges must have seemed absurd. To Reece and his fellow travelers, anything vaguely left of center was an object of suspicion. These suspicions had political payoff. The right wing was especially suspicious of the social sciences. Reece and the far right demanded blind adherence to certain tenets: the free market, orthodoxy in religion, and super-patriotism. Social science research made conservatives squirm. In their view, sociologists in particular were deadly enemies of these three pillars of American society.[43]

Politics is a complex phenomenon; it is easy to talk about "right wing" and "left wing," but these "wings" are themselves fragmented and inconsistent. Reece and McCarthy represented one facet of the American conservative movement: paranoid, deeply suspicious of government, sensing "socialism" in the most unlikely places, and hostile to "elites." But there are other facets too. The men who founded the great foundations were hardly left-wingers. Although the foundations ultimately tended to pass into the hands of academics and professional managers, these people were also hardly "reds." And they represented *private* wealth, privately endowed and privately managed, rather than an arm of any particular regime or government; and this was an important aspect of their ideology, as Katz and Karl have pointed out. Much later, Reece's spiritual descendants waged war on the National Endowment for the Humanities and federal support for the arts, modest though the amounts in question were. They discovered, however, that the men and women who sat on the boards of symphonies, opera companies, and art museums were, often enough, conservative Republicans deeply committed to these essentially private institutions.

Congress did put into effect some rules and regulations that were meant to curb certain actions of the foundations. The basis was not their political bias, though perhaps this played a minor role. The real problems attacked were financial abuse and misuse of the foundation form. The tax reform law of 1969 began requiring minimum pay-outs every year,[44] and it prohibited foundations from owning more than 20% of the stock of any particular business (in other words, using a foundation to continue family control of a business).[45]

CY PRES

Legally speaking, there is no reason why a charitable trust cannot go on forever. Most foundations, in fact, are set up to be perpetual, as I mentioned. Requiring a foundation to go out of business is rare. There have been, however, some notable instances: for example, the Rosenwald Foundation, established by Julius Rosenwald, president of Sears, Roebuck, & Co. In 1928, Rosenwald amended the by-laws of his foundation to provide that it had to spend itself down to zero within twenty-five years of his death. He wrote: "I am emphatically opposed to never-ending endowments."[46] He died in 1932, and in 1948 the foundation also came to an end. It had given all its money away. A more recent example was the John M. Olin Foundation, established in 1953. The foundation was supposed to spend all its money down within one generation after Olin died, which he did in 1982. And indeed, the foundation closed down in 2005.[47]

Most foundations, however, have immortal life. This is not a problem for the major foundations and trusts. They have very broad mandates that are unlikely to become obsolete. But some of the smaller, more narrowly focused foundations might, in the course of time, become useless, illegal, or impossible to sustain. Or the goals of a trust or foundation might be illegal or impossible to begin with. Robert Wallace Craig left $150,000 to the Sisters of Mercy of Arizona to build a hospital for the "exclusive care of tubercular cases." But the amount was woefully inadequate for that purpose.[48] It was impossible, then, to carry out his wishes—at least not literally. In another case, Frederick M. Thompson left money to be used to "acquire a farm of twenty-five acres or more" and build on it a "nonsectarian home for crippled and other children . . . to provide an outing and vacation home." But the "testator's dream of the Children's Outing Home" was "unattainable" because he left the mere sum of $88,000.[49] What should be done with these unworkable trusts? One obvious answer is to give the money back to the heirs. But this is not what usually happens. There is a fine and handy doctrine in the tool chest of the law, called *cy pres*, which can be invoked in such cases. This doctrine allows a court to change the terms of a charitable trust, in order to keep it alive, if the trust has become impossible or illegal. The court can modify the trust, though always with a view to keeping it as close as possible to the original terms. ("Cy pres" is old Law French for "so close.")

Some early American courts were skeptical about the doctrine; some even doubted that it existed at all in this country.[50] In part this was a reaction against the way the doctrine was used in England—especially "prerogative" cy pres. This was the power of the Crown to divert charities to other ends under certain circumstances. So, for example, in a 1754 case, a Jewish testator left money to found a Yeshiva where students could study Rabbinic law. The chancellor held that such a gift was void. It was a gift for a "superstitious use," that is, for "promoting a religion contrary to the established one." But in such a case the Crown could divert the gift to some other charity. The bulk of the money went to support a preacher at a Foundling Hospital, who would " instruct the children . . . in the Christian religion."[51] The poor testator must have been whirling in his grave. Clearly, no such doctrine was suitable in the United States. But the courts were even leery about ordinary ("judicial") cy pres, probably for a familiar reason—the general distrust of gifts to charity, which were imagined mostly to pass into the dead hand of the church.

This attitude is now history, as they say. One turning point was a Massachusetts case, *Jackson* v. *Phillips* (1867).[52] Francis Jackson died in 1861. He left money to trustees to be used to prepare and circulate "books, newspapers . . . speeches, lectures, and such other means, as . . . will create a public sentiment that will put an end to negro slavery in this country"; and also to be used "for the benefit of fugitive slaves who may escape from the slaveholding states of this infamous Union from time to time."[53] The 13th Amendment to the Constitution had put an end to slavery. So, the argument went, the trust could no longer be carried out and the money should be returned to the family. But the court disagreed. In a long and learned opinion, the court discussed, and applied, the doctrine of cy pres. "The negroes, though emancipated," said the court, "still stand in great need of assistance and education."[54] The court referred the case to a master, to frame a scheme for the proper disposition of the funds along these lines.

The cy pres doctrine is now in full flower. This illustrates, once more, how much the law smiles on charities—and on the dynasts who create charitable trusts and foundations. The doctrine gives courts the power to alter the terms of these trusts and foundations in such a way as to preserve the basic intent of the men and women who created them. And the court will use the doctrine whenever it decides that the testator had a "general charitable intent." This is, essentially, an assumption—that the dead man or woman would have preferred some sort of modification of the trust, rather than see it die and let the money pass into the hands of the testator's relatives.

In theory, the court will change the terms as little as possible, just the bare minimum needed to keep the intent alive. But this is not always easy to do.

Who can tell what arrangements are the right ones, the closest ones, the most appropriate ones? In one interesting Arizona case in 1971,[55] James Kidd left a holographic will, in which he recited that he had no heirs, left $100 to "some preacher of the gospel to say fare well at my grave," and then gave the rest of his property to support "a research or some scientific proof of a soul of the human body which leaves at death I think in time their can be a photograph of soul leaving the human at death." The estate amounted to some $175,000. No fewer than 103 eager claimants tried to get their hands on the money. These included one Emma G. Clausser, who "claims she saw her soul leave her body during a volunteer experiment in Stuttgart, Germany, in 1937." The trial court ignored her and others like her, and gave the money to Barrow Neurological Institute, which did purely medical research. The appeal court disagreed. The court felt that Kidd had set up a valid charitable trust and that cy pres was appropriate, but that Barrow Neurological Institute was not the right place to put the money. The court made some sneering remarks about "modern secularism" and told the lower courts to look for a more suitable taker. The trial court, on remand, gave the money to the American Society for Psychical Research in New York City, an organization which studied such things as "crisis apparitions" and "deathbed visions" and also had an interest in "physical changes in the surroundings at death, such as the stopping of a clock when its owner died."[56]

The trusts and foundations most likely to need cy pres, of course, are those whose goals are quite specific. They are thus the opposite of the great foundations that have extremely broad and vague charters. A small but interesting group of founders took the opposite tack. Stephen Girard was one of these; Tilden was another. Another member of this group was Colonel John McKee, who died in 1902. McKee was said to be, at the time of his death, the richest African American in the country.[57] His will was a long, complicated document.[58] McKee was obviously familiar with the will of Stephen Girard, and in some ways he modeled his own will after Girard's. In the will, he left rather small annuities to his daughter and other relatives. Part of the estate was to be held in trust until the death of all his children and grandchildren living at the time of his death. At that time, it was to be used to establish "Colonel John McKee's College," a kind of Annapolis for "poor colored male orphan children and poor white male orphan children" (and by "orphan" he meant "fatherless children") born in Philadelphia. The buildings were to be "durable" and "fireproof." They had to accommodate at least two hundred of these "male children." And McKee's name was to appear on a "large marble slab in the front wall of said college building"; a statue of McKee was also to be placed in front of the college.

The college, according to McKee, had to be surrounded by a stone wall. The will specified its height and thickness. It went into elaborate detail about other matters too: the pupils were to be given an education similar to the education at the United States Naval Academy. It was to have a full music and drum corps. On Memorial Day the band would parade and decorate McKee's grave, along with the graves of white and colored soldiers and sailors. McKee even gave instructions about what the students would wear: buttons on their coats and caps would be made out of brass, with "McKee" embossed on every button. The college would be managed by a board of ten members chosen by Roman Catholic priests of the Diocese of Philadelphia (though McKee himself was not a Catholic).[59]

McKee was a rich man, but not as rich as Girard; or perhaps his investments did not do as well. At any rate, when the last grandchild died, there was about a million dollars available. This was not enough to build the college McKee wanted and support it out of the income from the trust. The matter fell into the hands of the Pennsylvania courts. Some of McKee's descendants wanted the court to throw the whole plan out and give them the money. But the court rejected this idea and upheld the trust. This meant that cy pres would have to come into operation. As was true of Kidd's will, a whole gaggle of claimants appeared—institutions that argued they were just the ones to get McKee's money. Some were naval training schools, but without many African American boys (let alone orphans). Another claimant, Downington Industrial School and College, had a student body of "about 100 boys and girls, coming mainly from families of low income in the so-called slum areas of Philadelphia and vicinity"; many were "either orphans or fatherless." But this institution had "no white boys or girls attending," while McKee clearly wanted an interracial school; and Downington did not give any "naval training" at all. Among the other Philadelphia candidates was "Spring Garden Institute and Automotive Training Center," where almost half of the students in the "Automotive Training Center" were "colored." Fair enough; but "automotive training" was pretty remote from naval training. A Baptist church and a Muslim institution in Connecticut also made a case for themselves. The court rejected all of the institutional claimants and accepted a quite different scheme: the money was to be held by the trustee and used as a scholarship fund for white and African American orphan boys who wanted a naval education; and the trustee was also authorized to try to raise more money to add to the fund, so that perhaps someday the college could be built. This will probably never happen; in the meantime, the "McKee Scholarships" are a going concern.

The dispute over the McKee estate had everything: the rich, eccentric donor; quarreling family members; a will contest; even some mysterious family history. The trust for the family was supposed to end when the last grandchild died; but when the trustees *thought* this had happened, another grandson suddenly appeared out of nowhere. The rest of the family, apparently, had had no idea he even existed. This grandson had been passing for white all his life. A lawsuit was brewing over disposition of the estate. If it succeeded, the grandson would come into considerable money. It was this chance that brought him out of the race closet. In fact, this grandson died a bit later; and in any event, the court upheld the will; the family's lawsuit failed.[60]

Cy pres cases are not usually as colorful as McKee's. But sometimes the court has to make a delicate judgment, choosing between two or more claimants, or, as in the case of the Kidd estate, a whole flock of them. In one New Jersey case the testator left money to the Seton Hall College of Medicine.[61] The college was part of Seton Hall University, a Catholic university. Seton Hall later sold the medical school to the New Jersey College of Medicine, a state institution. Could the New Jersey College take over the fund; or should it be diverted, under the cy pres doctrine, to some other Catholic hospital or charitable institution? In other words, if the testator came back from beyond the grave, what would he want? If only one could ask him the crucial question: when you left money to Seton Hall College of Medicine, was it more because it was a Catholic institution, or more because it was a college of medicine in New Jersey? Of course, dead people do not answer such questions. Courts do. This particular court gave the fund to the New Jersey College of Medicine.[62]

An important cluster of cy pres cases have dealt with race and sex discrimination. Suppose that a donor leaves money to his university to be used for scholarships for white Protestant boys. Is this now illegal? If the gift is to a state university, the gift clearly is. Even if it is a gift to a private university, so long as the university refuses to carry out the gift as written (because race discrimination is against the school's policy), then the trust, legal or not, is impossible to carry out. In either case, cy pres can come to the rescue. In theory, in the case of a private university, a court could say, you, the university, have made this trust impossible; we will shift it to another institution less squeamish about racism, which will carry out the donor's wishes. In practice, it would be hard to find such a school, and the courts have not indulged in this kind of noxious behavior. In practice, they have simply granted cy pres in these cases and removed conditions that are now seen as against school (and public) policy.

But not always. A donor who was a dyed-in-the-wool bigot could say in his will: I want this fund to be used for white people, and if that can't be done, then give the money to my relatives. A court would feel obliged to respect his wishes. Hardly anybody is that blunt and explicit. Senator A. O. Bacon of Georgia, however, gave property, in 1911, to the city of Macon to be used as a "park and pleasure ground" for white people; and in his will he said that, while he felt very kindly toward "Negroes," including "sincere personal affection," he also felt that "the two races (white and negro) should be forever separate." By the 1960's, it was perfectly clear that the city of Macon could not run a park for white people only. Nor could the city transfer it to private owners to run a segregated park. Could a court apply cy pres and remove the racial restriction? The Georgia courts said no, and the Supreme Court of the United States agreed. Segregation was "an essential and inseparable part of the testator's plan." His charitable intent was not "general," but "specific"; and since it could not be carried out, the park land would revert to Senator Bacon's heirs.[63]

This, however, is not the usual result. Probably many donors *were* bigots; but times have changed, and courts hate to give property back to the heirs, especially if a long time has passed. Courts also hate to lose a public facility, like a park, by handing it over to family members; in this regard too, Senator Bacon's case was deviant. Only a few years after the Bacon affair, the Georgia Supreme Court dealt with the will of one Clem Boyd. Boyd left money for a scholarship fund in his parents' memory, at three colleges, for "deserving and qualified poor white boys and girls." The Georgia court applied cy pres and got rid of the racial restriction. The law favors charitable trusts and does not want them to fail, said the court. Would the dead donor prefer to kill the scholarship fund, rather than open it up to African Americans? Maybe; but the court would not presume any such thing unless there was a "clear, definite, and unambiguous" expression of this biased intent.[64]

Sometimes it is perfectly clear that a charitable trust is illegal or impossible to carry out. At other times, it is much less obvious. Historically, courts have been pretty insistent on leaving charitable trusts alone unless the trust really is illegal or impossible to carry out. One notable case concerned the Buck Trust, in northern California. Beryl Buck, who lived in Marin County, California, died in 1975. She left the bulk of her estate to the San Francisco Foundation, a community trust, to be "used for exclusively non-profit charitable, religious or educational purposes in providing care for the needy in Marin County, California, and for other non-profit charitable, religious, or educational purposes in that county."

The gift was worth about $7 million. It consisted primarily of stock in an oil company. By 1979 the stock had increased enormously in value—and by 1984 it was worth more than $400 million and was producing more than $30 million a year. The San Francisco Foundation decided it was "impractical" to spend all that money in Marin County, a fairly ritzy county just across the Golden Gate Bridge from San Francisco. There is no question that many people in Marin County are rich, though by no means all. The foundation wanted to spend the money throughout the San Francisco Bay Area. And it wanted court permission, which it did not get. The doctrine of cy pres, said the court, would be "distorted" if such "nebulous standards" as "ineffective philanthropy" were recognized; and if courts allowed trustees to "vary the terms of a trust simply because they believe that they can spend the trust income better or more wisely elsewhere."[65]

Nothing in Beryl Buck's will even hinted at the possibility of using the money outside of Marin County. And $30 million a year, even in a rich county, can surely be spent on worthwhile causes in a county with a substantial population. This, at any rate, was what the court felt: the income "could continue to be spent effectively and efficiently in Marin County."[66] Indeed, the Buck Trust and its subsidiaries have had no trouble spending the money; in 2004, according to its website, the Marin Community Foundation gave Buck money to the Hospice of Marin Foundation, Rock'n Blues by the Lake, the Muir Beach Quilters, the Cloverdale Citrus Fair, and a host of other organizations; the Marin Institute, working to "reduce alcohol problems," was a "special project" of the Buck Trust; and many of the grants seemed to have implications or benefits that went far beyond Marin County. Still, it would be wonderful if one could only bring back the ghost of Beryl Buck, and ask, would you still restrict your generosity to Marin County, now that the value of your estate has exploded the way it has?

The court in the Buck case was cautious, in other words; and it interpreted cy pres strictly. Impossible means impossible, illegal means illegal; they do not mean unwise or inefficient or insufficiently practical. A lot of legal scholars think the court in the Buck case was *too* cautious. They think there is an argument for giving the courts (or perhaps the trustees themselves) more power.[67] The issue is a familiar one: how much power to allow the dead hand to exercise? Why should we pay so much attention to the *literal* wishes of a testator, especially a testator who has been dead for a very long time? The courts (so the argument goes) should look for the most "efficient" or "socially beneficial" use of the money, even if this is not the one closest to the dead man's wishes. Cy pres should not be confined to the impossible or the illegal; it should also be used where the trust is obsolete, or wasteful, or inefficient.

The Buck case was, in any event, quite exceptional. Cy pres applies, and can apply, primarily to small trusts and foundations. The big ones, as we mentioned, have broad mandates and charters; they do not need cy pres. A Ford Foundation or a Gates Foundation can shift from goal to goal, whether urban planning, vaccination of African children, reform of the school system of New York, or support for ballet companies, without blinking an eye. Indeed, this was true of the Buck Trust as well—except as to geography.

There is, of course, a case for expanding the concept of cy pres. As the world turns, as the climate of opinion changes, the big foundations shift their emphasis. Overpopulation, AIDS, global warming—these issues were not on the agenda in 1900 or 1950. Also, as the donors die and their families lose interest, the foundation's personnel changes, and this has an impact on what they try to do. Perpetual life, for an estate or an institution, comes at a price—the original intent, like the original staff, vanishes into history.

United States v. *Cerio* (1993)[68] was one of the rare cases in which the problem was too much money, rather than too little.[69] It was a case of "looking the gift horse in the mouth and finding it too good to accept as is." The gift in question came from the estate of Robert T. Alexander, a retired Coast Guard captain. He was a childless widower. He left the bulk of his estate to establish a scholarship fund at the Coast Guard Academy; the income from the fund was to be "awarded and paid to the graduating cadet who has attained the highest grade average in chemistry and physics while enrolled in the academy."

The problem was the size of the estate. The corpus of the trust was worth more than $1 million; and the proposed cadet award "would range from $65,000 to $130,000" each year. The Coast Guard balked at this. This prize would jeopardize the mission of the academy; it would "engender intense, unhealthy competition . . . distort the competition to major in the sciences at the expense of other majors . . . erode, if not destroy, the class and interpersonal relationships . . . so vital to the Academy's goal . . . and . . . serve to teach cadets, wrongly, that the reward for a job well done in a life of public service . . . is cash." The district court agreed and applied the doctrine of cy pres. The court outlined an elaborate plan for spending the money. The cash award was reduced to $750 for physics and $750 for chemistry; other modest cash awards were to be paid out; money was allocated to "senior projects in science"; other money would go to graduate fellowships and visiting lecturers; and if all this did not soak up the entire income, money could be used "to purchase or repair special scientific equipment or machinery."

In one sense, this is an ordinary case of cy pres. The trust was impossible to carry out because the Coast Guard refused to accept it. On the other hand, the *reasons* for refusing the gift were not that the gift was illegal or impossible, but that it was wasteful and economically inefficient. This type of consideration may become more common in the future. Meantime, partly in response to the problems of the Buck Trust, the scholars and lawyers who drafted the Uniform Trust Code put in a provision that allowed cy pres not only when a trust's goals were illegal or impossible, but also when they were "impracticable" or "wasteful." A number of states have adopted the code.[70] How this will play out in the future is impossible to say.

MONITORING CHARITABLE TRUSTS

In a normal trust, if the trustee misbehaves, there are beneficiaries who have the right to go to court and enforce the trust. The enforcement of charitable trusts and foundations is a trickier proposition. Suppose there is a large charitable trust whose mandate is "medical research to alleviate human suffering." As we mentioned, no particular person has "standing," that is, the right to complain in court about the actions of the trustees. Just because a person is ill or suffering does not mean that the trust is for his or her individual benefit, such that this particular human being has the right to monitor the trustees. At any rate, the courts have so held.

Who then has the power? How about the original donor? In most states, the answer is no. The original donor is just somebody who used to own the property; he or she no longer has any say in the matter. This rule is pretty firmly established, but there are some signs of change. Wisconsin law, for example, provides that a "proceeding to enforce a charitable trust" could be brought by any "settlor or group of settlors who contributed half or more of the principal."[71] In *Smithers v. St. Luke's–Roosevelt Hospital Center*,[72] a New York case, Adele Smithers, the plaintiff, was the widow and administrator of the estate of R. Brinkley Smithers. Smithers was not only rich; he was also a recovered alcoholic. He gave $10 million to the hospital to set up a center to treat alcoholism. The family quarreled with the hospital over the way the hospital used (or misused) the funds. The state, through its attorney general, intervened, but in the end not to the satisfaction of Mrs. Smithers. The New York court allowed Mrs. Smithers to bring her lawsuit. The donor of a charitable gift, said the court, is in the best position to be "vigilant." The donor also has a profound interest in seeing to it that the trustee complies with the terms of the gift.

But this kind of holding is still quite exceptional. Courts are afraid of a plague of lawsuits against charities and charitable trusts brought by irascible and discontented donors. And note that neither the Smithers case nor the Wisconsin statute would allow a donor's children, grandchildren, great-grandchildren, or other friends and relations to bring any such lawsuit. The court did allow the donor's widow to sue, but probably only because she was administering the donor's estate.

Who then has any authority over charitable trusts, if the public has none and neither does the donor or his family? The answer is, the state—more precisely, the attorney general of the state in which the trust has its headquarters. This official, to quote the California statute, has "primary responsibility for supervising charitable trusts," for "ensuring compliance" with the terms of the trust, and for "protection of assets" in trusts and foundations.[73] Indeed, in the Smithers case the family had complained to the attorney general, and the attorney general had jumped in and investigated.

How much does the attorney general of a typical state actually do to monitor charitable trusts and foundations? Normally, very little. Normally, he or she pretty much leaves charitable trusts and foundations alone. Of course, when a controversy erupts the attorney general's office will be roused from its torpor and may take action. In many states too, charitable trusts are required to file reports with the attorney general's office. In New Hampshire, charitable trustees have to furnish a copy of the trust instrument and make "periodic written reports, under oath," listing the assets of the trust and giving financial information.[74] Under a statute of this type, there will be a staff somewhere in the capital of the state that takes a look at these reports, files them, and if necessary deals with them. This probably does some good. A trust that has been dormant, or has been frittering away its money, might be flushed out and induced to mend its ways.

Still, the staffs that oversee charitable trusts and foundations within the offices of attorneys general tend to be small. A study in 1994 found that Connecticut had four attorneys in its charity division; Massachusetts had seven; New York had seventeen. What triggers investigations are not the reports that charities file, but "inquiries or complaints from dissenting board members, employees, beneficiaries or other members of the public, or the press."[75] The state will do something if it gets complaints, or if the woes of the charitable trust or foundation are noisy enough to reach the ears of the public, or if a lot of money or some famous institution is involved, but not otherwise.[76]

There have been a number of notable examples, however, in recent years. The tale of the Barnes Foundation is one of the best known. Dr. Albert C. Barnes made a fortune selling a compound of silver and protein he called Argyrol, mainly used as eyedrops. He spent a good deal of the money buying French impressionist paintings. The paintings passed to the Barnes Foundation. The Foundation displayed the paintings in a gallery in suburban Philadelphia. The Barnes Foundation operated under rather strict rules. The public was allowed to look at the paintings only two days a week. The works could never be lent out, or moved from Lower Merion, Pennsylvania. (The trustees violated the no-tour rule in the 1990's by sending eighty-three paintings to Washington, Paris, Tokyo, and other cities.) There were five trustees, all of them chosen by Lincoln University, a historically black university in the Philadelphia area.

In the course of time, the foundation ran into financial troubles. It petitioned the local Orphans' Court (the quaint Pennsylvania name for a probate court) for the right to expand the board of trustees and to move the gallery to a prominent site in Philadelphia. Three foundations pledged money to make the move possible. At first Lincoln University objected, and the fate of the foundation was fought over bitterly in the courts. Later, Lincoln University withdrew its objections, in exchange for an expanded role on the board; and in December 2004, a judge ruled that the Barnes collection could be moved to Philadelphia.[77] This was called, by one writer, a "triumph of accessibility over isolation."[78] The public, arguably, was the winner in this battle. The loser, most obviously, was Albert Barnes. Here too, arguably, the decision was in line with old and well-established doctrines—if the foundation was really facing bankruptcy, something had to be done. But this was no ordinary case of cy pres, where the idea is to change the terms of the trust as little as possible. This was clearly *not* done in the case of the Barnes Foundation.

Museums are open to the public and have important constituencies. The Museum of the American Indian, "the world's foremost repository of Indian art of the Western Hemisphere" got into trouble: its building in New York City was "lamentably inadequate," its finances a mess, objects were missing, and the trustees seemed derelict in their duties. This made enough noise to arouse the sleeping giants in Albany; the attorney general stepped in, the board was reconstituted, new money was raised, and a new home for the museum was found.[79]

Perhaps the most spectacular blow-up of a foundation occurred in Hawaii and involved the Bishop estate, which presided over an enormous charitable trust. Bernice Pauahi Bishop was born a Hawaiian princess. She married an American, Charles Bishop. Bernice Bishop owned, at her death, a vast tract of land, part of the royal patrimony of the Hawaiian monarchy. She died childless and left the land in trust to "erect and maintain in the Hawaiian Islands two schools . . . one for boys and one for girls," to be known as the Kamehameha Schools. The schools were duly established; the lands Bernice Bishop had owned became, in time, enormously valuable. The trust was therefore flush with money, and the trustees and officers treated it as a kind of cash cow. They paid themselves obscenely large salaries, appointed cronies to sinecures, and in general, pillaged and mismanaged the trust. In the 1990's, investigative journalists began to strip away the curtains of secrecy and exposed the misdeeds of the scoundrels who sat on the board of trustees. A series of exposés and audits set off a huge uproar in the state. Some of the trustees were thrown out of office, and at least one went to jail.[80] The story has, in a way, a happy ending; but on the other hand, that the "broken trust" could last so long and cause so much damage is disheartening, to say the least.

Benjamin Ferguson, in his will dated November 28, 1904, set up a fund whose tangled history points up another moral tale. Ferguson's trust had about a million dollars in assets—a very sizable sum for the time. The fund was to be called the B. F. Ferguson Monument Fund. Income from the trust was to be paid to Chicago's great museum, the Art Institute of Chicago. The Art Institute was told to use the money to put up "enduring statuary and monuments" of stone, granite, or bronze in parks, along boulevards, and in other public places. These were to commemorate "worthy men or women of America, or important events in American history."[81] Ferguson was a friend of the sculptor Lorado Taft, and had been "enthralled and intrigued by the quantity and quality of the sculpture" in Europe, including great monuments. For example, as a columnist for the *Chicago Tribune* asked, what would Trafalgar Square be without the monument to Lord Nelson?[82]

For some years, the Art Institute duly followed the terms of the trust, using the money to support sculpture in public places in Chicago. Then, rather abruptly, it stopped this practice cold; instead, it began to let the money accumulate. In 1933 the institute went to court and rather slyly asked the judge to explain exactly what the word "monument" might mean in Ferguson's will? Could it possibly mean a *building*? Maybe a new wing for the Art Institute? And wasn't it true that there was quite enough sculpture around parks and boulevards in Chicago? It artfully suggested that progressive cities no longer went in for that kind of art, and that the Art Institute badly needed a new wing. Nobody raised much of an objection, and the court was only too happy to oblige the great Art Institute. The depression of the 1930's put the plans on hold; but eventually the Art Institute did go ahead with plans for an administrative wing, which it was happy to name after Benjamin Ferguson, another donor who perhaps was whirling in his grave. Along the way, there were indeed some protests, from the city and from sculptors, but to no avail. The courts consistently sided with the Art Institute, and in the end the Benjamin Ferguson Memorial wing was built.[83]

It is hard to resist the conclusion that the Art Institute, which was, after all, *not* the beneficiary of the trust, but rather the trustee, decided to use the trust funds, income and principal, for its own purposes. It simply ignored the wishes of the donor. This is not supposed to happen, but in this case it did. The Art Institute is a powerful and important institution, one of the jewels in the crown of Chicago's cultural life. The losers in the battle—sculptors, artists, and the citizens of Chicago—had no say in the matter, legally speaking. The state of Illinois also paid no attention. None of the judges who dealt with the case saw any reason to intervene. Perhaps they thought the best thing for Chicago and its citizens was to give the Art Institute what it wanted. In the long run, one might argue, the Ferguson wing might be more beneficial to the public than, say, another solemn statue of Abraham Lincoln, sitting, standing, lying down, or splitting rails.

Apparently, the story did not end when the museum opened its new administrative wing. A campaign got under way in the 1960's to reopen the matter. The campaign was led by two organizations—the Chicago Heritage Committee and Artists Equity Association of Chicago. A new attorney general, William G. Clark, joined in. As a result of this pressure, the Art Institute agreed to use some of the accumulated income of the fund—about $1 million—for the original purpose, that is, putting up statues.[84] Still, it seems that at most one new statue has been commissioned; instead the money has been spent on restoring old monuments and sculptures, including the Fountain of Time, a notable piece of sculpture in Chicago; this was a massive job that cost the fund $950,000.[85]

Poor Benjamin Ferguson's mistake, but an understandable one, was trusting the integrity of the Art Institute of Chicago. But in the end two things doomed his trust. One was simply the passage of time, which led to a change in artistic fashions. Another was the law (and practice) about enforcement of charitable trusts. Those who went to court to ask for change were politically powerful; their power was not counterbalanced in any way; rules of standing shut out most of the opposition; and the state government yawned and stayed away. True, the case was reopened in the 1960's. But what was decisive was not Benjamin Ferguson's intention, but changing politics and the formation of new interest groups.

In contemporary times, a kind of artistic nationalism has become noisy and salient. The old days of digging up antiquities and pillaging archaeological sites seem to be over. In the United States the individual states seem to share in this ethos. The judge in the Barnes case, I imagine, would never have agreed to let the collection move to New Jersey or Arizona, no matter how much money was offered. The Terra Museum, in Chicago, was a small institution on Michigan Boulevard with a "modest collection of American impressionist art."[86] The board proposed moving the museum to Washington, D.C., but two directors objected. In this case, the attorney general jumped in, insisting that the charitable corporation that ran Terra had a duty to act for the benefit of the "people of Illinois." No such words, of course, appeared in the charter of the corporation. In the end, the collection stayed in Chicago—given over, for the most part, on long-term loan, to the Art Institute of Chicago. The attorneys general of other states have also stepped in to keep charitable funds at home. When the directors of the Dan and Margaret Maddox Charitable Trust, in Nashville, Tennessee, moved its assets to Hernando, Mississippi, Tennessee sent up a howl of protest; the issue was settled in December 2007, when $54 million in assets were returned to Tennessee.[87]

The travails of the Hershey trust show how a charitable trust can become entangled in local and state politics.[88] Milton Hershey, who made his fortune in chocolate, had a wife, Catherine, but no children. He and Catherine set up a trust to support a Hershey Industrial School, for "poor white male orphans." When Hershey died in 1945 (his wife was already dead), he gave the trust a large tract of land and all of his stock in the Hershey Chocolate Company. The trust flourished financially. But it worried the trustees that they had put all their eggs in one basket, even though this was a chocolate basket, and very profitable. Gradually, they diversified their holdings; but finally, in 2002, the trustees decided to sell their controlling interest in the company.

Hershey had been a very paternalistic boss; and Hershey, Pennsylvania, was practically a company town. Charity supposedly begins at home, and home was Hershey, Pennsylvania. The locals were horrified at the thought that Hershey might sell out. They worried about their jobs and the fate of their town. The company itself was opposed to the sale. The storm over Hershey reached the ears of the governor, and the attorney general (who was in fact running for governor). The attorney general came out strongly against the sale and went to court to try to prevent it. He asked for a temporary restraining order; a local judge granted a preliminary injunction forbidding the sale, and this was upheld on appeal. The board of the trust never made the sale, and many of the members were later replaced. The legislature then entered the picture. A new law made it the duty of charitable trusts—if "a majority of its beneficiaries" lived at a particular place in Pennsylvania, and if the trust had as one of its assets "voting control of a publicly traded business corporation"—not to "consummate any transaction" that would give up that control, without notice to the attorney general—and to the "affected employees."[89] In the "case of a charitable trust," a fiduciary making investment and management decisions was supposed to consider "the special relationship" of an asset, "and its economic impact as a principal business enterprise on the community in which the beneficiary of the trust is located"; and the "special value of the integration of the beneficiary's activities with the community" where the business might be located."[90] The language is quite general, but obviously was aimed squarely at the Hershey situation.

Most charitable trusts and foundations never make headlines. They are honestly administered—or not—and nobody knows or, for the most part, cares. Smaller trusts, when the original donors die, become "orphans" and pass into the hands of banks and lawyers; the desires of the founders can easily get lost.[91] On a larger scale, this is the fate of the big foundations as well. They are hardly "orphans," but the power of the donor's dead hand diminishes radically as time goes by.

The giant foundations have had their share of political grief, to be sure. But those days too are over. The Ford Foundation, the Gates Foundation, the Hewlett Foundation, the Carnegie Foundation, and the rest pursue their goals and spend their money without much outside control. There are no stockholders and no outsiders with the right to complain. They are not under the discipline of the competitive market. Management must answer to the board of directors; but the board itself is not accountable to anybody; and the members of the board choose their own successors. Foundations, like charities in general, are "favorites of the law." The cases endlessly repeat this phrase. This then seems to be an area in which the dead hand most definitely has its way, in one regard: an "estate" goes on forever, but without, apparently, much real control, either by the original dead hand or by anybody else.

Yet this much is undeniable: dead hands have helped to create a sort of third force in the United States. The foundations are one branch of this third force, along with a host of nongovernmental organization (NGO's) with missions, like the Sierra Club, Greenpeace, and the NAACP. They represent neither the power of the state nor the power of the market and private enterprise. NGO's like the Sierra Club depend directly on public support. They may or may not have endowments. For the most part, they have to raise money or die. The great foundations, on the other hand, do have endowments, and what is more, eternal life.

The role of the foundations in society is undeniable. Yet it would be a bit misleading to assign this role to the grip of the dead hand. That grip may not be quite as tight as it appears. Changes in public policy, together with the doctrine of cy pres, have led to alterations in terms that are at the very heart of certain trusts. And the foundations evolve. As the family members die off, as we said, professional managers replace them. It thus cannot be really said that they are ruled from the grave by rich, dead men of the past.

This fact has not escaped the beady eyes of conservatives. Ironically, one bitter criticism of the great classic foundations has come from the leaders of a right-wing foundation, the Washington Legal Foundation. In December 2007 the foundation placed an ad in the *New York Times* warning Americans to be "very careful" before writing "that next check to charity." Philanthropy has "too little respect for donor intent." Men like Carnegie, Rockefeller, and Ford "were passionate believers in market capitalism"; but their foundations have been "hijacked by special interests to fund social engineering and legal assaults on economic rights." These institutions "use their benefactor's financial legacy to bankroll professional activist organizations that despise free enterprise ... hundreds of foundations ... have been turned into cash cows for radical causes."[92]

Would Carnegie, Rockefeller, and Ford really disapprove of what their foundations are doing? Perhaps; perhaps not. Are foundations supporting "radical" causes? That depends on one's definition of "radical." What the Washington Legal Foundation considers radical, most people (I would guess) would label as middle of the road or mildly liberal. But the foundations do escape from the control of donors, and descendants of donors. They evolve, they change, they move on. Meanwhile, foundations continue to be born; new money foundations jostle the old money foundations and vie with them for power and prestige. The new founders—people like Bill Gates—still control these infant foundations, proud and cocky with their billions of fresh dollars. They add to the strength and the legitimacy of foundations, and most likely make them politically and socially invulnerable, at least for now.

CHAPTER 9

DEATH AND TAXES

LIVING PEOPLE have to pay an income tax on their earnings, year in and year out. They also pay sales taxes and property taxes. When a rich person dies, another cluster of taxes comes into play. The most significant of these "death taxes" has been the *estate tax*. The federal government imposes this tax on the estate, that is, on everything a person owned or controlled when he or she died—money in the bank, houses, stocks and bonds, as well as interests in "living trusts" and certain other assets.

The present estate tax has been part of federal law since 1916.[1] There were two earlier attempts to tax the dead. During the Civil War, the federal government imposed an inheritance tax on bequests. This tax was repealed in 1870. The War Revenue Act of 1898 was the second federal death tax. It applied solely to personal property. Gifts to a surviving spouse were tax-free. Only estates over $10,000 were subject to the tax. The top rate under this law, on estates over $1 million, was 15%. This tax too had a short life. It was repealed in 1902.

The law of 1916 was destined to last much longer. In its original version, the first $50,000 of the estate was exempt from tax, and the top rate was 10% on estates over $5 million. This would probably be equivalent to an estate of about half a billion dollars today. Under this estate tax law, only big estates were required to pay any money at all; and only *very* big estates would have to pay appreciable amounts. But the rates were destined to grow; and the scope of the tax also increased over the years. A gift tax was enacted in 1924, repealed in 1926, and enacted again in 1932. In the 1920's, the taxable estate began to include revocable transfers in trust. Before 1976 the gift tax rates were lower than the estate tax rates; but in 1976 the two taxes were unified.

The estate tax, like most taxes, was and is primarily a device to raise money for the federal government. In fiscal year 2004 the federal government collected over $24 billion from estate taxes. This is, of course, only a tiny percentage of the money the federal government takes in, and an even tinier percentage of what it spends. It is, in one sense, a lot of money; but the government would suffer very little, fiscally speaking, if Congress did away with the estate tax. But the estate tax has always been more than a way to fill the government's coffers. It also expressed an important policy: the great dynastic fortunes had to be cut down in size. The ethos was not too different from the notion underlying the rule against perpetuities, or perhaps the rule against accumulations. The estate tax was explicitly a tax on the rich. The average person never had to pay it. In 1934, less than 1% of the people who died left behind an estate that had to file a return. This rose to a high of 7.65% in 1976—some 139,115 tax returns in all. Even so, this was not a great number of estates. And only a decade or so later, the situation had changed dramatically: in 1987 the estates of only 0.88% of those who died had to file a return; the total number of returns was 18,059.[2]

To say that there is a tax on the whole estate glosses over a mare's nest of complexities. First there is the question, what is in the estate, and what is not? Answering this question is anything but easy. A person's house, stocks and bonds, cash in the bank, jewelry, and the like are obviously part of the estate. The tax laws also try to scoop up a number of additional and less obvious items. Any money I have given away to my children (or to anybody else) is no longer part of the estate. This is true whether it is an outright gift or a gift in the form of a solid, unchangeable trust. On the other hand, if I keep control—if I can change the terms of the trust, or take the money back—then the government will treat the assets of this trust as part of my estate when I die.[3]

The tax is also not really a tax on the whole estate. There are exemptions and deductions. Money given to charity is not taxed. Money left to a spouse is not taxed. If I leave an estate of $100 million, half to my wife and half to my university, there is no tax on the estate at all. And if my wife, after I die, marries some gigolo and leaves him her $50 million, this too escapes tax entirely. I do not even have to leave the money to my wife outright; I can leave it in trust for her, although there are special rules about this—the trust has to qualify, by following certain rules (which give the surviving spouse a good deal of power over the trust).[4]

As I said, any money that I gave away while I was alive is not part of my estate when I die, with some exceptions not worth going into here. But large gifts were subject to another tax, the *gift tax*, more or less parallel to the estate tax. (No gift tax is required, and no tax is assessed, on gifts up to $12,000 per donee, as of 2008; and a married couple can give $24,000. This applies to as many separate people as a person chooses to give money to; hence it is possible to give away millions without paying a tax or filing a tax return, provided the money is spread around to enough people.)

The person who gets the gift, by the way, pays nothing. It might seem odd that if I hand my son a check for $10 million, I will pay a tax on the gift and he will pay nothing at all. People have to pay income tax on their hard-earned money; but if a rich uncle gives someone a substantial gift, or a dead grandmother leaves him a fortune, he will pay absolutely nothing in federal taxes. Only the generous donor will pay, if anybody has to. Why? Because otherwise, there would be too large a hole in the estate tax. And the estate tax, after all, is paid by the (dead) donor, not by the heirs who actually receive the money. The gift tax brings in much less money than the estate tax—in fiscal year 2004, the total take for the federal government was about one and a half billion dollars.

In addition to the estate and gift taxes, since 1976 the federal government has imposed a tax on generation-skipping transfers, as I mentioned in an earlier chapter. Suppose, in my will, I leave $10 million in trust; I direct the trustee to pay the income from this sum of money to my son for as long as he lives; then, when he dies, the trustee will pay the income to my son's children, in equal shares. When I die, my estate will have to pay estate tax. But what happens when my son dies? What is actually *in* his estate? His right to collect the income from the trust was a valuable asset; but it died with him. So, at the moment of death, this right was worth exactly nothing. By this logic, his estate would not owe the government any tax, and the money would go to the children tax-free.

This struck some people as a serious loophole. Here was this rich guy, living in luxury off the income that this trust fund of ten million dollars generated, yet when he died, his estate owed nothing to the federal government. To plug this loophole—if you considered it a loophole—the code was amended to impose a special tax on "generation-skipping" transfers, including transfers in trust. The transfer is taxed at the highest estate tax rate in effect for the year the "skip" takes place. This tax, however, is imposed primarily on people who are seriously rich. For each "skip"—for each gift across generations—there is a generous exemption. It began at $1 million, but has been going up; in 2007 it was $2 million. The generation-skipping trust also applies to a "direct skip": an outright gift, for example, to a grandchild, bypassing the grandchild's parent. The details of the tax are so involute that I sometimes doubt if anybody really understands all of the GST details; but the main idea is clear enough.

For most of the twentieth century, a majority of the states also took their tax bite from estates of the dead. Some states had actual estate taxes—taxes on the whole estate. But others had something rather different, an *inheritance tax*. The key distinction between an estate tax and an inheritance tax is this: putting aside gifts to spouses and to charities, the estate tax falls on whatever else is in the estate. It makes no difference who inherits under an estate tax; if a woman dies, and leaves nothing to charity or to a husband, the tax will be exactly the same whether she leaves the estate to her children, a brother-in-law, friends she met while bird-watching, second cousins, or her next-door neighbor. Under an inheritance tax, the amount of tax *does* depend on who the money is left to. Under the Maryland version, for example, gifts to spouses, children, and grandchildren (and their spouses), and to parents, brothers, and sisters, are exempt from tax. Gifts to other people carry a 10% burden.[5] In Pennsylvania, under the current law, money left to spouses is tax-free; money left to parents, children, and grandchildren, and to *their* spouses, pays a tax of 6%; everybody else pays 15%.[6]

Taxes on estates are common in Western societies. They raise money, but they have also reflected an ideology of hostility to great dynastic fortunes. A truly democratic society, many people thought, should treat inherited wealth with suspicion. Dynastic money was associated in England and elsewhere with the nobility, the landed gentry, and the bad old times before the common man or woman had a say in the affairs of society. Heavy death duties in England were one of the weapons in the project to destroy the power of the old aristocracy. In the United States, the estate tax was associated with a somewhat different battle. The enemies here were the mighty fortunes of the robber barons and other enormously wealthy men who had the power to distort policy, pull the strings of government, and drive the small merchant, farmer, and worker to the edge of destruction. The enemies were the obscenely rich, the moneyed aristocracy, men like John D. Rockefeller with his tight grip on the oil industry. As I said, the early forms of the estate tax had only modest rates. But the rates kept going up; and the top rate, during the Second World War, was 77%. The British rates were even higher, and in a way, almost confiscatory. Since the end of the Second World War the rates have declined significantly, even in England; the rate in England, today, above a certain minimum, is 40%.

For a long time, not many people in the United States questioned the philosophy behind the estate and inheritance taxes. Life is unfair; it seemed particularly unfair when spoiled young heirs inherited fortunes that they had done nothing to earn or deserve. And there was nothing wrong with the idea of putting some sort of brake on the power of the big fortunes—the monopolists who controlled giant corporations. There were, of course, those who opposed the estate tax; and there was a campaign in the 1920's to get rid of it, when Calvin Coolidge was president and Andrew Mellon secretary of the Treasury. But this campaign ended in failure.[7]

In the 1970's, however, the old ideology began to lose some of its vigor. The states were first to make a move. They began to back away from inheritance and estate taxes.[8] A few states had no such taxes to begin with. Others now joined this camp. New Mexico acted in 1976, and by the early twenty-first century only about ten states had retained the inheritance tax as such. California had abolished it in 1982, Texas in 1983, New York in 2000.[9]

Why did this happen? One explanation is "interstate tax competition." In a very mobile society, a state may feel it can attract rich elderly people if it gets rid of the burden of its death taxes.[10] The states that lacked these taxes, before the 1970's, were mostly in the South—Florida, very notably. But why would North Dakota get rid of its succession taxes, which it did in 1979? Perhaps to keep at least some of its elderly citizens from moving to Florida; North Dakota could do nothing about its harsh winters, but it could ease the burden of its taxes. Since some states were passing laws to attract people, and other states to counteract this attraction, the movement became a kind of stampede.

No doubt tax competition was a powerful motive; and this kind of race (to the bottom, perhaps) is something we have met before, in the discussion of the rule against perpetuities. But tax competition cannot be the only motive. California is an interesting case in point. The good citizens of California got rid of their inheritance tax by referendum, or popular vote. Countless voters, whose estates would never have to pay a penny of tax, trooped to the polls and voted for Proposition 6 in June 1982, which abolished the inheritance tax. That they were thinking of tax competition with Florida or Nevada is extremely unlikely. What then *were* they thinking of?

To begin with, enemies of the inheritance tax ran a clever and misleading campaign. They poured in money to defeat the tax.[11] They played on a popular fear that taxes would gobble up the average man's estate. They wept crocodile tears over small farmers whose farms would be wrenched away, or the struggling small businessperson whose precious pizza parlor or sweet little factory would be swept away by the tax man. A Republican assemblywoman in California wrote that the tax "on death itself" was "ruining too many families both financially and emotionally. For many survivors, the grim reaper is too often their own tax collector." Families "have to sell their homes and possessions," their "family farms, ranches, and businesses." And this was "a tax upon a tax," something between "double jeopardy and grave robbing."[12]

These were totally specious arguments, but they seemed to work. More than 60% of the voters in California voted in favor of Proposition 6.[13] I suspect that the campaign reflects, also, something deeper seated and more fundamental—an aspect of American culture I noted before, that is, a radical change in attitudes toward wealth. No longer was great wealth associated with the likes of John D. Rockefeller—powerful, crafty, malevolent men. Nor was it associated with idlers living lives of empty luxury, huge parties, and yachts, on inherited money. The new image of the rich was the image of self-made men like Bill Gates and celebrities, stars of stage and screen, rock and roll musicians, basketball players, football heroes, and the like.[14]

The campaign against the federal estate tax—conveniently labeled the "death tax"—was quite similar. The same, equally specious chestnuts were trotted out: family farms, small businesses. Yet the estate tax is paid only by the rich. The average person has very little chance of leaving behind enough money to face the federal tax collector. In 2002 only 1.17% of the people who died left behind a taxable estate—a total of just over 28,000 estates. In 2006 there were only 22,798 taxable returns. Nor do many people have a chance to inherit enough money to worry about the tax. In 2004, median inheritances came to about $29,000, which actually represents a decline over the previous generation or so.[15]

The campaign against the estate tax rests on a heavy dose of misinformation; but, even more than the state campaigns, it rests on cultural and political factors, very likely on changes in attitudes toward wealth. Obviously, tax competition between states cannot be a factor in explaining why the federal estate tax is in trouble. Yet the federal campaign has been astonishingly successful.[16] A small group of people, ideologically opposed to the tax, have worked tirelessly to promote their cause. Some of these people are in fact millionaires who would gain a great deal from repeal; but there are also very rich people who are on the other side, and some of the zealots are not themselves particularly rich. The group includes anti-tax crusaders who hate the welfare-regulatory state and want to "starve the beast"; anything that reduces its income is fine with them. For most of the population, the estate tax is not a big issue. Surprisingly, however, polls show huge majorities *against* the estate tax. People apparently consider it "unfair." In part, people simply do not understand the issues. Polls show that most people think they or somebody in their family will have to pay the tax; in fact only 2% or less will actually have any liability at all. And another poll, in 2003, showed that more than half the population thought, quite wrongly, that "the estate tax is assessed on transfers to a surviving spouse."[17] Many Americans have a visceral reaction against anything that smacks of redistribution of income. Many people, too, do not grasp the difference between probate costs and "death taxes"; they mix them up in their minds. This may be one reason why they imagine that they or their families will have to pay huge amounts of money when they die.

The Republican Party beat the drums for repeal throughout the 1990's. They had some support, too, among Democrats. When the George W. Bush administration took over the White House in 2000, it moved quickly to enact a drastic cut in the taxes wealthy people had to pay. Part of the program was repeal of the estate tax. Congress voted in 2001 to phase out the tax. In 2010 it is supposed to vanish altogether.[18] To be sure, for complicated reasons the changes made by the 2001 law disappear at the end of 2010. In theory then, in 2011 the estate tax roars back to life, in the same form, and with the same rates and provisions as was true before the enactment of 2001. But nobody expects this miraculous resurrection to take place. At this writing in 2008, it is impossible to predict the ultimate fate of the federal estate tax. It might be abolished completely; more likely, it will be eliminated for all but the very largest estates. The exempt amounts will go up, and fewer estates will feel the bite than did in, say, 1990. If the estate tax disappears, inequality of wealth in the United States may increase.[19] By how much is impossible to say. If the estate tax goes, there will also be less incentive for people to leave money to charity. Here too it is impossible to gauge how big an impact this would have on universities, hospitals, churches, and charities in general.

CHAPTER 10

CONCLUSIONS

WE HAVE TAKEN A QUICK LOOK, over time, at some aspects of the law of succession. This branch of law has immense importance socially, culturally, and economically. And it has suffered greatly from scholarly neglect—particularly with regard to its social and economic role in society, and how that role has changed over time. With this book I have tried, rather modestly, to fill some of the gaps, at least on the social history of the subject.

I have not made any proposals for changes in the law. Certainly there is room for improvement. The law of wills is surely still too rigid. There are too many formalities. The whole process of "probating an estate" is still too bureaucratic and complex. Most countries seem to manage to transfer enormous sums from generation to generation without the fuss and formality of American law. But American law is moving in the direction of greater simplicity and flexibility. The spread of the holographic will is one example. It used to be valid only in the southern and western states, but it is now found in many states outside its natural habitat. One could also point to the "self-proved" will, and to states that now grant forgiveness and indulgence to people who make some minor mistake in drafting or executing a will. The courts are more willing to stretch a point, to correct mistakes, to search for clues to what the testator actually wanted, and to forgive small flaws in execution. Still, the process of change is glacially slow.

One important development has been the (partial) dethronement of the last will and testament. This document is no longer the centerpiece of succession. It has powerful rivals. People have alternatives—will substitutes. These have become more and more popular, for rich and poor alike. The Totten trust is flourishing. This is within the reach of anybody with a bank account. Estate planners are vigorously, and successfully, peddling "living trusts," which bypass the probate court. There are, in short, alternative ways of disposing of one's earthly goods. Of course, the will remains important. And it remains, in most regards, still rather rigid and formal; but less than it was. The change may be in part because of a general decline in "formalism." But it also reflects the rise of will substitutes, which are much less formal. Also, wills no longer seem to be vital documents of title, especially title to land. Land is less important in the economy than it was; and in any event, we have other, better ways to guarantee title and clear up ownership. In the future then, wills may become even less formal. The courts may go further in excusing mistakes. And we might get to see electronic wills, on-line wills, or video wills.

The law reflects its social context, of course. Changes in family structure have had a major impact on this field of law. Families have gotten smaller; the extended family is not what it used to be (and perhaps never was); and the welfare state has taken over *some* of the job of caring for old folks and worn-out family members. People are living longer, a fact that changes the social meaning of inheritance.

One of the strongest trends in the law has been away from exclusive emphasis on the bloodline family and toward what I call the "family of affection and dependence." Of course, bloodline is still important. It would be easy to imagine a system that gave a person's estate (if there was no last will and testament) to whomever the dead person cared about the most, or was closest to. This might be a friend or a neighbor instead of an uncle or a cousin the deceased had not seen in many years. No such system exists. But over the course of the past two centuries or so, spouses (and other partners), who are not after all blood relatives, have gained legal rights, at the expense of direct descendants and more remote relatives. The surviving spouse (mostly a she) began our period in a very subordinate position. Now she bestrides the world of intestacy like a colossus. She is the only person in the family who cannot be disinherited (at least not easily). And there is a strong trend toward getting rid of the "laughing heirs"—remote relatives. There are societies where the kinship system is strong, and where distant cousins mean something to a person. But not the United States. This has always been an immigrant society, a society of rolling stones. The nuclear family means a great deal to most people; but the extended family has come to mean less and less. Many European societies are somewhat different, though they too are moving in the same direction. Everywhere the nuclear family counts most; but the nucleus is shrinking.

The definition of "family" has also changed. Millions of couples live together without getting married. Some of these couples mate for years, or for life. Some produce or adopt children. Some of these couples are gay. Of course, one could always provide for a partner by will. But today, in some places, the law will do this for you, even without a will. The "family" is thus both broader and narrower than it once was: narrower in that it excludes more distant relatives, broader in that it tends to include (unmarried) partners. It also includes illegitimate children, who would have had no claim in the nineteenth century unless "acknowledged" by the father. In this regard, one might argue, bloodline is *more* important than before. This somewhat paradoxical development follows from the broader definition of "family." Still, the trend is clear: away from traditional notions of bloodline, and toward a stronger emphasis on the family of affection and dependence.

Our society, like other modern societies, recognizes the right of the dying to do what they wish with their property—within limits, of course. Throughout this book I asked: How much power does the dead hand have, under law? How much can the dead hand control? Is the dead hand getting weaker or stronger? This theme—to what extent the dead can rule over the living—raises the question of the legal fate of dynastic, long-term arrangements.

The story here is fairly complex. In the early republic there were strong feelings against dynastic wealth. Dynastic wealth meant land monopolies and the dead hand of the church. These feelings weakened over the course of the nineteenth century and into the twentieth; and then they declined almost to the vanishing point. Dynastic wealth was no longer associated with control of land. Long-term and charitable trusts were not viewed as enemies of the land market. Prejudice against the dead hand of the church lost its bite. Charities and churches became favorites of the law. Mortmain statutes gradually disappeared. The rich set up huge foundations; legal barriers to these entities were swept away. The rule against perpetuities, the guillotine for long-term trusts, is tottering; some states have abolished it outright. The spendthrift trust doctrine, and the Claflin rule, protected the integrity of long-term private trusts. The cy pres doctrine allowed courts to make changes in charitable trusts, but only when this was necessary to keep the trust alive, and (theoretically at least) in such a way as to preserve, as much as possible, the original goals of the trust.

In short, in the late nineteenth and early twentieth centuries a strong legal trend favored the dynastic trust. The dead hand got stronger in that period. And in some ways this trend continues today. Inequality of wealth is growing; and the thrust of public policy, at least in the past generation or so, has helped this inequality along. Death taxes might be in their death throes. Taxes on the rich have been slashed and slashed again. Fifty years ago, nobody thought a perpetual trust (other than a charity) was either possible or desirable. But in recent years there has been a massive assault on the rule against perpetuities. A rich man can now, in some states, set up a private trust that lasts forever. All these trends—which of course might be reversible—suggest even greater sympathy to the dead hand, certainly to the dead hand of the rich and the powerful.

But this trend might be somewhat misleading. In the late nineteenth century the law of trusts did evolve in ways that favored rich individuals, rich dynasts; the law extended their power beyond the grave. In the late twentieth century, and into the twenty-first, the law smiled much more on rich *institutions*: notably the banks and trust companies. These institutions formed a powerful lobby. They were a strong and focused interest, and they were usually able to get their way. Individuals, even rich individuals, were a more diffuse interest. It is a maxim of political science that, in the legislative halls, even a small, focused interest beats out a larger but diffuse interest. Not that rich individuals are hurting. The legal changes that benefit banks and trust companies do not, on the whole, hurt the interests of their wealthy clients.

The brutal fact remains: the dead are definitively dead. The dead "control" beyond the grave only insofar as living people let them do so. In the long run, the dead run nothing. Even in a supposed perpetual trust, charitable or not, the dead hand reigns but does not rule. Like modern kings and queens, its power ebbs away. The evolution of the cy pres doctrine; the decay of the Claflin doctrine; the hegemony of professional managers in the large foundations—these all demonstrate that, practically speaking, the living rule the dead, not vice versa.

One thing is clear: as society changes, the law of succession will change with it. Whatever the future might bring, this one simple fact is the only thing we can take for granted.

NOTES

CHAPTER 1: INTRODUCTION

1. See Liesl Schillinger, "Astor's Place," *New York Times*, August 13, 2007, Sunday Book Review.

2. "Banta: His Character Still Under Official Investigation," *Los Angeles Times*, June 20, 1889, p. 3.

3. "The Banta Case Still: A Witness Who Saw the Old Man Stark Crazy," *Los Angeles Times*, June 26, 1889, p. 2.

4. "The Will Sustained: Son-in Law Pierce Will Administer the Estate," *Los Angeles Times*, July 11, 1889, p. 2.

5. *Los Angeles Times*, August 29, 1889, p. 6.

6. This information is from the website of the Cryonics Institute, http://www.cryonics.org/become2.html, visited September 18, 2007.

7. John J. Havens and Paul G. Schervish, "Millionaires and the Millennium: New Estimates of the Forthcoming Wealth Transfer and the Prospects for a Golden Age of Philanthropy," Boston College Social Welfare Research Institute, Report, released October 19, 1999; John J. Havens and Paul G. Schervish, "Why the $41 Trillion Wealth Transfer Estimate Is Still Valid: A Review of Challenges and Questions," *Journal of Gift Planning* 7: 11 (2003).

8. George E. Marcus with Peter Dobkin Hall, *Lives in Trust: The Fortunes of Dynastic Families in Late Twentieth-Century America* (1993).

9. On this "regression to the mean," see Jenny B. Wahl, "From Riches to Riches: Inter-

generational Transfers and the Evidence from Estate Tax Returns," *Social Science Quarterly* 84: 278 (2003).

10. Roy Williams and Vic Preisser, in *Preparing Heirs: Five Steps to a Successful Transition of Family Wealth and Values* (2003), estimate that there is a 70% "failure rate" for wealth transfers. That means that in only 30% of the cases of great wealth transfers does the wealth stay in the hands of the beneficiaries for any really significant period of time.

11. Stephen J. McNamee and Robert K. Miller, Jr., "Estate Inheritance: A Sociological Lacuna," *Sociological Inquiry* 59: 7 (1989); Clifton D. Bryant and William A. Snizek, "The Last Will and Testament: A Neglected Document in Sociological Research," *Sociology and Social Research* 59: 219 (1975); Remi Clignet, *Death, Deeds, and Descendants* (1992).

12. Edward V. Carroll and Sonya Salamon, "Share and Share Alike: Inheritance Patterns in Two Illinois Farm Communities," *Journal of Family History* 13: 219 (1988).

13. See James W. Deen, "Patterns of Testation in Four Tidewater Counties in Colonial Virginia," *American Journal of Legal History* 16: 154 (1972); Lawrence M. Friedman, "Patterns of Testation in the 19th Century: A Study of Essex County (New Jersey) Wills," *American Journal of Legal History* 8: 34 (1964); David Narrett, "Preparation for Death and Provision for the Living: Notes on New York Wills (1665–1760)," *New York History*, October 1976, p. 417.

14. Allison Dunham, "The Method, Process and Frequency of Wealth Transmission," *University of Chicago Law Review* 30: 241 (1962). Steuart Henderson Britt, "The Significance of the Last Will and Testament," *Journal of Social Psychology* 8: 347 (1937); Edward H. Ward and J. H. Beuscher, "The Inheritance Process in Wisconsin," *Wisconsin Law Review* 1950: 393.

15. Carole Shammas, Marylynn Salmon, and Michel Dahlin, *Inheritance in America: From Colonial Times to the Present* (1987). Jens Beckert's *Inherited Wealth* (2008) is a translation from German of a comparative study of some aspects of the law of succession in France, Germany, and the United States.

16. The Cuyahoga County study is by Marvin B. Sussman, Judith N. Cates, and David T. Smith, *The Family and Inheritance* (1970); the San Bernardino study is by Lawrence M. Friedman, Christopher J. Walker, and Ben Hernandez-Stern, "The Inheritance Process in San Bernardino County, California, 1964: A Research Note," *Houston Law Review* 43: 1445 (2007). Other studies using 1960's data include Olin L. Browder, Jr.'s, "Recent Patterns of Testate Succession in the United States and England," *Michigan Law Review* 67: 1303 (1969); and John R. Price's, "The Transmission of Wealth at Death in a Community Property Jurisdiction," *Washington Law Review* 50: 277 (1975).

17. Stuart Banner, *How the Indians Lost Their Land* (2005).

18. William Blackstone, *Commentaries on the Laws of England*, Book 2 (1765–1769), p. 433.

19. If the will fails to name an executor, or if it names an executor who dies or quits or refuses, then the court will appoint an administrator, called an "administrator with the will annexed."

20. In some states, the probate court goes by a different name: "surrogate's court" in New York and New Jersey; "orphan's court" in Maryland and Pennsylvania. In some states, there is a separate probate court; in others (California, for example), the probate court is a division of a trial court of general jurisdiction.

21. See William Fratcher, *Probate Can Be Quick and Cheap: Trusts and Estates in England* (1968).

22. Texas Probate Code §145 (b). In addition, the "distributees," if they all agree, can make the executor an independent administrator. See §145 (c).

23. In part, this is due to people who peddle trusts and other devices to avoid probate. Norman Dacey's book *How to Avoid Probate*, which I mention again later on, has sold over 15 million copies and is partly responsible for this widespread but erroneous idea.

24. California Probate Code §6602.

25. The Uniform Probate Code includes a provision for "universal succession," modeled after the European systems. This would make the process much more streamlined than the Texas arrangement. Uniform Probate Code §3-312.

26. See, in general, Ralph C. Brashier, *Inheritance Law and the Evolving Family* (2004).

27. John H. Langbein, "The Twentieth-Century Revolution in Family Wealth Transmission," *Michigan Law Review* 86: 722 (1988). Modern medicine is one reason why we are living longer; but modern medicine also makes it possible for people to stay "alive" when "alive" means an existence little better than that of a vegetable. For this reason many people make out "living wills," telling the world what they want done in this situation.

28. Edward N. Wolff, "Bequests, Saving, and Wealth Inequality: Inheritances and Wealth Inequality, 1989–1998," *American Economic Review* 92: 260 (2002).

CHAPTER 2: DISTRIBUTION AFTER DEATH

1. Willard Hurst, *Law and Economic Growth* (1964), p. 9.

2. On this practice, see Chapter 5.

3. Children, however, can be freely disinherited in our system; minor children may have minor (and temporary) rights, but for the most part a testator can ignore his children. There is one exception: Louisiana, where children under age 24 normally have a right to inherit a share of the estate. And even in common law jurisdictions rules about homestead and family allowance give *some* protection to dependent children. On the other hand, in many European systems, and even some common law jurisdictions (England, Australia), the law is wobbling a bit; and children have more rights. I will return to this topic.

4. James Kent, *Commentaries on American Law*, Vol. IV, 2nd ed. (1832), p. 383.

5. Laws and Liberties of Massachusetts, 1648 (1929 ed.), p. 53.

6. Kent, *Commentaries*, Vol. IV, 2nd ed., p. 385.

7. Stanley N. Katz, "Republicanism and the Law of Inheritance in the American Revolutionary Era," *Michigan Law Review* 76: 1 (1977).

8. Kent, *Commentaries*, Vol. IV, 2nd ed. pp. 14–15.

9. On the classic law of dower, see William Blackstone, *Commentaries on the Laws of England*, Book 2 (1765–1769), pp. 129–39.

10. England did not provide for official formal adoption until 1926. 16 and 17 Geo. V, ch. 29; see Stephen Cretney, *Family Law in the Twentieth Century: A History* (2003), pp. 598–606. Before 1926 there was adoption "in the sense of providing a home for a child," that is, a "social institution"; but the adoptive parents and the child were "legally strangers"; and there was no "effective machinery to prevent the natural parents exercising their common law right to remove the child." Ibid., p. 598.

Most of the American states had recognized adoption of children long before this. The pioneer American statute—from Massachusetts—was enacted in 1851. Laws of Massachusetts 1851, ch. 324, p. 815. There were private acts of adoption before 1851; see Lawrence M. Friedman, *Private Lives: Families, Individuals, and the Law* (2004), p. 99. On the history of adoption, see Julie Berebitsky, *Like Our Very Own: Adoption and the Changing Culture of Motherhood, 1851–1950* (2000); Jamil Zainaldin, "The Emergence of a Modern American Family Law: Child Custody, Adoption, and the Courts," *Northwestern University Law Review* 73: 1038 (1979). Other states followed Massachusetts rather quickly. See, for example, Laws of Iowa 1858, ch. 67, p. 102.

11. Blackstone, *Commentaries*, Book 2, ch. 8.

12. See, for a discussion of settlements in England, Eileen Spring, *Law, Land, and Family: Aristocratic Inheritance in England, 1300 to 1800* (1993).

13. Suzanne Lebsock, *The Free Women of Petersburg: Status and Culture in a Southern Town, 1784–1860* (1984), p. 60. Most of these were set up by relatives of the woman *after* marriage, when it appeared to a man (for example) that his son-in-law was a spendthrift, or was bankrupt. There is also material on settlements in the nineteenth-century United States in Hendrik Hartog, *Man and Wife in America: A History* (2000).

14. Revised Statutes. N. Y. 1829, Vol. 1, p. 751.

15. Some states at the time did distinguish between half-blood and whole-blood relatives; a few still do. See, for example, Kentucky Revised Statutes §391.050.

16. Revised Statutes N. Y., 1829, Vol. 1, p. 753.

17. Michigan Revised Statutes 1846, Title XV, p. 273; similarly, Revised Statutes of Arkansas 1838, p. 330.

18. See Ariela Dubler, "In the Shadow of Marriage: Single Women and the Legal Construction of the Family and the State," *Yale Law Journal* 112: 1679 (2003).

19. Revised Statutes of Indiana 1852, ch. 27, §§16, 17.

20. Kansas Statutes 1862, ch. 83.

21. Dower and curtesy are still part of the law of Arkansas, but in a modified form. Interestingly, the "inchoate" feature of dower and curtesy are preserved: "If the heir alienates lands of which a surviving spouse is entitled to dower or curtesy, he or she shall still be decreed his curtesy or her dower in the lands so alienated, in whosoever hands the land may be." Arkansas Statutes §28-39-307.

22. Oregon Revised Statutes §112.025. For simplicity, I used the word "children"; the

statute says "issue," which includes (for example) grandchildren, if their parent—the testator's child—is dead. Other states—Florida, for example—use the term "lineal descendants."

23. Florida Statutes §732.102. In Illinois too, if there are no children, the surviving spouse will inherit the whole estate. 755 ILCS 5/2-1 (a). See also Colorado Revised Statutes §15-11-102; the surviving spouse gets everything if there are no children or parents of the deceased.

24. *Newman v. Dore*, 275 N. Y. 371, 9 N. E. 2d 966 (1937). Straus died in July 1934; *New York Times*, July 3, 1934, p. 19.

25. In recent years, some states have adopted a new approach. Under these statutes a widow is entitled to a share of the "augmented" estate. The "augmented" estate includes not only the probate estate, but also certain lifetime transfers of property. This approach was accepted by the Uniform Probate Code §2-202. Different states, however, have different versions of the general idea.

26. Georgia Code §53-4-1. A testator, by will, can "make any disposition of property" to whomever the testator wishes, to the "exclusion of the testator's spouse and descendants."

27. California Probate Code §6401.

28. Another possibility, to be sure, was to ask for a divorce and hope to get rights to the property that way. But divorce was not common in this period; and in the southern states it also required a private act. On divorce, see Norma Basch, *Framing American Divorce: From the Revolutionary Generation to the Victorians* (1999); Richard H. Chused, *Private Acts in Public Places: A Social History of Divorce in the Formative Era of American Family Law* (1994).

29. See, on the origins of this particular law, Megan Benson, "*Fisher v. Allen*: The Southern Origins of the Married Women's Property Acts," *Journal of Southern Legal History* 6: 97 (1998). On the married women's property laws there is something of a literature; see Norma Basch, *In the Eyes of the Law: Women, Marriage, and Property in Nineteenth-Century New York* (1982); Richard H. Chused, "Married Women's Property Law: 1800–1850," *Georgetown Law Journal* 71: 1359 (1983).

30. Laws of Maryland 1842–43, ch. 293, §§1, 6. The statute also provided that "no will under this act shall be valid unless made at least sixty days before the death of the testatrix." Ibid., §6. This is a so-called mortmain provision, which I discuss in more detail in Chapter 3.

31. See Douglas Woodruff, *The Tichborne Claimant: A Victorian Mystery* (1957); Geddes MacGregor, *The Tichborne Impostor* (1957).

32. *In re Wood*, 299 N. Y. S. 195 (Surr. Ct., 1937).

33. *Garrett Estate*, 372 Pa. 438, 94 A. 2d 357 (1953).

34. *In re Estate of Wendel*, 287 N. Y. S. 893 (Surr. Ct., 1936).

35. "Heir hunters" might also be attracted to a situation in which, for example, the deceased's will names Cousin Mary as an heir but nobody knows where she is, whether she is alive or dead, living in Tasmania, or whatever.

36. *Estate of Denis Griswold*, 79 Cal. App. 4th 1380, 94 Cal. Rptr. 2d 638 (2000).

37. This ad is from the company's website, www.lostheir.com, which I consulted in April 2007.

38. David V. DeRosa, "Intestate Succession and the Laughing Heir: Who Do We Want to Get the Last Laugh?" *Quinnipiac Probate Law Journal* 12: 153 (1997).

39. This is the case in Florida, for example; the statute did, however, allow descendants of the decedent's great-grandparents to inherit, if the great-grandparents were Holocaust victims. This particular provision lapsed on December 31, 2004. Florida Statutes §732.103 (6).

40. See Alan Friedman, "Heir Hunt Agreements: Recommendations for the Extension of Probate Court Jurisdiction," *Connecticut Probate Law Journal* 6: 87 (1991). The business goes back more than a century. See Note, "Heir Hunting—A Profession or a Racket," *Vanderbilt Law Review* 7: 104 (1953); DeRosa, "Intestate Succession and the Laughing Heir," pp. 153, 174–82.

41. Lawrence W. Waggoner, "The Multiple-Marriage Society and Spousal Rights under the Uniform Probate Code," *Iowa Law Review* 76: 223 (1991).

42. *Neiderhiser Estate*, 2 Pa. D. & C. 3d 302 (1977); see, on this point, Ralph C. Brashier, *Inheritance Law and the Evolving Family* (2004), pp. 9–10.

43. Uniform Probate Code §2-202.

44. Arkansas Code Annotated §28-39-401 (a).

45. *Shaw v. Shaw*, 337 Ark. 530, 989 S. W. 2d 919 (1999).

46. In *Artz v. Artz*, 198 N. J. Super. 585, 487 A. 2d 1294 (1985), Jay Artz was charged with murdering his mother. At a bench trial he was acquitted "on the basis of insanity." Both the trial court and the appellate court felt he could inherit, and also benefit from her life insurance, under the terms of the local statute.

47. California Probate Code §250. The code makes a "final judgment of conviction of felonious and intentional killing . . . conclusive." But what if there is no "final judgment"? This would be the case, for example, if a man killed his father and then committed suicide. Here the court can "determine by a preponderance of evidence" if the "killing was felonious and intentional." California Probate Code §254.

48. Here California law is clear; the killing "effects a severance of the interest of the decedent"; the share of the decedent "passes as the decedent's property and the killer has no rights by survivorship." California Probate Code §251.

49. *United States v. Burns*, 103 F. Supp. 690 (D.C. Md., 1952). In *State Farm Life Insurance Company v. Smith*, 66 Ill. 2d 591, 363 N. E. 2d 785 (1977), Rosa Mae Smith shot and killed her husband, Jesse Lee Smith. A grand jury refused to indict her. She sued to collect on two insurance policies. The Illinois Supreme Court went over the evidence carefully, and in the end she got her money; but the court clearly felt the failure to indict her was not binding; it made its own decision on whether or not she had acted "intentionally" and wrongfully in killing her husband.

50. In California as we noted, in a civil suit, absence of a conviction is *not* conclusive, and the court can decide whether the defendant did in fact "feloniously and intentionally" kill, according to a preponderance of the evidence. California Probate Code §254. The reader will recall the famous case of O. J. Simpson, who was acquitted of murdering his ex-wife

and another man and yet lost a civil suit for damages for "wrongful death" brought against him by the man's family.

51. California Probate Code §259. The section applies only if the person to be disinherited "acted in bad faith," was "reckless, oppressive, fraudulent, or malicious" in committing the abusive acts, and the decedent was, "at the time those acts occurred and thereafter until the time of . . . death . . . substantially unable to manage his or her financial resources." This is probably a unique statute, at least at this writing. See Seymour Moskowitz, "Golden Age in the Golden State: Contemporary Legal Developments in Elder Abuse and Neglect," *Loyola of Los Angeles Law Review* 36: 589, 654–55 (2003).

52. Revised Statutes of Indiana 1843, p. 430, ch. 28, §93.

53. Note that the statute says "living in adultery," which is not the same as just plain adultery. In *Gaylor v. McHenry*, 15 Ind. 383 (1860), the wife, Many Ann Hayden, had left her husband. There was some evidence she had committed adultery. The court said: "While it is true that a single act would make the plaintiff an adulteress, it does not follow . . . that . . . she would be living in adultery, within the meaning of this statute." The adultery laws in the nineteenth century often criminalized only "open and notorious adultery," which meant more or less the same as "living in adultery," rather than adultery plain and simple. See Lawrence M. Friedman, *Crime and Punishment in American History* (1993), p. 130.

54. Connecticut General Statutes §45a-436 (g).

55. *Estate of Scott*, 90 Cal. App. 2d 21, 202 P. 2d 357 (1949).

56. *Estate of O'Keefe*, 583 N.W. 2d 138 (So. Dak., 1998).

57. *Hotarek v. Benson*, 211 Conn. 121, 557 A. 2d 1259 (1989).

58. 755 ILCS 5/18-1.1 (2007). The statute was held constitutional in *Porter v. Jolliff*, 199 Ill. 2d 510, 771 N. E. 2d 346 (2002).

59. California Probate Code §6609 (b).

60. Kent, *Commentaries*, Vol. 4, 2nd ed., p. 61.

61. Ohio Code §2106.15.

62. California Probate Code §6524.

63. Louisiana Civil Code Art. 1493; see Kathrun Venturatos Lorio, "Forced Heirship: The Citadel Has Fallen—Or Has It?" *Louisiana Bar Journal* 44: 16 (1996)

64. Quoted in *Succession of Lauga*, 624 So. 2d 1156 (La., 1993).

65. *Succession of Lauga*, 624 So. 2d 1156 (La. 1993).

66. See Hendrik Hartog, "Someday All This Will Be Yours: Inheritance, Adoption, and Obligation in Capitalist America," *Indiana Law Journal* 79: 345 (2004).

67. On the Hillblom saga, see Philip D. Witte, "Heir Wars," *California Lawyer* (2003), p. 22; Robert Frank, "The Fatherlode," *Wall Street Journal*, March 20, 2000, p. A1; Mary Curtius, "Asian Children Finally Get Part of $550-Million Estate," *Los Angeles Times*, May 20, 1999, p. A1.

68. Witte, "Heir Wars," p. 22.

69. Claudia Dreifus, "A Math Sleuth Whose Secret Weapon Is Statistics," *New York Times*, August 8, 2000, p. F3.

70. California Probate Code §21621. The child does not take, also, if the decedent made some other financial arrangements, and there is evidence that these arrangements were meant to be "in lieu of a provision" in the will.

71. Julius Cohen, Reginald A. Robson, and Alan P. Bates, *Parental Authority: The Community and the Law* (1958), pp. 76–78.

72. See Luke Cooperrider's review of Cohen, Robson, and Bates's *Parental Authority*, in *Michigan Law Review* 57: 1119 (1959).

73. Mary Louise Fellows, William Rau, and Rita J. Simon, "An Empirical Study of the Illinois Statutory Estate Plan," *University of Illinois Law Forum* 1976: 707, 728.

74. Carole Shammas, Marylynn Salmon, and Michel Dahlin, *Inheritance in America: From Colonial Times to the Present* (1987), p. 184.

75. Lawrence M. Friedman, Christopher J. Walker, and Ben Hernandez-Stern, "The Inheritance Process in San Bernardino County, California, 1964: A Research Note," *Houston Law Review* 43: 1458 (2007).

76. Shammas, Salmon, and Dahlin, *Inheritance in America*, pp. 196–97.

77. David Margolick, in *Undue Influence: The Epic Battle for the Johnson & Johnson Fortune* (1993), tells the story.

78. *Estate of Marshall G. Gardiner*, 42 P. 3d 120 (Kansas, 2002).

79. The Inheritance (Family Provision) Act, 1938, 1 & 2 Geo. VI, ch. 45.

80. F. R. Crane, "Family Provision on Death in English Law," *New York University Law Review* 35: 984 (1960).

81. Joseph Gold, "Freedom of Testation," *Modern Law Review* 1: 296, 300 (1938).

82. The act, which is extremely long and detailed, is Chapter 63 of the statutes of 1975. See Gareth Miller, "Provision for Adult Children under the Inheritance (Provision for Family and Dependants) Act 1975," *Conveyancer and Property Lawyer* (Jan.–Feb. 1995), p. 22.

83. *Heatley v. Doherty*, [1983] 8 NIJB; this case came out of Northern Ireland, under an order that extended the reach of the English statute to Northern Ireland.

84. *Lambeff v. Farmers Co-operative Executors and Trustees*, [1991] South Australian State Reports, p. 323.

85. *In re Estate of Jetter*, 570 N. W. 2d 26 (S. Dak. 1997).

86. Mary Louise Fellows, William Rau, and Rita J. Simon, "A Comparison of Public Attitudes about Property Distribution at Death to Intestate Succession Laws in the United States," *American Bar Foundation Research Journal* 1978: 321, 333–34. That was also the message of the 1958 study by Cohen, Robson, and Bates, *Parental Authority*.

87. Allison Dunham, "Sixty Different Succession Laws in Illinois," 46 *Ill. B. J.* 742 (1958).

88. Also ex-spouses, if they were married for at least ten years before the divorce.

89. Connecticut General Statutes Annotated §51-295a (c).

90. On common law marriage, see Michael Grossberg, *Governing the Hearth: Law and the Family in Nineteenth-Century America* (1985), ch. 3; Lawrence M. Friedman, *Private Lives: Families, Individuals, and the Law* (2004), pp. 17–27; Ariela R. Dubler, "Wifely Behavior: A Legal History of Acting Married," *Columbia Law Review* 100: 957 (2000).

91. 26 Geo. II, ch. 33; see Stephen Parker, "The Marriage Act 1753: A Case Study in Family Law-Making," *International Journal of Law and the Family* 1: 133 (1987).

92. On these laws, see Lawrence M. Friedman, *Private Lives: Families, Individuals and the Law* (2004), pp. 51–54. A Wisconsin statute, for example, passed in 1913, required all "male persons" who wanted to marry to undergo a physical examination and get a certificate from a doctor stating that they were free from "acquired venereal disease." Laws of Wisconsin 1913, ch. 738.

93. See Friedman, *Private Lives*, p. 44.

94. New Hampshire Revised Statutes §457.39. In Oregon, a statute passed in 1993 defined as a "surviving spouse" a person who had lived together with the deceased "for at least ten years" if the couple had "represented themselves, and conducted their affairs, as husband and wife" and were not legally married to somebody else. Laws of Oregon 1993, ch. 598, §4. The act was amended in 1995 and then repealed in 1999.

95. Pennsylvania Consolidated Statutes Annotated, 23 §1103.

96. Kaja Whitehouse, *What Your Lawyer May Not Tell You about Your Family's Will* (2006), p. 147.

97. The courts made it clear that New Hampshire did not recognize the doctrine of common law marriage, *except* insofar as a relationship conformed to this statute. In *Joan S. v. John S.*, 121 N. H. 96, 427 A. 2d 498 (1981), Joan and John lived together for nearly fifteen years and had four children. When they split up, Joan wanted alimony. But the court denied it. Alimony depends on divorce, and divorce depends on marriage. This was not a real marriage under the statute, because the statute requires the couple to "acknowledge" each other as a spouse, but John had always insisted he would never marry Joan. Of course, under classic common law marriage doctrine, the couple was supposed to have agreed to be married; if they insisted they were not, there could be no common law marriage.

98. *Callen v. Callen*, 365 S. C. 618, 620 S. E. 2d 59 (2005). The trial court had held that there was a valid common law marriage; the appellate court reversed on various grounds and sent the case back for retrial.

99. *Jennings v. Hurt*, 554 N. Y. S. 2d 220 (Sup. Ct. N.Y., App. Div., 1990). The case arose in New York, but the court applied South Carolina law.

100. In May 2008, the California Supreme Court overturned the state's ban on gay marriages, in a hotly contested 4 to 3 decision. *In re Marriage Cases* 43 Cal. 4th 757, 183 P. 3rd 384 (2008). As of this writing, however, the fate of this case is unknown. A proposed amendment to the Constitution of California will be on the ballot in November 2008; if it succeeds, it will nullify the Supreme Court's decision.

101. The study is Mary Louise Fellows et al., "Committed Partners and Inheritance: An Empirical Study," *Law & Inequality* 16: 1 (1998).

102. *Oliver v. Fowler*, 126 P. 3d 69 (Wash. App., 2006).

103. *Vasquez v. Hawthorne*, 145 Wn. 2d 103, 33 P. 3d 735 (2001).

104. Vermont Statutes Annotated 15 §1201–7 is the civil union statute; registration is governed by 18 §5160–69. There are civil union statutes in New Jersey, Connecticut, and

New Hampshire as well. New Jersey Statutes Annotated, Title 37, Art. 6, §§37-1-28 to 37-1-36; Connecticut General Statutes Annotated, Title 46B, Ch. 185F, §§46b-38aa to 46b-38pp; Revised Statutes Annotated of New Hampshire, Title XLIII, Ch. 457-A, §§457-A-1 to 457-A-8.

 105. California Family Code §§297 (a), (b); and 297.5.

 106. Ann E. Marimow, "California Extends Inheritance Rights," *San Jose Mercury-News*, September 11, 2002, p. 19.

 107. Maine Revised Statutes Annotated 22 §2710 (2).

 108. *Vasquez* v. *Hawthorne*, 145 Wn. 2d 103, 33 P. 3rd 735 (2001).

 109. *Braschi* v. *Stahl Associates Co.*, 74 N. Y. 2d 201, 543 N. E. 2d 49 (1989).

 110. "The rights [of a bastard] are very few . . . for he can inherit nothing, being looked upon as the son of nobody, sometimes called filius nullius." Blackstone, *Commentaries*, Book 1, p. 446.

 111. *Stanley* v. *Illinois*, 405 U.S. 645 (1972).

 112. On this general theme, see Lawrence M. Friedman, *Guarding Life's Dark Secrets* (2007).

 113. Laws of Massachusetts 1851, ch. 324, p. 815.

 114. Laws of Mississippi 1844, ch. 154, p. 339, ch. 173, p. 353. A more elaborate statute changed the names of two minors, James Vinyard and Frances Vinyard, who were "now in the care of Dempsey Blanks," to James Blanks and Frances Blanks. Dempsey was given the "full paternal care and custody" of these two children, against the claims of anybody else; it gave a slave, Lucy, and her four children "in fee simple" to James and Frances, "to be equally divided between them, when the youngest, to-wit, Frances, attains the age of twenty-one years." Laws of Mississippi 1844, ch. 179, pp. 357–58.

 115. Laws of Mississippi 1846, ch. 60, p. 231.

 116. Laws of Texas 1850, ch. 39, p. 36.

 117. Colorado Revised Statutes Annotated, §19-5-211 (1).

 118. Yet another consequence is that the adopted child by and large *loses* the right to inherit from its "natural" parents. This, however, is not universally the case. Suppose a man dies, his wife remarries, and the new husband adopts the child of the dead spouse. In this case, under a Florida statute, for example, the adoption "has no effect on the relationship between the child and the family of the deceased natural parent." Florida Statutes Annotated §732.108. The same is true in Florida if the child is adopted by a "close relative" of dead parents.

CHAPTER 3: THE LAST WILL AND TESTAMENT

 1. Each state has a statute that sets out the formalities required for a will. In California, for example, it is Probate Code §6110. There are separate provisions, of course, for holographic wills; see California Probate Code §6111.

 2. 1 Victoria ch. 26, §9 (1837). The Wills Act required a will to be signed "at the foot or end thereof"; the Statute of Frauds, 29 Charles II, ch. 3, §5, had no such requirement.

 3. See Joseph H. Smith, ed., *Colonial Justice in Western Massachusetts (1639–1702): The*

Pynchon Court Record (1961), p. 266: Henry Burt of Springfield died on April 30, 1662, "not leavinge any will . . . yet for that he did by words express his mind therein before Ensigne Thomas Cooper and Jonathan Burt who by a writing under their hands presented the Same unto this Courte."

4. Revised Statutes of New York 1852, Vol. II, p. 243.

5. Burns Indiana Code Annotated §29-1-5-4 (2006); see also Mississippi Code Annotated §91-5-15 (2007), which is even more restrictive; in New York, NY CLS EPTL §3-2.2 (2007), the nuncupative will is still recognized, but is, as before, valid only for "members of the armed forces" and only "during a war, declared or undeclared," or for a "mariner while at sea."

6. At one time, many states required three witnesses. New Hampshire was one of the last holdouts; but it now asks only for two witnesses, like the other states. New Hampshire Revised Statutes §551.2. In Vermont and Louisiana three witnesses are still required.

7. Today, in almost all states, a testator can execute a "self-proved will," which is a witnessed will together with a notarized affidavit; in the affidavit, the testator and the witnesses swear that the will has been properly executed. The self-proved will can be admitted to probate without calling in the witnesses and hearing their testimony.

8. Mary Louise Fellows, William Rau, and Rita J. Simon, "A Comparison of Public Attitudes about Property Distribution at Death to Intestate Succession Laws in the United States," *American Bar Foundation Research Journal* 1978: 319, 336–37.

9. Lawrence M. Friedman, Christopher J. Walker, and Ben Hernandez-Stern, "The Inheritance Process in San Bernardino County, California, 1964: A Research Note," *Houston Law Review* 43: at 1453 (2007).

10. Carole Shammas, Marylynn Salmon, and Michel Dahlin, *Inheritance in America: From Colonial Times to the Present* (1987), p. 17.

11. *Fleming v. Morrison*, 187 Mass. 120, 72 N. E. 499 (1904). The will had three witnesses, but the court decided that two of them did not count because the testator did not intend the document to be a real will when they signed it; that left only one witness, which, of course, would not be enough in any case.

12. *Eaton v. Brown*, 193 U.S. 411 (1904).

13. *Smith v. Nelson*, 227 Ark. 512, 299 S. W. 2d 645 (1957).

14. The proponents of the will then argued that the letters were valid holographs, but this argument did not work. There was nothing in the letters to show they were intended to be wills or anything other than "family correspondence."

15. In Smith, *Colonial Justice in Western Massachusetts*, p. 212.

16. J. Hall Pleasants, ed., *Archives of Maryland, LIV: Proceedings of the County Courts of Kent (1648), Talbot (1662–1674) and Somerset (1665–1668) Counties* (1937), p. 13. This pattern was common: see, for example, the will of John Salter, also of Kent County, in 1661: ". . . beinge very sicke and week of body but of sound and perfett memory. . . . I Commett and Commend my soule to god my Maker and to Jesus Christ my sauioure. . . . I Commett my body to the Earth. . . ." Ibid., p. 219.

17. *In re Fish's Will*, 88 Hun. 56, 34 N. Y. Supp. 536 (1895).

18. However, the courts were somewhat understanding on what constituted a "signature." If an illiterate person signed with an "X," that was good enough; for example, see *Reed* v. *Hendrix*, 180 Ky. 57, 201 S. W. 482 (1918). In a letter that the court was willing to treat as a holographic will, the signature "Father" was held to be enough of a signature to satisfy the legal requirement. *Kimmel's Estate* 278 Pa. 435, 123 A. 405 (1924).

19. *Stevens* v. *Casdorph*, 508 S. E. 2d 610 (W. Va. 1998).

20. *Walker* v. *Walker*, 342 Ill. 376, 174 N. E. 541 (1930).

21. *Burns* v. *Adamson*, 313 Ark. 281, 854 S. W. 2d 753 (1993).

22. See California Probate Code §6111. This is a modernization of the law, which was at one time extremely strict, and required everything in the will to be in the testator's handwriting.

23. General Statutes North Carolina §31-3.4 (3) (2005).

24. These states, and others, have adopted provisions that appear in the Uniform Probate Code. A will, according to the code, may be valid, even if it lacks the usual formalities, if the "signature and material portions of the document are in the testator's handwriting." UPC §2-502 (b). See, for example, North Dakota Statutes §30.1-08-02; New Jersey §3B:3-2. In New York, a holograph is valid only when a nuncupative will would be valid, which means only for soldiers and sailors on active duty in time of war. NY CLS EPTL §3-2.2 (2007).

25. Friedman, Walker, and Hernandez-Stern, "The Inheritance Process in San Bernardino County," pp. 1464–65.

26. Probate Records Nos. 33767, 33714, San Bernardino County, Calif. (1964).

27. *Maines* v. *Davis*, 227 So. 2d 844 (Miss., 1969).

28. *Kimmel's Estate*, 278 Pa. 435, 123 A. 405 (1924).

29. *Estate of Charles Kuralt*, 303 Mont. 335, 15 P. 3d 931 (2000). A codicil requires the same formalities as a will. But there can be a holographic codicil to a nonholographic will, and vice versa.

30. *Trim* v. *Daniels*, 862 S. W. 2d 8 (Tex., 1992).

31. *Button* v. *Button*, 209 Cal. 325, 287 Pac. 964 (1930).

32. There were a number of other legal problems in this case. For example, instead of a signature, the note or letter ended with "Love from 'Muddy.'" "Muddy" was the name she was "affectionately known by" to her ex-husband and children; many cases have held that it is not necessary for a "signature" to consist of the "legal or true name," and "Muddy" was held good enough.

33. *In re Thorn's Estate*, 183 Cal. 512, 192 Pac. 19 (1920).

34. California Probate Code §6111(a).

35. See Gerry W. Beyer and William R. Buckley, "Videotape and the Probate Process: The Nexus Grows," *Oklahoma Law Review* 42: 43 (1989); in *Estate of Reed*, 672 P. 2d 829 (Wyo., 1983), Robert Reed left behind a tape recording in a sealed envelope. On the envelope were the words "Robert Reed To be played in the event of my death only!" and his signature. The court refused to admit the tape as a will.

36. Burns Indiana Code Annotated §29-1-5-3.2 (2006).

37. This is from the website of Pilot Video Productions, LLC, http://www.pilot-video.com/legal.html, viewed June 27, 2007; another company, Top Legal Video Services, also claims that proof of "due execution" of the will "becomes more certain when substantiated by a video recording," http://www.toplegalvideoservices.com/ols.html, viewed June 27, 2007; of course these companies also make videos for many other purposes, for example, "Pre-Construction Video Surveys," depositions, and "day-in-the-life" documentaries that outline a typical day of a "plaintiff who has sustained injuries," to be used in tort cases.

38. *Hultquist* v. *Ring*, 301 S. W. 2d 303 (Ct. of Civil Appeals, Texas, 1957).

39. Nevada Revised Statutes Annotated (2003), §133.085.

40. In 2000, Congress enacted the Electronic Signatures in Global and National Commerce Act 114 Stat. 464 (2000), which requires states, under certain conditions, to recognize electronic signatures as valid. The act does not apply to wills and testamentary trusts. But this situation may change.

41. If a later will disposes of *some* but not all of the estate, it may revoke the earlier will only to the extent that will number two is inconsistent with will number one. Lawyer-drafted wills almost always begin with a clause expressly revoking all older wills.

42. California Probate Code §6120.

43. The case is *Thompson* v. *Royall*, 163 Va. 492, 175 S. E. 748 (1934).

44. *Kronauge* v. *Stoecklein*, 293 N. E. 2d 320 (Ohio, 1972).

45. It was, and is, possible to revoke *part* of a will by physical act—for example, by crossing out a single clause. But if the testator, after crossing out the clause, writes in a new one, this could be a big mistake: the revocation might be valid, but the new clause almost certainly will not be, because it lacks witnesses and other formalities.

46. Uniform Probate Code §2-507.

47. See Kansas Statutes Annotated §59-610: "If after making a will the testator marries and has a child, by birth or adoption, the will is revoked."

48. Administration of Justice Act, 1982, ch. 53, creating §18A of the Wills Act; after a divorce or an annulment, devises or bequests to a former spouse lapse; and appointments as executor or trustee also disappear.

49. See, for example, Kentucky Revised Statutes §394.092. This section, and comparable sections in many other states, provides that divorce also wipes out any designation of the ex-spouse as executor or trustee under the will.

50. *Pepper* v. *Peacher*, 742 P. 2d 21 (Okla., 1987).

51. This case was *Clymer* v. *Mayo*, 393 Mass. 754, 473 N. E. 2d 1084 (1985). The court also decided that provisions in a will leaving money to the ex-spouse's *relatives* were not automatically revoked by a divorce.

52. *Egelhoff* v. *Egelhoff*, 532 U.S. 141 (2001). The lower federal court cases had split on the issue of preemption in the case of nonprobate transfers. See, for example, *Emard* v. *Hughes Aircraft Co.*, 153 F. 3d 949 (C.A. 9, 1998), which held that ERISA did not preempt the state rules.

53. Washington Revised Code §11.07.010(2)(a).

54. What about state statutes that prevent a murderer from inheriting? Does ERISA preempt these statutes? Well, said the Court, bobbing and weaving, those "statutes are not before us, so we do not decide the issue." Anyway, "nearly every State" had such a statute; and those murdering-heir statutes had "a long historical pedigree." *Egelhoff v. Egelhoff.*, p. 152.

55. See Georgia Code 1933, §113-107; see also *Kelley v. Welborn*, 110 Ga. 540, 35 S. E. 636 (1900).

56. Maryland Constitution 1776, Art. XXXIV. But a gift or devise of land "not exceeding two acres, for a church, meeting, or other house of worship, and for a burying-ground," was not subject to this stricture.

57. One of those that survived was California Probate Code §41; it was repealed by Laws of California 1970, ch. 1395, p. 2747.

58. *Estate of Cavill*, 459 Pa. 411, 329 A. 2d 503 (1974); see also *In re Estate of Kinyon* 189 Mont. 76, 615 P. 2d 174 (1980).

59. *Shriners Hospital for Crippled Children v. Zrillic*, 563 So. 2d 64 (Fla., 1990).

60. *Estate of Cavill*, 459 Pa. 411, 329 A. 2d 503 (1974).

61. Laws of New York 1860, ch. 360, p. 607.

62. Laws of New York 1929, ch. 229, §3, p. 570.

63. *Estate of Rothko*, 71 Misc. 2d 74, 335 N. Y. Supp. 2d 666 (Surr. Ct., N.Y. County, 1972) was one of a whole series of tangled cases arising out of the messy affairs of the estate of Mark Rothko, the artist. He left the bulk of his estate to a foundation; a challenge was brought under the mortmain statute. A "skilled draftsman," the court pointed out, can prevent such a challenge if the testator slips in a provision leaving any "failed gift to charity to some unrelated person." Rothko's will, however, never had the benefit of such a "skilled draftsman."

See also *Shriners Hospital for Crippled Children v. Zrillic*, 563 So. 2d 64 (Fla., 1990), where the court remarked that "artful will drafting easily defeats the effect of the statute: If the testator names anybody other than a spouse or lineal descendent to take the charitable devise in the event the charitable devise fails, nobody would have standing to petition to avoid the charitable devise."

64. *In re Estate of Bertha W. Fitzgerald*, 339 N. Y. Supp. 2d 333 (Surr. Ct. N. Y. County, 1972). The estate was worth more than $2 million. The testatrix explained that she made no provision for her son (who had been adjudged incompetent and was in an institution) because he had money from a grandparent.

65. *In re Estate of Shameia*, 257 So. 2d 77 (Fla. App., 1972), Saba George Shameia, in his will, made certain charitable bequests; he left the residuary estate to relatives in the Middle East. His "natural daughter," Lillie, objected. Lillie, the court held, had no standing. If the charitable bequests lapsed, they would fall into the residue, and thus in no event could Lillie inherit.

66. *Mahoney v. Grainger*, 283 Mass.189, 186 N. E. 86 (1933).

67. *Hunt v. Hunt*, 3 Bro. C. C. 312, 29 Eng. Rep. 554 (1791). See also *Asten v. Asten* [1894] 3 Ch. 260; Robert Asten built four new houses on a certain street. He had four sons and clearly intended to give a house to each one of them. But he left the addresses blank in the will, so that,

as far as the will was concerned, it was impossible to tell which house he left to which son. The court refused to admit "extrinsic" evidence and declared the bequests "void for uncertainty."

68. Anybody, that is, except the trial judge, who awarded the estate to UCLA and felt there was no ambiguity at all. Maybe he was a loyal alumnus. The appeals court actually called the ambiguity "latent." The argument here was that "University of Southern California" could refer to *location*, not the name of a school, in which case it simply told us where UCLA was located. Hence there was no "patent" ambiguity at all. Only when you discovered there *was* a University of Southern California did the problem appear. The case was sent back to the trial court to sort things out. *Estate of Cora Black v. University of Southern California*, 211 Cal. App. 2d 75, 27 Cal. Rptr. 418 (1962).

69. *Succession of Bacot*, 502 So. 2d 1118 (La., 1987).

70. *Estate of Russell* 69 Cal. 2d 200, 444 P. 2d 353 (1968).

71. Actually, what the court decided is this: it was correct to admit evidence to show the ambiguity—that is, that Roxy Russell was a dog. But there was no way you could twist the words of the will itself. They seemed plainly to suggest that she wanted the dog to take half her estate.

72. *Hultquist v. Ring*, 301 S. W. 2d 303 (Ct. of Civil Appeals, Texas, 1957).

73. *Patch v. White*, 117 U.S. 210 (1886).

74. The Wisconsin case is *In re Gibbs' Estate*, 14 Wis. 2d 490, 111 N.W. 2d 413 (1961). In another case, *Moseley v. Goodman*, 195 S. W. 590 (Tenn., 1917), E. J. Halley left $20,000 to "Mrs. Moseley." Halley was a merchant who sold, among other things, cigars, which he bought from a man named Trimble, who in turn worked for a Mr. Moseley. Halley was quite fond of Trimble's wife, whom he habitually called "Mrs. Moseley," perhaps because of the business connection between Trimble and Moseley. There *was* a Mrs. Moseley; but Halley did not know her. The court was willing to find a kind of latent ambiguity and affirmed a judgment giving the money to Mrs. Trimble.

75. *In re Estate of Pavlinko*, 394 Pa. 564, 148 A. 2d 564 (1959).

76. *Matter of Snide*, 52 N. Y. 2d 193, 418 N. E. 2d 656 (1981).

77. *Estate of Herceg*, 193 Misc. 2d 201, 747 N. Y. S. 2d 901 (2002).

78. *Knupp v. District of Columbia*, 578 A. 2d 702 (D. C. Ct of App. 1990).

79. John H. Langbein, "Substantial Compliance with the Wills Act," *Harvard Law Review* 88: 489 (1975). See also James Lindgren, "The Fall of Formalism," *Albany Law Review* 55: 1009 (1992); Bruce H. Mann, "Formalities and Formalism in the Uniform Probate Code," *University of Pennsylvania Law Review* 142: 1033 (1994).

80. *Will of Russell G. Ranney*, 124 N. J. 1, 589 A. 2d 1339 (1991).

81. Administration of Justice Act, 1982, ch. 53, Part IV. The statute also allows "extrinsic evidence" if any part of a will is "meaningless," or "ambiguous on the face of it," or "ambiguous in the light of surrounding circumstances."

82. See R. Kerridge and A. H. R. Brierley, "Mistakes in Wills: Rectify and Be Damned," *Cambridge Law Journal* 62: 750 (2003).

83. Queensland Succession Act 1981, Division 4, Subdivision 1, §18, applying to a docu-

ment that "purports to state the testamentary intentions of a deceased person," even though it does not comply with the usual requirements. The act also allows a court to "rectify a will to carry out the intentions of the testator" because of a "clerical error" or because the will does not comply with the "testator's instructions." Ibid., §33.

84. For a discussion, see Emily Sherwin, "Clear and Convincing Evidence of Testamentary Intent: The Search for a Compromise between Formality and Adjudicative Justice," *Connecticut Law Review* 34: 453 (2002).

CHAPTER 4: BREAKING A WILL

1. Edward H. Ward and J. H. Beuscher, "The Inheritance Process in Wisconsin," 1950 *Wisconsin Law Review* at 415–16.

2. Jeffrey A. Schoenblum, "Will Contests—an Empirical Study," *Real Estate, Probate and Trust Journal* 22: 607 (1987).

3. Lawrence M. Friedman, Christopher J. Walker, and Ben Hernandez-Stern, "The Inheritance Process in San Bernardino County, California, 1964: A Research Note," *Houston Law Review* 43: at 1467 (2007); see also Jeffrey P. Rosenfeld, "Will Contests: Legacies of Aging and Social Change," in Robert Miller and Stephen McNamee, eds., *Inheritance and Wealth in America* (1998), pp. 173, 184–85.

4. Some courts, and many who write about these issues, do not seem to like no-contest clauses very much. Under §3-905 of the Uniform Probate Code, a no-contest clause is "unenforceable" if the contestant had "probable cause" to challenge the will, even if the contestant loses. But this is not the rule in California, for example; under §21303 of the California Probate Code, the clause is "enforceable." On the other hand, in "determining the intent of the transferor, a no contest clause" is to be "strictly construed" and is not to be enforced if the contestant claims, "with reasonable cause," that the will was forged; or if the contestant contests a provision that benefits the drafter of the will or a witness. California Probate Code §§21304, 21306, 21307.

5. Probate Record No. 33513, San Bernardino County, Calif. (1964); see Friedman, Walker, and Hernandez-Stern, "The Inheritance Process in San Bernardino County, pp. 1467–68. Mrs. Moster was an heir-at-law. Theoretically, she did have standing: she could have challenged all of Mrs. Straisinger's wills; but her chances of overturning a string of wills must have been close to zero. Ironically, there was a contest in this case: the charity, which lost out in the later will, contested, but lost.

6. Schoenblum, "Will Contests—An Empirical Study," pp. 615–16.

7. *Estate of Ernest J. Torregano*, 54 Cal. 2d 234, 352 P. 2d 505 (1960).

8. Rosenfeld, "Will Contests," pp. 177–83, is the source of the information on motives for will contests.

9. See David Margolick, *Undue Influence: The Epic Battle for the Johnson & Johnson Fortune* (1993).

10. Other grounds for will contests also reflect what has been happening to the family

and to family structure. In some cases, elderly people, no longer cared for by their families, disinherit their children or other relatives and leave money to caregivers, or to neighbors or friends; this is a situation that might well provoke a will contest.

11. Martin L. Friedland, *The Death of Old Man Rice: A True Story of Criminal Justice in America* (1994). Friedland takes the position that Patrick was not guilty of murder, and he doubts the chloroform story; but he does think that Patrick forged the will.

12. See "What It Disposed Of: The Alleged Forged Will of Mrs. Dunton in Court," *Chicago Tribune*, April 23, 1892, p. 3.

13. On this celebrated case, see Suzanne Finstad, *Heir Not Apparent* (1984).

14. A second will surfaced in 1976; but mistakes in the text made it clear from the outset that this will was a fake. Al Delugach, "Second Hughes 'Will' Surfaces but Flaw Is Noted," *Los Angeles Times*, May 12, 1976.

15. Las Vegas: "'Will' in Hughes Case Is a Fake, Jury Declares," *Los Angeles Times*, June 9, 1978; Los Angeles: "'Dummar Will' Ruled a Fake," *Los Angeles Times*, December 5, 1978. There were many people who found the story of Melvin Dummar and Howard Hughes exciting and romantic—a kind of male Cinderella story—and who believe he was telling the truth. See Gary Magnesen, *The Investigation* (2005). A 1980 movie, "Melvin and Howard," directed by Jonathan Demme, dealt mostly with Melvin Dummar's life, and Hughes appears in it only briefly.

16. This information is from an article by Mike Cowling, headed "Dixieland Bash for Mlle. Liberte," *Los Angeles Times*, June 24, 1986, Part 1, p. 1.

17. James R. Phelan and Lewis Chester, *The Money: The Battle for Howard Hughes's Billions* (1997), p. 189.

18. William Herbert Page, *The Law of Wills*, 2nd ed. (1926), p. 313.

19. *Orth v. Orth*, 145 Ind. 184, 42 N. E. 277 (1895). The more substantial claim was that the letter, in conjunction with the will, created a kind of trust for the benefit of all three children, including William. But the court refused to so hold.

20. Page, *The Law of Wills*, p. 310.

21. *Hildreth v. Marshall*, 51 N. J. Eq. 241, 27 Atl. 465 (1893).

22. Schoenblum, "Will Contests—An Empirical Study," p. 648. Fraud was alleged in six cases, duress or coercion in two, forgery in two.

23. Georgia Code §53-4-10.

24. *Barnes v. Marshall*, 467 S. W. 2d 70 (Missouri, 1971).

25. "Duryea Family Fight in Court," *Chicago Tribune*, November 11, 1900, p. 5. Two witnesses testified that they had never seen him sober, and that he drank as much as forty drinks of whiskey a day. It was also claimed that Walter Duryea, the testator's son and principal beneficiary, had "exerted an undue influence over his father" and "encouraged his father in his drinking habits and was his companion in his carousals." "Duryea's Will in Court," *New York Times*, November 18, 1900, p. 5.

26. "Delusions Cited in Pratt Will Case," *New York Times*, June 6, 1934, p. 43; "Nurse

Says Pratt Feared His Wife," June 20, 1934, p. 14. The Surrogate admitted the will to probate, *New York Times*, June 23, 1934, p. 15. He felt she was "of sound mind. . . . The alleged acts of eccentricity recited by witnesses may be built up in any man's or woman's life." See also "Fight on Pratt Will Reviewed by Court," *New York Times*, October 10, 1935, p. 10 (the case in the Appellate Division).

27. Rajeev Syal, Francis Elliott, and Dominic Kennedy, "Son's Fight for £10m Bequest His Deluded Father Left to the Tories," *Times* (London), July 18, 2007, p. 3.

28. Thomas J. Reed, "Breaking a Will in Indiana," *Indiana Law Review* 14: 865, 879 (1981).

29. *Estate of Killen*, 188 Ariz. 562, 937 P. 2d 1368 (1996).

30. *In re Hongiman's Will*, 8 N. Y. 2d 244, 168 N. E. 2d 676 (1960).

31. *Addington v. Wilson*, 5 Ind. 153 (1854).

32. *Bonard's Will*, 16 Abb. Pr. N. S. (N. Y.) 128 (1872); *New York Times*, November 9, 1872, p. 2.

33. See Susanna L. Blumenthal, "The Deviance of the Will: Policing the Bounds of Testamentary Freedom in Nineteenth-Century America," *Harvard Law Review* 119: 959 (2006).

34. *Anderson v. Anderson*, 210 Ga. 464, 80 S. E. 2d 807 (1954).

35. *Wilson v. Mitchell*, 101 Pa. 495 (1882).

36. *Will of Shanks*, 172 Wis. 621, 179 N. W. 747 (1920).

37. *In re Newhall's Estate*, 190 Cal. 709, 214 Pac. 231 (1923).

38. George E. Gardner, *Handbook of the Law of Wills* (1903), p. 182.

39. Margolick, *Undue Influence*, tells the tale.

40. *Estate of Hamm*, 262 N. W. 2d 201 (So. Dak., 1978).

41. When Green E. Roberts, a "well-known citizen of Atlanta," died, his three children attacked his will, claiming that "their mother exerted undue influence over him" in making the will. "Roberts Will to Be Fought," *Atlanta Constitution*, February 2, 1904, p. 6.

42. Reed, "Breaking a Will in Indiana," pp. 892–97.

43. "Two Contested Wills: Clergymen Charged with Unduly Influencing Testators," *New York Times*, July 7, 1890, p. 5. This article also mentions a contest over the will of the ex-mayor of New Brunswick, Garret Conover. Conover's sons claimed the Rev. John Handley, pastor of St. James's Church, was guilty of using undue influence to induce Mr. Conover to neglect his sons; the pastor, however, said it was Mr. Conover himself who complained about the disgraceful conduct of his sons and their "fast living," and said "he did not wish them to get control of the property," which was left in trust.

44. See *Estate of Evelyn Maheras*, 897 Pac. 2d 268 (Okla., 1995). The testatrix, who was very old and an alcoholic, left most of her money to a Baptist church. It was set aside as the product of undue influence.

45. *Olsen v. Corporation of New Melleray*, 245 Iowa 407, 60 N. W. 2d 832 (1953).

46. The cases are: *Farr v. Thompson*, 25 S. C. L. (Chev.) 37 (1839); *Thompson v. Farr*, 28 S. C. L. (1 Speers) 93 (1842); *O'Neall v. Farr*, 30 S. C. L. (1 Rich.) 80 (1844).

47. *Farr* v. *Thompson*, 25 S. C. L. (Chev.) 37 (1839).
48. *Lamborn* v. *Kirkpatrick*, 97 Colo. 432, 50 P. 2d 542 (1935).
49. 247 N. Y. Supp. 2d 664 (Sup. Ct., N.Y., App. Div., 1964); affirmed, 15 N. Y. 2d 825, 205 N. E. 2d 864 (1965). The opinions never *say* that the two men were lovers; but there are hints that point in that direction, though not unambiguously.
50. *Evans* v. *May*, 923 S. W. 2d 712 (Tex. App., 1996).
51. This was Georgia Code §53-2-9(b); the present statute is Georgia Code §53-4-1.
52. *In re Estate of Strittmater*, 140 N. J. Eq. 94, 53 A. 2d 205 (1947).
53. *In re Wright's Estate*, 7 Cal. 2d 348, 60 P. 2d 434 (1936).

CHAPTER 5: WILL SUBSTITUTES

1. Edward H. Ward and J. H. Beuscher, "The Inheritance Process in Wisconsin," 1950 *Wisconsin Law Review* 393: 396, 411.
2. Lawrence M. Friedman, Christopher J. Walker, and Ben Hernandez-Stern, "The Inheritance Process in San Bernardino County, California, 1964: A Research Note," *Houston Law Review* 43: 1453 (2007).
3. See Carole Shammas, Marylynn Salmon, and Michel Dahlin, *Inheritance in America: From Colonial Times to the Present* (1987), p. 16.
4. Hendrik Hartog, "Someday All This Will Be Yours: Inheritance, Adoption, and Obligation in Capitalist America," *Indiana Law Journal* 79: 345, 352 (2004).
5. Augustus Peabody Loring, *A Trustee's Handbook*, 2d ed. (1900), p. 22: "The trustee's estate consists in the ownership of the property itself; and the beneficiary's in his right in a court of equity to compel the trustee to carry out the provisions of the trust, but not in any estate in the property itself."
6. See, for example, California Probate Code §825: "Except as otherwise expressly provided in this code, there is no right to a jury trial in proceedings under this code." (The California Probate Code covers both wills and trusts.) Some states, however, provide for a jury trial in will contests.
7. The trust, however, will be irrevocable, unless the settlor expressly says otherwise.
8. See, for example, *Nutt* v. *Morse*, 142 Mass. 1, 6 N. E. 763 (1886); *McEvoy* v. *Boston Five Cents Savings Bank*, 201 Mass. 50, 87 N. E. 465 (1909).
9. Norman F. Dacey, *How to Avoid Probate*, 5th ed. (1993), Prologue, p. 1.
10. Ibid., p. 23.
11. Kaja Whitehouse, *What Your Lawyer May Not Tell You about Your Family's Will* (2006), p. 77. She adds: "Indeed, the cost of setting up a living trust can be higher than that to write a will and settle the estate, especially for people with small estates."
12. Another possible advantage—at least a *claimed* advantage—is that you cannot contest a living trust; to be sure, a "disgruntled heir" could try to "break" the trust, but "the legal fees would be high and chances of success very slim." Alexander A. Bove, Jr., "Breaking a Will," *Worth* 2 no. 8: 96, 98 (1993). This is probably true, especially since the living trust is

more likely to be executed when the testator is younger and healthier than when she executes her last will. Still, we have to remember that the risk of a will contest is always very small, and if the provisions of a trust and will are "natural" (that is, the money is left to the closest relatives), the risk is *very* small.

13. Whitehouse adds two other advantages: if you "want to keep the value of your assets private," this might be the way to go. Probate documents are public, and anybody who wants to can find out what you owned and who your heirs are. Also, if you own property in several states, probate can get messy and expensive, since your estate might have to be probated in each state where you owned land, a house, or a farm. Whitehouse, *Your Family's Will*, pp. 76–77. Neither of these is a factor for most people. The privacy factor might be important, though, for celebrities and others in the public eye.

14. John Price, "The Transmission of Wealth at Death in a Community Property Jurisdiction," *Washington Law Review* 50: 338–39, n. 179 (1975).

15. *Matter of Totten*, 179 N. Y. 112, 71 N. E. 748 (1904).

16. See, for example, Florida, in *Seymour v. Seymour*, 85 So. 2d 725 (Fla. 1956).

17. *Truax v. Southwestern College*, 214 Kan. 853, 522 P. 2d 412 (1974).

18. The statutes are KSA §9-1215 (banks); KSA §17-2263 (credit unions); and KSA §17-5828 (savings and loan associations).

19. *Estate of Nona E. Morton*, 241 Kan. 698, 769 P. 2d 616 (1987).

20. *Farkas v. Williams*, 5 Ill. 2d. 417, 125 N. E. 2d 600 (1955).

21. For federal estate tax purposes, a transfer at death *might* be taxable, if certain conditions are met. If the joint tenants are husband and wife, of course, the issue is moot—transfers to a surviving spouse are not subject to estate tax.

CHAPTER 6: DYNASTIC AND CARETAKER TRUSTS

1. Carol A. Engler-Bowles and Cary S. Kart studied a small sample of wills in rural Woods County, Ohio, for the period between 1820 and 1967. Up to 1910, they found twenty-three wills that left a life estate to a widow, and only one that left a fee simple. In the twentieth century, most testators left property to a spouse outright. "Intergenerational Relations and Testamentary Patterns: An Exploration," *The Gerontologist* 23: 167, 169 (1983).

2. Joan R. Gundersen, "Women and Inheritance in America: Virginia and New York as a Case Study, 1700–1860," in Robert K. Miller, Jr., and Stephen J. McNamee, eds., *Inheritance and Wealth in America* (1998), pp. 91, 101; James W. Deen, "Patterns of Testation in Four Tidewater Counties in Colonial Virginia," *American Journal of Legal History* 16: 154 (1972).

3. Carole Shammas, Marylynn Salmon, and Michel Dahlin, *Inheritance in America: From Colonial Times to the Present* (1987), p. 112.

4. Lawrence M. Friedman, "Patterns of Testation in the 19th Century: A Study of Essex County (New Jersey) Wills," *American Journal of Legal History* 8: 43 (1964).

5. Probate Record No. 2630, Salt Lake County, Utah (1897). The "widow" in question was the third wife of a polygamous testator. I am indebted for this reference to a term paper

by Clark Asay, Stanford Law School 2007, examining the 1897 probate records of Salt Lake City, Utah.

6. Friedman, "Patterns of Testation in the Nineteenth Century," at 43.

7. On San Bernardino, see Lawrence M. Friedman, Christopher J. Walker, and Ben Hernandez-Stern, "The Inheritance Process in San Bernardino County, California, 1964: A Research Note," *Houston Law Review* 43: 1445 (2007). On Cuyahoga County, see Marvin B. Sussman, Judith N. Cates, and David T. Smith, *The Family and Inheritance* (1970), pp. 92–93. See also *Hill's Estate*, 432 Pa. 269, 247 A. 2d 606 (1968): Edward Hill left his estate in trust for the benefit of his wife "as long as she has no other means of support or remains unmarried." (In the actual case, the wife died before the testator.)

8. The marital deduction is spelled out in Internal Revenue Code §2056.

9. Suppose, for example, a massive gift of millions of dollars is made, on which the giver pays a gift tax of $5 million. This has to be paid immediately, so this particular $5 million will not be part of the estate at death, and will not be subject to estate tax.

10. See Lawrence M. Friedman, "The Dynastic Trust," *Yale Law Journal* 73: 547 (1964); a rather different interpretation of the history of the dynastic trust is offered by Gregory S. Alexander in "The Dead Hand and the Law of Trusts in the Nineteenth Century," *Stanford Law Review* 37: 1189 (1985).

11. *Harvard College v. Amory*, 26 Mass. (9 Pick.) 446 (1830).

12. A leading case was *King v. Talbot*, 40 N. Y. 76 (1869). Charles W. King left money to his three minor children; the executors of his will (in effect, trustees) invested in canal, railroad, and bank stocks. They were held liable for losses.

13. This was also the rule in England.

14. For example, Illinois Revised Statutes, ch. 148, §32 (1957); see also Minnesota Statutes Annotated §501.125 (1946).

15. 133 Mass. 170 (1882). Adams, the defendant, was the beneficiary of a trust set up by his brother. The income payments were to be made "to him personally . . . free from the interference or control of his creditors."

16. There are other exceptions in California, including "restitution judgments," defined as judgments "awarding restitution for the commission of a felony." California Probate Code §§15305, 15305.5. See the odd case of *Young v. McCoy*, 147 Cal. App. 4th 1078, 54 Cal. Rptr. 3d 847 (2007), discussed below, n. 20.

17. See, for example, Michigan Compiled Laws, §501.14; Oklahoma Statutes Annotated, title 60, §140.

18. John Chipman Gray, *Restraints on the Alienation of Property*, 2d ed. (1895), Preface, p. ix.

19. The general rule, however, was that a person cannot set up a spendthrift trust for himself—that is, a person cannot transfer property to a trust that would pay him the income, and also provide that no creditor could reach that income. See, for example, *Bank of Dallas v. Republic National Bank of Dallas*, 540 S. W. 2d 499 (Ct. of Civil Appeals, Texas, 1976). But as we will see, some states have now done away with this limitation as well.

20. *Young v. McCoy*, 147 Cal. App. 4th 1078, 54 Cal. Rptr. 3d 847 (2007).

21. Lucile died in 2005. The facts suggest strongly that she preferred her black sheep son, Steven, over his victim, her only other son. She set up a trust for Steven but not for Richard; indeed, she specified that Richard was not to be allowed into her home after she died; and she left him $5,000, but only on condition that he release her, Steven, and the trust from all claims. Naturally, he refused. The trust, incidentally, also had a spendthrift clause.

22. *Claflin v. Claflin*, 149 Mass. 19, 20 N. E. 454 (1889).

23. *Estate of Brown*, 148 Vt. 94, 528 A. 2d 752 (1987).

24. This point is underscored by an apparent exception to the Claflin doctrine: if the settlor is still alive, he can terminate the trust if all the beneficiaries consent. Claflin applies most rigorously if the settlor is dead.

25. For a review of cases up to the 1980's, see Gail Boreman Bird, "Trust Termination: Unborn, Living, and Dead Hands—Too Many Fingers in the Trust Pie," *Hastings Law Journal* 36: 563 (1985).

26. Revised Statutes of Missouri §456.590 (2007).

27. In California, a court can "modify or terminate" a trust if it believes there is a good reason to do so and that this reason "outweighs the interest in accomplishing a material purpose of the trust." But this power is not terribly important, since it does not apply to spendthrift trusts. California Probate Code §15403.

28. Kansas Statutes Annotated §58a-415 (2006).

29. This is Uniform Trust Code §415; see *In the Matter of the John P. Harris Testamentary Trust*, 275 Kan. 946, 69 P. 3d 1109 (2003).

30. See *Estate of Bonardi*, 376 N. J. Super 508, 871 A. 2d 103 (2005). Bonardi set up a trust. The trustee was to pay his wife, Donna, all the net income as long as she lived, and also the principal, at the trustee's discretion. When she died, the trust would be distributed to their two daughters. Bonardi added that his "expectation" was that the trust should *not* be Donna's main source of income; she should, in the main, support herself. He wanted the corpus to go, if possible, to the daughters. The two daughters and Donna agreed to terminate the trust and distribute the money to Donna. The trustee refused. The court sided with the trustee, and refused to terminate the trust.

31. See *Estate of Somers*, 277 Kan. 761, 89 P. 3d 898 (2004).

32. See, for example, *Estate of Brown*, n. 23 above.

33. "An Act to Amend the Trustee Act," Statutes of Manitoba 1982–84, ch. 38 (August 18, 1983).

34. 15 & 16 Geo. 5, c. 19, §33; see Gary Watt, *Trusts and Equity* (2003), pp. 211–13.

35. There is a big literature on this point. See, for example Michael T. Johnson, "Speculating on the Efficacy of 'Speculation': An Analysis of the Prudent Person's Slipperiest Term of Art in Light of Modern Portfolio Theory," *Stanford Law Review* 48: 419 (1996); Paul G. Haskell, "The Prudent Person Rule for Trustee Investment and Modern Portfolio Theory," *North Carolina Law Review* 69: 87 (1990). Haskell says, for example, that the "prudent

person rule may make it illegal for a trustee to invest in a market fund because some of the components may be speculative. This is unsound . . . " Ibid., p. 111.

36. Haskell, in "The Prudent Person Rule," p. 87, does recognize that portfolio theory is not for everybody: "The . . . traditional prudent person rule needs some retuning, but . . . for family trusts it remains essentially a sound rule." And he concludes that the "trustee of the family trust should not be permitted to use portfolio theory to justify selective diversification involving volatile stocks." Ibid., p. 111.

37. See, for example, California Probate Code §16047 (b) (2007); and Alabama Code, §19-3B(b)-1002 (2007), using the exact language of the Uniform Act.

38. Survey results are found in Martin D. Begleiter, "Does the Prudent Investor Need the Uniform Prudent Investor Act?—An Empirical Study of Trust Investment Practices," *Maine Law Review* 51: 27, 72–85 (1999).

CHAPTER 7: CONTROL BY THE DEAD

1. This is the plan followed in the Uniform Statutory Rule against Perpetuities, which was drafted in the late 1980's and adopted by a substantial number of states.

2. Quoted in the classic article by W. Barton Leach, "Perpetuities in a Nutshell," *Harvard Law Review* 51: 638, 639 (1938). Almost fifty years later, Jesse Dukeminier summed up the state of the law in "A Modern Guide to Perpetuities," *California Law Review* 74: 1867 (1986).

3. Leach, "Perpetuities in a Nutshell," p. 643. The leading case was *Jee* v. *Audley*, 29 Eng. Rep. 1186 (Ch., 1787). The rule, as Jesse Dukeminier put it in 1986, has "been the subject of many gibes as well as more affectionate raillery. Nonetheless, it continues to be followed in perpetuities cases." Dukeminier, "A Modern Guide to Perpetuities," p. 1877.

4. Leach, "Perpetuities in a Nutshell," p. 644.

5. In all these cases, it is extremely easy to avoid the rule, just by sensible draftsmanship. In the case of the 90-year-old sister, you could simply name the children, or specify that you are referring only to existing children; similarly, you can exclude unborn widows by naming your son's wife: "upon the death of Roderick, the income to be paid for life to his widow, Tiffany." In practically every state today, even this would not be necessary, because the rule against perpetuities, where it still exists, has been thoroughly tamed. One way or another, these excrescences have been removed.

6. Mr. Bumble, of course, was not referring to the rule against perpetuities, but the rule that assumed that, if a wife committed a crime, it must have been at the instigation of her husband.

7. See, on this point about the evolution of (more or less) quantitative rules by courts, Lawrence M. Friedman, "Legal Rules and the Process of Social Change," *Stanford Law Review* 19: 786 (1967).

8. A bad lawyer, on the other hand, might be completely confused by the rule against perpetuities. In one notorious case, *Lucas* v. *Hamm*, 56 Cal. 2d 583, 364 P. 2d 685 (1961), defendant Hamm, a lawyer, prepared a will for one Eugene H. Emmick. The plaintiffs

were beneficiaries under the will; but they lost out because the will violated the rule against perpetuities. Was Hamm liable to them for this mistake? No, said the court. This is an area of law full of "traps for the unwary draftsman," thus it would not be "proper to hold that defendant failed to use such skill, prudence, and diligence as lawyers of ordinary skill and capacity commonly exercise."

9. John Chipman Gray, *The Rule against Perpetuities* (1886), Preface, p. v.

10. It is possible to leave, say, a house to your son for life, then to his eldest son for life, and then to the grandchildren. But these chains of "legal life estates," which do not put the house in trust, are rare to the point of extinction.

11. For example, Michigan Compiled Laws §554.72; §554.74 (the fourth section of the Uniform Rule) gives courts a limited power to reform instruments that might violate the rule.

12. Smith-Hurd Illinois Compiled Statutes, 765/305/4 (3).

13. This is true not only in the United States. The province of Alberta, Canada, Revised Statutes of Alberta, 2000, ch. P-5, enacted a law under which every "contingent interest . . . capable of vesting within or beyond the perpetuity period is presumptively valid until actual events" show whether it will or will not vest "within the perpetuity period." The statute also sets up a presumption that "a female" will not be "able to have a child . . . over the age of 55 years."

14. Perpetuities and Accumulations Act 1964 (UK Statutes 1964, ch. 55, as amended).

15. Lewis M. Simes and Allan F. Smith, *The Law of Future Interests*, Vol. 3, by John A. Borron Jr. (2004), §1288, p. 294.

16. Delaware Code Annotated, Title 25, §503 (a), (b). For a discussion, see Richard W. Nenno, *Delaware Dynasty Trusts, Total Return Trusts, and Asset Protection Trusts* (2004).

17. See Angel M. Vallario, "Death by a Thousand Cuts: The Rule against Perpetuities," *Journal of Legislation* 25: 141 (1999). See also Jesse Dukeminier and James E. Krier, "The Rise of the Perpetual Trust," *UCLA Law Review* 50: 1303 (2003).

18. Rhode Island Statutes §34-11038.

19. Washington Revised Code §11.98.130.

20. Wyoming Statutes Annotated 2007, §34-1-139 (b). Nevada, a state not usually known for modesty in legislation, also found the ordinary rule too restrictive and passed the Uniform Act, with trusts allowed to last 365 years. But Nevada has a constitutional provision, of a rather common type, which states, "No perpetuities shall be allowable except for eleemosynary purposes." Attempts to get rid of this provision in 2002 ended in failure. Thus the status of the law in Nevada is not at all clear. Lewis M. Simes and Allan F. Smith, *The Law of Future Interests*, Vol. 3, by John A. Borron Jr. (2004), pp. 448–50.

21. New Hampshire Revised Statutes §564:24.

22. Why not? Because the estate tax is a tax on *estates*, on the value at death of what a person owns. But my daughter, under the trust, had a life interest only. When she died, the value of her interest was zero; there was nothing about the trust, then, that made her estate liable to tax.

23. The Wyoming statute, already mentioned, which lets trusts last a thousand years, adds the proviso that this great boon applies only if the trust "is governed by the laws of this state and the trustee maintains a place of business, administers the trust in this state or is a resident of this state." Wyoming Statutes Annotated 2007, §34k-1-139 (b) (iii).

24. The firm is Oshins & Associates, LLC. Estate-planning firms have placed newspaper ads in the *New York Times* offering dynasty trusts. And see also Carole Gould, "Shifting Rules Add Luster to Trusts," *New York Times*, October 29, 2000, p. B11. This article, incidentally, is full of legal inaccuracies.

25. Robert H. Sitkoff and Max M. Schanzenbach, "Jurisdictional Competition for Trust Funds: An Empirical Analysis of Perpetuities and Taxes," *Yale Law Journal* 115: 356 (2005).

26. Adam J. Hirsch, "Fear Not the Asset Protection Trust," *Cardozo Law Review* 27: 2685, 2687 (2006).

27. Ibid. For a discussion, see Nenno, *Delaware Dynasty Trusts*, pp. 75–137. There are some limits: if the transfer is, or can be labeled, fraudulent, creditors may still be able to reach the assets.

28. Rachel Emma Silverman, "States Court Family-Trust Business," *Wall Street Journal*, June 22, 2006, p. D1.

29. Joel C. Dobris, "The Death of the Rule against Perpetuities, or the RAP Has No Friends—an Essay," *Real Property Probate & Trust Journal* 35: 601, 614–15 (2000–2001).

30. On the celebrity culture and its impact, see Lawrence M. Friedman, *The Horizontal Society* (1999), pp. 27–43.

31. The extensive revisions of New York's property laws in 1828 were a glaring exception.

32. Friedman, "The Dynastic Trust," p. 565.

33. Even big trusts that still named individual trustees expected these trustees to hire professional managers to do the actual work—subject, of course, to the supervision of the individual trustees.

34. The Perpetuities and Accumulations Act, Statutes of Manitoba, 1982–84, ch. 43, p. 551 (August 18, 1953). The statute also got rid of the "Accumulations Act . . . so far as it is part of the law of Manitoba" (§2).

35. Ruth Deech, "The Rule against Perpetuities Abolished," 4 *Oxford Journal of Legal Studies* no. 3, p. 454(1984).

36. Dukeminier and Krier, "The Rise of the Perpetual Trust," p. 1316.

37. See, on this point, Dukeminier and Krier, "The Rise of the Perpetual Trust," discussing ways in which courts, or the documents themselves, can make these trusts more flexible.

38. *Thelluson* v. *Woodford*, 11 Ves. Jun. 111, 32 E. R. 1030 (1805).

39. 40 Geo. III, ch. 98 (1800). It may seem odd that the statute is five years earlier than the case; but it must be recalled that Thellusson died in 1797, and the lawsuit concerning his estate was not finally decided until eight years later.

40. See Karen J. Sneddon, "The Sleeper Has Awakened: The Rule against Accumula-

tions and Perpetual Trusts," *Tulane Law Review* 76: 189 (2001); Robert H. Sitkoff, "The Lurking Rule against Accumulations of Income," *Northwestern University Law Review* 100: 501 (2006).

41. See Delaware Statutes 25 §506: "No provisions directing or authorizing accumulations of trust income shall be invalid."

42. The basic provision on the income taxation of trusts is IRC §641 and the following sections.

43. Sitkoff, "The Lurking Rule against Accumulations of Income," p. 514.

44. *James Estate,* 414 Pa. 80, 199 A. 2d 275 (1964).

45. *Trusts of Holdeen* 486 Pa. 1, 403 A. 2d. 978 (1979).

46. The case is *Marsh* v. *Frost National Bank,* 129 S. W. 3d 174 (Tex. App., 2004); the Texas Supreme Court denied a petition for review.

47. *Mercantile Trust Company National Association* v. *Shriners' Hospital for Crippled Children,* 551 S. W. 2d 864 (Ct. App. Mo., 1977).

48. On the requirement of payout, see 83 Stat. 487 (act of December 30, 1969).

CHAPTER 8: CHARITABLE GIFTS AND FOUNDATIONS

1. For an overview, see Joel L. Fleishman, *The Foundation: A Great American Secret* (2007).

2. PNN Online: The Nonprofit News and Information Resource, http://www.pnnonline.org/article.php?sid=6645&mode=thread&order=0, visited November 2, 2007.

3. Steuart Henderson Britt, "The Significance of the Last Will and Testament," *Journal of Social Psychology* 8: 347 (1937).

4. T. P. Schwartz, "Testamentary Behavior: Issues and Evidence about Individuality, Altruism and Social Influence," *Sociological Quarterly* 34: 337, 345 (1993).

5. Olin L. Browder, Jr., "Recent Patterns of Testate Succession in the United States and England," *Michigan Law Review* 67: 1303, 1314 (1969).

6. Lawrence M. Friedman, "Patterns of Testation in the 19th Century: A Study of Essex County (New Jersey) Wills," *American Journal of Legal History* 8: 47 (1964).

7. John R. Price, "The Transmission of Wealth at Death in a Community Property Jurisdiction," *Washington Law Review* 50: 317 (1975).

8. This information is from an unpublished term paper by Hiro Aragaki, "Testamentary Behavior in Alameda County: Evidence from the Late Nineteenth and Early Twentieth Centuries" (1996), on file with the author of this book.

9. Lawrence M. Friedman, Christopher J. Walker, and Ben Hernandez-Stern, "The Inheritance Process in San Bernardino County, California, 1964: A Research Note," *Houston Law Review* 43: 1449, 1461 (2007).

10. Dwight Macdonald, *The Ford Foundation: The Men and the Millions* (1956), p. 3. The book is based on articles that earlier appeared in *The New Yorker.*

11. Information from the Foundation Center, http://www.fndcenter.org/findfunders/top100 assets.html, visited April 17, 2006.

12. Karen Richardson, "Warren Buffett Gives $30 Billion to Gates Foundation," *Wall Street Journal*, June 26, 2006, p. B1. See also Rachel Breitman and Del Jones, "Should Kids Be Left Fortunes, or Be Left Out?" *USA Today*, July 26, 2006, "Money," Section B.

13. Upheld in *Guaranty Trust Co. of New York v. The New York Community Trust*, 141 N. J. Eq. 238, 56 A. 2d 907 (1948).

14. The fellowships are so described on the website of the John D. and Catherine T. MacArthur Foundation.

15. Information from http://www.schalkenbach.org/, visited April 18, 2006.

16. *Detwiller v. Hartman*, 37 N. J. Eq. 347 (1883).

17. *In re Shaw, Public Trustee v. Day*, 1 All E. R. 745 (1957). The attorney general and the public trustee appealed, but the appeal was dismissed when the parties reached a settlement. Under the settlement, a certain amount of money was "to be devoted to the purposes which the testator had expressed in his will regarding a new alphabet," *In Re Shaw, Public Trustee v. Day*, 1 All E. R. 245 (1958); but, for better and for worse, the old alphabet is still with us.

18. The so-called cy pres doctrine, discussed later in this chapter, permits the modification of trusts that become illegal or impossible to carry out.

19. *Morsman v. Commissioner*, 90 Fed. 2d 18 (8th Cir., 1937) is often cited on this point. Occasionally, courts have voided trusts, because the language describing the beneficiary or beneficiaries seems too vague. In *Clark v. Campbell*, 82 N. H. 281, 133 A. 166 (1926), the deceased left property to trustees to distribute to "such of my friends as they, my trustees, shall select." The court felt that "friends" was too indefinite a category, and the trust failed. But see *Rowland's Estate*, 73 Ariz. 337, 241 P. 2d 781 (1952); here the gift was to Mr. and Mrs. Cuthbert "to distribute to any of my close friends," though they were also told to "give generously to Maria Discombe." The court held that the Cuthberts had a "power coupled with a trust in favor of Maria Discombe."

20. In *Estate of Searight*, for example, 95 N. E. 2d 779 (Ohio Ct. App. 1950), George Searight left his dog, Trixie, to Florence Hand, and set aside a fund of $1,000; the executor was to use the money "to pay Florence Hand at the rate of 75 cents per day for the keep and care of my dog as long as it shall live." Florence was willing, and the court allowed the gift.

A trust for animals might conceivably also run afoul of the classic rule against perpetuities; a dog or cat cannot be a measuring life. Of course, in fact, pets do not have long lifespans, with the exception of elephants and giant tortoises; but as we saw, the rule against perpetuities does not exactly track actual probabilities.

21. The case is *In re Roger Fouts*, 176 Misc. 2d 521, 677 N. Y. S. 2d 699 (1998). The statute is EPTL §7-8-1 (a): "A trust for the care of a designated domestic or pet animal is valid"; if the instrument does not name a trustee, the court can appoint one.

22. See Alan Feuer, "Helmsley, through Will, Is Still Calling the Shots," *New York Times*, August 30, 2007, p. B2; Manny Fernandez, "A Newly Minted Multimillionaire Can't Buy Herself a Friend," *New York Times*, September 3, 2007, p. B3. The will itself does not spell out the terms of the trust for the dog. I am indebted to Joanna Grossman for a copy of the will.

23. *Trustees of the Philadelphia Baptist Association* v. *Hart's Executors*, 17 U.S. (4 Wheat.) 1 (1819).

24. See 43 Eliz. I, ch. 4 (1601).

25. *Vidal* v. *Girard's Executors*, 43 U.S. (2 How.) 127 (1844).

26. Two blacks applied, in 1954, for admission to Girard College. In *Pennsylvania* v. *Board of Directors of City Trusts*, 353 U.S. 230 (1957), the Supreme Court held that the board which operated the college was "an agency of the State of Pennsylvania" and that the refusal to admit the blacks was a violation of the 14th Amendment. The Pennsylvania Supreme Court had upheld the right to exclude blacks, 386 Pa. 548, 127 A. 2d 287 (1956); but the U.S. Supreme Court reversed this decision.

27. *Vidal* v. *Girard's Executors*, p. 186.

28. See Stanley N. Katz, Barry Sullivan, and C. Paul Beach, "Legal Change and Legal Autonomy: Charitable Trusts in New York, 1777–1893," *Law and History Review* 3: 51 (1985). This is an excellent piece of work, although I disagree with the conclusion of the authors that the story of the charitable trust in New York is, up to a point, an example of legal "autonomy."

29. *Tilden* v. *Green*, 130 N. Y. 29, 28 N. E. 880 (1891).

30. James Barr Ames, "The Failure of the 'Tilden Trust,'" *Harvard Law Review* 5: 390 (1891–92). Ames was extremely critical of the New York decision, which (he argued) was unnecessary, in that there were adequate legal grounds for upholding the trust. On the other hand, James L. High, in "The Tilden Trust, and Why It Failed," *Atlantic Monthly* (October 1893), p. 481, argued that the will had been badly drafted, and the trust was "properly defeated by reason of the . . . uncertainty, and lack of precision" in the draftsmanship.

31. Ames, "The Failure of the 'Tilden Trust,'" p. 391.

32. Laws of New York 1893, ch. 701: "No . . . bequest or devise to . . . charitable . . . uses . . . shall or be deemed invalid by reason of the indefiniteness or uncertainty of the persons designed as the beneficiaries thereunder." If the bequest or devise names a trustee, "the legal title to the lands or property given . . . for such purposes shall vest in such trustee"; and if no trustee is named, then the title to the property "shall vest in the supreme court."

33. Quoted in *Crerar* v. *Williams*, 145 Ill. 625, 34 N. E. 467 (1893); see also High, "The Tilden Trust," p. 485, contrasting the Crerar and Tilden cases.

34. *Crerar* v. *Williams*, at 638.

35. Barry D. Karl and Stanley N. Katz, "Foundations and Ruling Class Elites," *Daedalus* 116: 1, 5 (1987).

36. Barry D. Karl and Stanley N. Katz, "The American Private Philanthropic Foundation and the Public Sphere, 1890–1930," *Minerva* 19: 236, 241 (1981).

37. Ibid., pp. 242–43.

38. Laws of New York 1913, ch. 488. In furtherance of this goal ("the well-being of mankind") the foundation was authorized to use "as means to that end, research, publication, the establishment and maintenance of charitable, benevolent, religious, missionary,

and public educational activities, agencies, and institutions . . . and any other means and agencies which . . . shall seem expedient to its members or trustees."

39. See Francis X. Sutton, "The Ford Foundation: The Early Years," *Daedalus* 116 (Winter): 41 (1987).

40. Ibid., p. 42.

41. Macdonald, *The Ford Foundation*, pp. 27–35. In 1953 the Cox Committee took a similar position.

42. B. Carroll Reece, "Tax-Exempt Subversion," *American Mercury* (July 1957), p. 56. The news about Moscow's "direct orders" came from one Maurice Malkin, who had been a member of the Communist Party until 1937, at which point he was expelled.

43. As was the New Deal itself. See Harry D. Gideonse, "A Congressional Committee's Investigation of the Foundations," *Journal of Higher Education* 25, no. 9: 457 (December 1954).

44. 83 Stat. 487 (act of December 30, 1969).

45. See, on this law, K. Martin Worthy, "The Tax Reform Act of 1969: Consequences for Private Foundations," *Law and Contemporary Problems* 39: 233 (1975).

46. Julius Rosenwald (as told to Elias Tobenkin), "The Burden of Wealth," *Saturday Evening Post*, January 5, 1929, p. 12.

47. "Goals Reached, Donor on Right Closes Up Shop," *New York Times*, May 29, 2005, p. 1.

48. *Estate of Craig*, 174 Ariz. 228, 848 P. 2d 313 (1992).

49. *In re Estate of Thompson*, 414 A. 2d 881 (Maine, 1980).

50. See, for example, *White v. Fisk*, 22 Conn. 31 (1852).

51. *Da Costa v. De Pas*, Amb. 228 (1754).

52. *Jackson v. Phillips*, 96 Mass. (14 Allen) 539 (1867).

53. The case turned on the validity of these provisions. Interestingly, in another clause of the will, Jackson left money to be spent to "secure the passage of laws granting women, whether married or unmarried, the right to vote; to hold office; to hold, manage, and devise property; and all other civil rights enjoyed by men."

54. Ibid., p. 596.

55. *Estate of Kidd*, 106 Ariz. 554, 479 P. 2d 697 (1971).

56. Note, "Society to Search for Evidence of Human Soul with Money Left by Prospector," *Trusts and Estates* 110: 1058 (1971).

57. See "McKee's Will Probated," *New York Times*, May 22, 1902, p. 3, referring to him as "the colored millionaire"; "Richest Colored Man Passes Away," *Philadelphia Inquirer*, April 8, 1902, p. 4.

58. Details of the will are found in *Estate of John McKee*, 378 Pa. 607, 108 A. 2d 214 (1954), which is discussed below; the whole will is available at a website, www.Mckeescholars.org, visited August 17, 2006.

59. According to one account, when McKee was "taken ill, he was nursed by two

Catholic sisters"; and though he continued to pay "pew rent" in his local Presbyterian church, he "evinced a preference for the Catholic faith." "Negro Millionaire's Kin to Fight for His Estate," *Philadelphia Press*, April 12, 1902.

60. See "Death of Claimant Ends Estate Fight," *New York Times*, August 19, 1948, p. 19. T. John McKee, an attorney, "who lived as a white man for forty-five years," had entered the picture when a "routine legal advertisement caused Mr. McKee to reveal that he was a Negro." The "routine legal advertisement" was a "notice that his grandfather's estate was up for final disposition." See also Lawrence Otis Graham, *The Senator and the Socialite* (2006), pp. 180–82, 384–86.

61. *Mt. Clair National Bank* v. *Seton Hall College of Medicine*, 90 N. J. Super. 419, 217 A. 2d 897 (1966).

62. See also *Estate of Crawshaw*, 249 Kan. 388, 819 P. 2d 613 (1991), where the testator left money to Marymount College to establish a fund to make loans to nursing students, and the college went out of existence shortly after he died.

63. *Evans* v. *Abney*, 396 U.S. 435 (1970). Two justices dissented.

64. *Trammell* v. *Elliott*, 230 Ga. 841, 199 S. E. 2d 194 (1973).

65. *Estate of Buck*, Superior Court of Marin County, California, August 15, 1986, Case No. 23259, The case is unreported, but is reprinted in full in *University of San Francisco Law Review* 12: 691 (1986–87), with the permission of the Superior Court of Marin County. The quote is from p. 752.

66. Ibid., p. 760. The decision also criticized the San Francisco Foundation, which "did not perform its duties in conformity with Mrs. Buck's expressed wishes" (p. 759).

67. See, for example, Rob Atkinson, "Reforming Cy Pres Reform," *Hastings Law Review* 44: 1111 (1993); C. Ronald Chester, "Cy Pres: A Promise Unfulfilled," *Indiana Law Journal* 54: 407 (1979).

68. *United States* v. *Cerio*, 831 F. Supp. 530 (E.D. Va., 1993).

69. In *Quinn* v. *Peoples Trust & Savings Company*, 223 Ind. 317, 60 N.E. 2d 281 (1945), Celia Foley left money for a scholarship, but only to "one person at a time"; and not more than $800 a year for four years. But Ms. Foley left a much larger estate, apparently, than she thought; and the estate produced more income than was needed for this scholarship. The court allowed the "excess income" to be used to carry out the "dominant charitable purpose of the testatrix," presumably to give out more scholarships. Another case that dealt with too much money for two scholarships created by will was *Estate of Puckett*, 111 Cal. App. 3d 46, 168 Cal. Rptr. 311 (1980).

70. See, for example, Utah Code Annotated §75-7-413 (1).

71. Wisconsin Statutes §701.10 (3)(a) (2006).

72. *Smithers* v. *St. Luke's–Roosevelt Hospital Center*, 281 A. D. 2d 127, 723 N. Y. S. 2d 426 (2001).

73. California Probate Code §12598.

74. New Hampshire Revised Statutes (2006), ch. 7: 28.

75. Susan N. Gary, "Regulating the Management of Charities: Trust Law, Corporate Law, and Tax Law," *University of Hawai'i Law Review* 21: 593, 623 (1999).

76. Thus, in California, there was a long investigation into the affairs of the J. Paul Getty Trust, "one of the world's richest cultural organizations," after allegations of improprieties; and the attorney general "appointed an independent monitor." Edward Wyatt and Randy Kennedy, "California Attorney General Appoints Overseer of Reforms at J. Paul Getty Trust," *New York Times*, October 3, 2006.

77. Carol Vogel, "Judge Rules the Barnes Can Move to Philadelphia," *New York Times*, December 14, 2004, p. A1.

78. Roberta Smith, "Does It Matter Where This Painting Hangs?" *New York Times*, December 15, 2004, p. E1.

79. Grace Glueck, "Museum of Indian: The Trouble's Over?" *New York Times*, January 17, 1980, p. C15.

80. For the story, see Samuel P. King and Randall W. Roth, *Broken Trust* (2006).

81. Eleanor Jewett, "Trust Fund Hearing Set for March," *Chicago Daily Tribune*, February 27, 1955, p. J6.

82. Eleanor Jewett, "Seek Ruling on Ferguson Trust Fund," *Chicago Daily Tribune*, January 30, 1955, p. E4.

83. "Art Institute Wins Battle to Use Bequest for Building," *Chicago Daily Tribune*, June 14, 1956, p. D10.

84. Luis Kutner, "The Desecration of the Ferguson Monument Trust: The Need for Watchdog Legislation," *De Paul Law Review* 12: 217, at 235–36 (1963).

85. This information is from *The C.A.C.A. Review* (a newsletter of the Chicago Art Critics Association) 5, no. 1 (April 2004), letter by Jeff Huebner, "The Art Institute's Ferguson Fund Must Always Be for Public Sculpture." Http://www.chicagoartcriticsassociation.org/P/no4.html, visited August 18, 2006.

86. On this incident, see Evelyn Brody, "Whose Public? Parochialism and Paternalism in State Charity Law Enforcement," *Indiana Law Journal* 79: 999–1003 (2004).

87. Stephanie Strom, "In Settlement, Charity Will Split Its Assets," *New York Times*, December 1, 2007, p. A.12.

88. On the Hershey trust, see Brody, "Whose Public?" pp. 937, 985–99; Mark Sidel, "The Struggle for Hershey: Community Accountability and the Law in Modern American Philanthropy," *University of Pittsburgh Law Review* 65: 1 (2003).

89. Pennsylvania Consolidated Statutes Annotated, 20: ch. 72, §7203 (d) (1)

90. Sidel, "The Struggle for Hershey," p. 40; Pennsylvania Consolidated Statutes Annotated, 20: ch. 72, §7203 (c) (6).

91. Stephanie Strom, "Donors Gone, Trusts Veer from Their Wishes," *New York Times*, September 29, 2007, p. A1.

92. "The Best of Intentions," *New York Times*, December 17, 2007, p. A29.

CHAPTER 9: DEATH AND TAXES

1. For a succinct history of these succession taxes, see Barry W. Johnson and Martha Britton Eller, "Federal Taxation of Inheritance and Wealth Transfers," in Robert Miller, Jr., and Stephen J. McNamee, eds., *Inheritance and Wealth in America* (1998), p. 61.

2. Ibid., p. 84.

3. A leading case was *Helvering* v. *Clifford*, 309 U.S. 331 (1940); the rules are now codified in Internal Revenue Code §§671–79. They are quite complex.

4. Provisions for marital deduction trusts are spelled out in §2056 of the Internal Revenue Code.

5. Michie's Annotated Code of Maryland, TG §7-203.

6. Pennsylvania Statutes 72-§9116.

7. Michael J. Graetz and Ian Shapiro, *Death by a Thousand Cuts: The Fight over Taxing Inherited Wealth* (2005), ch. 20.

8. Karen Smith Conway and Jonathan C. Rork, "Diagnosis Murder: The Death of State Death Taxes," *Economic Inquiry* 42: 537 (2004).

9. See Table 1, "Chronology of State Actions to Eliminate Their EIG Taxes," in Conway and Rork, "Diagnosis Murder," at 542. (EIG stands for Estate, Inheritance, Gift).

10. Conway and Rork, "Diagnosis Murder."

11. "Funds Flow in for Props. 6, 7," *Los Angeles Times*, June 4, 1982, p. 22.

12. Carol Hallett, "Propositions 5, 6: Should We Kill the Inheritance Tax?" *Los Angeles Times*, May 2, 1982, p. D3.

13. See Edward J. McCaffery, "The Uneasy Case for Wealth Transfer Taxation," *Yale Law Journal* 104: 283, 328, n. 166 (1994).

14. Lawrence M. Friedman, *The Republic of Choice: Law, Authority and Culture* (1990), pp. 112–32.

15. Eduardo Porter, "Inherit the Wind: There's Little Else Left," *New York Times*, March 26, 2006, section 4, p. 1.

16. The story of the campaign against the estate tax is brilliantly told in Graetz and Shapiro, *Death by a Thousand Cuts*.

17. Ibid., p. 122.

18. The generation-skipping trust tax would also vanish; but the gift tax was slated to remain.

19. Jenny B. Wahl, "From Riches to Riches: Intergenerational Transfers and the Evidence from Estate Tax Returns," *Social Science Quarterly* 84: 277, 294 (2003). Wahl argues that there is a "natural tendency of wealth to regress to the mean over time," and that this is a "counterbalancing force in the long run"; but "the long run may be long indeed."

INDEX

Accumulating trusts, 136–39
Actors Equity Association, 142
Addington v. Wilson, 91
Administrators, 9–10
Adoption: inheritance rights, 11–12, 56–57, 194n118; lack of in England, 22, 57, 188n10; laws, 11, 56–57, 188n10, 194n114
Alameda County, California, will study, 141
Alexander, Robert T., 160–61
Ambiguities, in wills, 74–76, 78
Ames, James Barr, 148, 149
Amory, Francis, 115
Amory, Jonathan, 115
Anderson, Burton, 92
Animals, *see* Pets
Annuities, 110
Arkansas: surviving spouses' rights, 31–32, 188n21; wills, 61–62, 64
Art Institute of Chicago, 165–66, 167
Artists Equity Association, 166

Asset protection trusts, 132–33
Assets, *see* Property
Asten, Robert, 198–99n67
Astor, Brooke, 1–2, 13
Australia, children's inheritance rights, 44

Bacon, A. O., 158
Bacot, Wilds, 75
Ball, J'Noel, 42
Banks: lobbying by, 131–32, 134, 182; P.O.D. (payable on death) accounts, 108–9; Totten trusts, 107–8, 109, 180. *See also* Trustees
Banta, Isaac, 2
Barnes, Albert C., 163, 164
Barnes Foundation, 163–64, 167
Baschi v. New York, 54
Bates, Alan P., 40, 41
Benson, Suzanne, 34
Bequests, *see* Charitable bequests; Wills
Beuscher, J. H., 100

B. F. Ferguson Monument Fund, 165–66
Bill and Melinda Gates Foundation, *see* Gates Foundation
Bishop, Bernice Pauahi, 164
Bishop estate, 164–65
Black, Cora L., 75, 199n68
Blackstone, William, 8, 22–23
Blanchard, Leslie, 54
Bleak House (Dickens), 102
Boeing Company, 70
Boyd, Clem, 158
Braden, Samuel, 97
Bradkowski, Keith, 53
Braschi, Miguel, 54
Breaking wills, *see* Will contests
Britain, *see* England
Broadway Bank v. *Adams*, 117
Browder, Olin, 141
Brown, Andrew, 120
Buck, Beryl, 159
Bucks County, Pennsylvania, study, 41, 100, 111
Buck Trust, 159–60, 161
Buffett, Warren, 141–42
Burns, Jewell, 64
Burns, Monette, 33
Burns, United States v., 33
Bush, George W., administration, estate tax cuts, 177–78
Button, Grace, 67
Button v. *Button*, 67

California: Alameda County, 141; charitable trusts, 162; community property, 16–17, 26; disinheritance of abusers, 33, 191n51; disinheritance of murderers, 190nn47–48; domestic partners' rights, 52–53; estate tax abolition, 175–76; homestead benefits, 36; intestacy, 26, 32, 34; Marin County, 159–60; Probate Code, 39, 68, 200n4; same-sex marriage, 53, 193n100; San Bernardino County study, 65, 82, 84, 100, 112, 141; small estates, 10, 36; trust modification and termination, 206n27
Callen, Page, 50–51
Callen, Sean, 51
Canada, provincial trust law, 134–35
Caretaker trusts, 113, 114, 115
Carnegie Foundation, 168
Catholic Church, 71, 73, 95–96
Cerio, United States v., 160–61
Chancery courts, 101–3
Charitable bequests: challenges by heirs, 73, 198n63; limits on (mortmain laws), 70–73, 149; potential effects of estate tax abolition, 178; proportion of wills including, 140–41
Charitable trusts and foundations: accumulation power, 137–39; company stock held, 150–51, 167–68; contested by relatives, 38–39, 147, 148; creation by wealthy, 135, 141–42, 149, 150–51, 182; criticism of, 169; cy pres doctrine, 153–61, 169; differences from other trusts, 143–45; diminishing power of donors, 168, 169; evolution of law, 145–52; favored by law and courts, 151, 168, 182; financial abuses, 152, 164–65, 215n76; grants by, 140; illegal, 159–60; image in nineteenth century, 149–50; independence, 168, 169; largest, 141–42, 168, 169; monitoring, 161–68; motives of creators, 150–51; number in United States, 142; payout rules, 139, 152; perpetual, 137–39, 144, 147, 152, 153; public perceptions, 181–82; purposes, 142–43, 150, 153, 155–57; Reece Committee investigation, 151–52; small and specialized, 142–43, 153; sunset provisions, 144, 152–53; tax exemptions for gifts to, 151; unworkable, 153, 214n69

Charities: favored by law and courts, 73, 143–45, 182; history in United States, 149–50; publicly supported groups, 169; tax exemption, 143, 151. *See also* Charitable trusts and foundations

Chicago: Art Institute of Chicago, 165–66, 167; Ferguson Monument Fund, 165–66; libraries, 148–49; Terra Museum, 167

Chicago Heritage Committee, 166

Children: born after will execution, 39; disabled, 36, 37, 43; disinheriting, 12, 38–41, 42, 94, 95; of earlier marriages, 42, 85, 94, 95; eldest son as heir (primogeniture), 11, 20, 21, 122; guardians of, 40, 113; as heirs, 36–44; illegitimate, 54–56, 96–97, 181; inheritance rights, 12, 27, 36, 43–44, 187n3; minor, 36, 37, 40, 43, 47, 113; partible inheritance rules, 20–21; restrictions on disinheritance, 38–39, 46; step-, 94; support during probate period, 37–38; trusts for, 113; unequal treatment, 38; of unwed parents, 55; wills contested by, 42, 85, 95, 96. *See also* Adoption

Christian Science, 95

Churches, *see* Religious bodies

Civil unions, 51, 52, 53, 193–94n104

Claflin doctrine, 119–20, 121, 206n24

Claflin v. *Claflin*, 119

Clark, William G., 166

Classes: in developed countries, 7; English nobility, 20, 122, 174–75; inheritance and, 5; landed gentry, 7, 9, 11, 20, 22, 23, 122. *See also* Wealth

Clausser, Emma G., 155

Clergy members, accused of undue influence, 95, 202n43. *See also* Religious bodies

Coast Guard Academy, 160–61

Cohabitation, *see* Domestic partners

Cohen, Julius, 40, 41

Collman, Jeff, 53

Colonial period: inheritance rules, 20–21; wills, 62–63

Colorado: adoption law, 57; surviving spouses' rights, 189n23; will contests, 97

Common law marriages, 48–51, 52, 54, 193n94

Communist influence, investigations in McCarthy era, 151–52

Community property states, 16–17, 26, 31, 109

Companionate marriages, 11, 12

Conditional wills, 61

Congress: estate tax cuts, 177–78; laws on charitable foundations, 152; Reece Committee, 151–52

Connecticut: disinheritance of spouse who abandoned decedent, 33; intestacy cases, 34–35; monitoring of charitable trusts, 163; public defenders' death benefits, 47

Conrad Cantzen Shoe Fund, 142

Contesting wills, *see* Will contests

Coolidge, Calvin, 175

Courts: of chancery, 101–3; changing terms of trusts (cy pres doctrine), 153–61; charities favored by, 73, 143–45, 151, 168, 182; correction of mistakes in wills, 62, 74, 76, 77–80, 180; enforcement of charitable trusts, 163–64; of equity, 101, 103; power to alter intestate succession, 42–44; trust modifications, 122, 154–61. *See also* Supreme Court

Coverture, 8, 23, 26–27

Craig, Robert Wallace, 153

Crerar, John, 148–49

Curtesy, 22–23, 188n21

Cuyahoga County, Ohio, study, 112

Cy pres doctrine, 153; applications, 154–61,

169; in English law, 153–54; expanding, 160; history, 154–55; interpretations, 160; judicial, 154; prerogative, 153–54; preservation of original intent, 154; race and sex discrimination cases, 157–58, 212n26

Dacey, Norman, *How to Avoid Probate*, 106
Dahlin, Michel, 5
Dan and Margaret Maddox Charitable Trust, 167
Dane County, Wisconsin, study, 82
Daniels, Bill Hayes, 67
Davidson County, Tennessee, study, 82, 84, 88
Dead hand: diminishing power over foundations, 168, 169; power, 4, 125, 181–83; restrictions on disinheritance, 18–19, 25–26, 31–32, 38–39, 44, 46; rights, 19
Death taxes, *see* Estate taxes; Taxes
Delaware trust law, 131, 133, 137
Dementia: assessing, 98; wills contested on grounds of, 89–92
Demographic change, 13
Dickens, Charles: *Bleak House*, 102; *David Copperfield*, 95; *Oliver Twist*, 128
Disabled people, 35, 36, 37, 43, 113
Discretionary trusts, 104, 117
Disinheritance: of abusers, 33, 191n51; of adulterous spouses, 33, 191n53; of children, 12, 38–41, 42, 94, 95; disputes over, 42, 85, 94, 95; of murderers, 32–33, 190nn47–48; restrictions, 18–19, 25–26, 31–32, 33–35, 38–39, 46; of spouses, 18–19, 25–26, 31–32, 33–34, 35, 46; unnatural wills, 93, 96, 98, 99
Disputes, inheritance: intestacy cases, 28; standard of proof, 33. *See also* Will contests
Divorce, 12, 30–31, 41, 70

Dobris, Joel, 133
Dogs, *see* Pets
Domestic partners: children of, 55; as family members, 181; inheritance rights, 12, 50, 51–53, 54
Dougal, David, 92
Dower rights, of widows, 22, 23, 24–25, 188n21
Dukeminier, Jesse, 135
Dummar, Melvin, 86, 201n15
Dunham, Allison, 47
Duryea, Edgar E., 89
Duryea, Walter, 201n25
Dynastic families: estate taxes on, 174–75; feudal, 128; law of succession and, 5. *See also* Wealth
Dynastic trusts: evolution, 121–23, 182; investment policies, 114–15; modification, 122; motives, 113–14; spendthrift trust doctrine, 182; spendthrift trusts, 116–18, 121, 123, 132; support trusts, 121; termination, 119–21. *See also* Perpetuities law; Trusts

Educational institutions: ambiguous bequests, 75, 199n68; detailed instructions in wills, 146–47, 155–57; Kamehameha Schools, 164; scholarship funds, 157, 160–61, 214n69
Egelhoff, David, 70
Electronic wills, 68, 197n40
Emmick, Eugene H., 207–8n8
Employee Retirement Income Security Act (ERISA), 47, 70, 197n52
England: death taxes, 122; lack of adoption laws, 22, 57, 188n10; Marriage Act, 48; nobility, 20, 122, 174–75; social change, 122
English inheritance law: charitable trusts, 145; correction of mistakes in wills, 80; cy pres doctrine, 153–54; distinction

INDEX   221

between real and personal property, 19–20; eldest son as heir (primogeniture), 11, 20, 21, 122; Family Provision Act, 43; influence on U.S. law, 8–9; Inheritance [Provision for Family and Dependants] Act of 1975, 43–44; interests of landed gentry and, 7, 9, 20, 22; mortmain law, 71; Perpetuities and Accumulation Act, 130–31; probate process, 9; Statute of Distributions, 20; taxes, 174–75; testaments, 19–20; trusts, 101–3, 121, 122, 123, 145; wills, 19–20, 59
Equity, courts of, 101, 103
ERISA (Employee Retirement Income Security Act), 47, 70, 197n52
"Esau and Jacob" cases, 95
Escheat, 27, 45–46
Essex County, New Jersey, study, 111–12, 141
Estate planning, business of, 5, 132. *See also* Living trusts; Trusts; Wills
Estate taxes, 173–74; avoided by charitable trust creation, 150–51; effects on charitable bequests, 178; English, 174–75; exemptions and deductions, 112, 172–73, 178; future of, 178, 182; history, 171–72, 175; on living trusts, 105–6; opposition to, 175–78; phase-out of federal, 177–78; proportion of estates subject to, 172, 176–77; public perceptions, 176–77; purposes, 172; rates, 18, 172, 175, 177–78; revenues, 172; social context, 176–77; state, 174, 175–76
Executors, 9–10

Families: of affection and dependence, 11–12, 19, 180–81; bloodline, 11, 19, 181; changing structure, 11–13, 29, 50, 180, 181; extended, 29, 180, 181; laughing heirs, 12, 30, 35, 181; nontraditional, 13, 181. *See also* Children; Marriages

Family Provision Act (U.K.), 43
Farkas v. *Williams*, 109
Farms, 38
Farr, William, 96–97
Fellows, Mary Louise, 51
Ferguson, Benjamin, 165, 166
Ferguson Monument Fund, 165–66
"Fertile octogenarian" doctrine, 127–28
Fish, Eliza, 63
Fitzgerald, Bertha, 73, 198n64
Florida: estate tax abolition, 175; intestacy law, 25; mortmain law, 72
Foley, Celia, 214n69
Forced heirship, 37
Ford Foundation, 141, 142, 150–51, 168
Ford Motor Company, 150–51
Forged wills, 86–87
Foundations, *see* Charitable trusts and foundations
Franklin, Benjamin, 144
Fraud: in execution of will, 87–88; in inducement, 87
Freedom of testation, 19, 44, 46–47, 96
Frost, Nettie, 64
Fugitive slaves, 154

Gardiner, Marshall, 42
Garrett, Henrietta, 28–29
Gates, Bill, 134, 135, 170, 176
Gates Foundation, 135, 141–42, 168
Gay couples, *see* Same-sex partners
Genealogists, forensic, 29–30
Generation-skipping transfers (GST), tax on, 131–32, 173–74
George, Henry, 143
Georgia: cy pres doctrine, 158; intestacy laws, 26; mortmain statute, 71; wills, 89, 92, 97, 189n26
Gift taxes: exemptions, 173; history, 172; on property put in trust, 113; provisions, 173; rates, 172; revenues, 173

Girard, Stephen, 146–47, 155
Girard College, 146–47, 212n26
Gray, John Chipman, 117, 129–30
Griswold, Denis, 29–30
GST, *see* Generation-skipping transfers
Guardians, 40, 113

Hall, Peter, 5
Halley, E. J., 199n74
Hamm, Billie Jean, 94
Hamm, Robert, 94
Handwritten wills, *see* Holographic wills
Hart, Silas, 145
Hartog, Hendrik, 38, 101
Harvard College v. *Amory*, 115, 116
Hawaii: Bishop estate, 164–65; domestic partners' rights, 52
Hazard, Laura, 148
Heir hunters, 29–30
Heirs: children as, 36–44; claimants, 29–30, 38–39, 45–46, 84–85; deserving, 35; forced, 37; under intestacy laws, 27, 28–29; laughing, 12, 30, 35, 181; murderers, 32–33, 190n46; pets, 75–76; standing to contest wills, 83–84, 200n5. *See also* Children; Disinheritance; Widows and widowers
Helmsley, Leona, 144
Hembree, Georgia, 75–76
Herceg, Eugenia, 79
Hershey, Milton and Catherine, 167
Hershey Chocolate Company, 167–68
Hershey Industrial School, 167–68
Hershey Trust, 167–68
Hewlett Foundation, 168
Hillblom, Larry, 38–39
Hogan, Lena, 108
Holdeen, Jonathan, 138
Holley, Caroline, 61
Holographic wills, 59, 61, 65–67, 179, 196n24

Holtquist, Otto, 76
Homestead provisions, 36
Honigman, Frank, 91
Hotarek, Kenneth, 34
How to Avoid Probate (Dacey), 106
Hughes, Howard, 28, 86–87
Hurst, Willard, 15
Hurt, William, 51
Husbands, control of wife's assets, 8, 17, 23, 26–27. *See also* Marriages; Widowers

Illinois: charitable trusts in, 148–49; intestacy laws, 35; succession, 47; surviving spouses' rights, 189n23
Income taxes: on spouses, 16–17; on trusts, 137
India, social position of widows, 17–18
Indiana: abolition of dower, 24; disinheritance of adulterous spouses, 33, 191n53; oral wills, 59; videotaped wills, 67–68
Inheritance [Provision for Family and Dependants] Act of 1975 (U.K.), 43–44
Inheritances, median amount, 177. *See also* Disinheritance; Succession; Wealth
Inheritance taxes, 171, 174, 175–76. *See also* Estate taxes
Insane delusions, 90–91, 93
Insanity, wills contested on grounds of, 89–92
Internal Revenue Code, 132. *See also* Taxes
Internal Revenue Service, information returns from foundations, 142
Intestacy laws, 4; alternatives, 42–44; in community property states, 26; decedents with no relatives, 27, 28–30, 45–46; deserving heirs, 35; development and evolution of, 19–27; disputes, 28; domestic partners' rights, 51–53, 54; English, 19–20; escheat, 27, 45–46; heirs, 27–28, 30, 34–35; marriage length

and, 31–32; "merit" and intestacy, 32–33; modern, 27–35; preferred heirs, 18, 19; proportion of intestate deaths, 60; real and personal property distinctions, 19–20; rigidity, 32, 34–35, 42; social change and, 12, 13; surviving spouses' rights, 19, 22–27, 30–31, 32–34; in United States, 20–22, 27–35
Italy, inheritance rights of children, 36, 42

Jackson, Francis, 154
Jackson v. *Phillips*, 154
Jacobs, William, 31
James, Frank, 137–38
Jennings, Sandra, 51
Jetter, Martin, 45–46
Jetter, Robert, 45–46
John M. Olin Foundation, 153
Johnson, Basia Piasecka, 42, 85, 94
Johnson, Seward, 42, 85, 94
Joint tenancy, 109–10
Jones, Charlie, 86
Jones, Jennifer, 69
Josh Butler & Co., 29–30
J. Paul Getty Trust, 215n76

Kamehameha Schools, 164
Kansas: P.O.D. (payable on death) accounts, 108–9, 110; widow's inheritance rights, 24, 42
Karl, Barry D., 149, 150, 152
Katz, Stanley N., 149, 150, 152
Kaufmann, Robert D., 97
Kent, James, 21
Kidd, James, 155
Killen, Dorothy, 90–91
Killough, David, 56
Killough, James T., 56
Kimmel, Harry, 66
King County, Washington, study, 141
Knickerbocker, Jack, 97

Kostic, Branislav, 90
Krier, James E., 135
Kuralt, Charles, 66

Land: agricultural, 38; coverture doctrine, 23; disposal by testament, 19–20; ownership in United States, 7–8, 9, 21–22
Landed gentry, English, 7, 9, 11, 20, 22, 23, 122
Langbein, John, 13, 80
Laughing heirs, 12, 30, 35, 181
Laws of succession: demographic change and, 13; evolution of, 19–27, 181–83; flexibility, 96, 179–80; future of, 182–83; for pensions and other benefits, 46–47; proposed improvements, 179; public attitudes, 46; scholarship on, 5–6; scope, 3, 4; small estates, 10, 36; social context, 6, 7–8, 11–13, 180; trend away from formalism, 80–81, 100–101, 110, 179–80. *See also* English inheritance law; Intestacy laws; Trust law; Wills
Lawyers, mistakes in wills made by, 78–80
Lebsock, Suzanne, 23
Libraries, 148–49
Life estates, 111–12. *See also* Trusts
Life insurance, 110
Lincoln University, 163, 164
Living trusts, 104–7; advantages, 105, 203–4n12, 204n13; costs, 106; importance, 13; popularity, 106–7, 180; taxes on, 105–6
Longevity, 13
Louisiana: constitution, 37; inheritance rights of children, 36–37, 187n3; wills, 65, 75
Lucas v. *Hamm*, 207–8n8

MacArthur Foundation, 142
Macdonald, Dwight, 141

Maddox Charitable Trust, 167
Mahoney v. Grainger, 74
Maine, domestic partnerships, 53
Manitoba trust law, 134–35
Marcus, George, 5
Marin County, California, 159–60
Marital deduction trusts, 112
Marriages: changing patterns, 12–13, 30–31, 41–42; common law, 48–51, 52, 54, 193n94; in community property states, 16–17, 26, 31, 109; companionate, 11, 12; divorces, 12, 30–31, 41, 70; as economic partnerships, 30; husband's control of wife's assets, 8, 17, 23, 26–27; joint income tax returns, 16–17; joint tenancy, 109–10; legal formalities, 48, 49–50, 53, 193n92; lengths before death, 31–32; levirate, 17; multiple, and will contests, 42, 85, 94, 95; rights of married women, 23, 27; same-sex, 53, 193n100; social customs, 17–18; undue influence claims, 93–94, 202n41; wills revoked by, 69–70. *See also* Widows and widowers
Married Women's Property Laws, 27
Marshall, A. H., 89, 90
Marshall, Anthony, 1
Marshall, John, 145
Marshall, Phillip, 1
Martin, James Isaac Thornton, 56
Maryland: constitution, 71; inheritance taxes, 174; Married Women's Property Laws, 27; mortmain law, 71, 189n30
"Mary Worth" cases, 95
Massachusetts: adoption law, 56; monitoring of charitable trusts, 163; pension plan death benefits, 70; professional trustees, 115; prudent investor rule, 115, 123; same-sex marriage, 53; trust law, 117, 119, 154; wills, 60, 62, 74

Massachusetts General Hospital, 115
May, Carl, 97
McCarthy era, 151–52
McCoy, Lucile, 117, 206n21
McCoy, Richard, 117, 206n21
McCoy, Steven, 117, 206n21
McGarrell, William, 43–44
McKee, John, 155–57
McKee, T. John, claim to McKee estate, 214n60
McKee Scholarships, 157
Meeker, Corry T., 138–39
Mehta, Deepa, 17
Mellon, Andrew, 175
Melton, John D., 56
Melton, William James, 56
Michigan: charitable bequests in wills, 141; widow's inheritance rights, 24
Miller, Homer, 64
Mississippi: adoption law, 56, 194n114; Married Women's Property Laws, 27; nuncupative wills, 195n5
Missouri: trust law, 121, 138–39; will contests, 89
M'Lean, John, 115
Morgan, J. P., 134
Mortmain laws, 70–73, 149, 189n30
Moster, Ester, 84, 200n5
Murderers, 32–33, 190nn46–49
Museum of the American Indian, 164

Neiderhiser, Robert, 31
Nelson, Harvey, 61–62
Nevada: constitution, 208n20; electronic wills, 68; Hughes will forgery, 86; trust law, 132, 208n20
New Hampshire: charitable trusts, 163; common law marriage, 50, 193n97; same-sex civil unions, 53; trusts, 131; wills, 195n6
New Jersey: Essex County, 111–12, 141;

Seton Hall College of Medicine, 157; wills, 65, 80, 98
New Mexico, estate tax abolition, 175
New York Public Library, 148
New York state: abolition of succession taxes, 175; attorney general, 164; charitable trust law, 147–48; domestic partners' rights, 54; intestacy laws, 24; laws on oral wills, 59; monitoring of charitable trusts, 163; mortmain law, 72–73
NGOs, *see* Nongovernmental organizations
Nicely, Naomi, 31
Nobility, English, 20, 122, 174–75
No-contest clauses, 83, 85, 200n4
Nongovernmental organizations (NGOs), 169
Normans, William James, 56
North Carolina, holographic wills, 65
North Dakota: estate taxes, 175; holographic wills, 65
Nuncupative wills, 59, 195n5

Ohio: Cuyahoga County, 112; surviving spouses' rights, 36; wills, 60, 69, 112
O'Keefe, Walter, 34
Oklahoma Teachers' Retirement System, 70
Olin Foundation, 153
Oliver Twist (Dickens), 128
Olsen v. Corporation of New Melleray, 95–96
Oral wills, 59, 195n5
Oregon: common law marriage, 193n94; domestic partners' rights, 52; intestacy, 25
Orphans, 56. *See also* Children
Orth, Godlove, 87
Orton, Arthur, 28

Partible inheritance, 20–21
Pastorino, Sergio, 79
Patrick, Albert, 86
Pauley, Debra, 64
Pavlinko, Vasil and Hellen, 79
Payable on death (P.O.D.) accounts, 108–9
Pennsylvania: attorneys general, 167; Barnes Foundation, 163–64, 167; Bucks County, 41, 100, 111; charitable trust law, 146–47; Girard College, 146–47, 212n26; Hershey Industrial School, 167–68; inheritance taxes, 174; mortmain law, 71–72; Orphans' Courts, 163–64
Pension plans: beneficiaries, 110; death benefits, 46–47, 49; effects of divorce on rights, 70
Perpetuities law: abolition of rule against perpetuities, 122, 130, 131, 132, 134–35, 182; accumulating trusts and, 136–37; avoiding limits of, 207n5; basics, 126–36; complexity, 126; contingent beneficiaries, 126; English, 130–31; evolution, 129, 182; "fertile octogenarian," 127–28; future of, 124, 136; rationale, 128, 130; reforms, 130–32; time limits, 114, 120, 124, 125, 126; "unborn widow," 128; Uniform Statutory Rule Against Perpetuities, 130, 207n1; violations, 127, 129–30
Pets: as heirs, 75–76; as trust beneficiaries, 144, 211n20
Philanthropy, distinction from charity, 149. *See also* Charitable trusts and foundations
P.O.D. (payable on death) accounts, 108–9
Portfolio theory, 123–24
Pratt, Florence, 89–90, 202n26
Pretermission statutes, 38–39
Price, John, 106–7
Primogeniture, 11, 20, 21, 122

Probate: avoiding with living trusts, 105, 106; bypassing, 10; costs, 10, 106, 177; criticism of process, 106; definition, 2; English law on, 9; problems with system, 10; process, 9–10; proportion of estates, 60, 100; Uniform Probate Code, 30, 31, 80, 196n24, 200n4. *See also* Wills

Promises, as will substitutes, 101

Property: defining, 15–16; distinction between real and personal property, 19–20; fee tail ownership, 21; joint tenancy, 109–10; ownership rights, 16; small estates, 10; societal definition of ownership, 15–18. *See also* Land

Protective trusts, 123

Prudent investor rule, 114–15, 116, 120, 123

Racial discrimination, 157–58, 212n26

Reanimation Foundation, 3

Reece, Brazilla Carroll, 151–52

Reece Committee, 151–52

Reed, Thomas J., 90, 95

Relatives, *see* Children; Families; Heirs

Religious bodies: bequests to, 71, 73, 95–96; clergy members accused of undue influence, 95, 202n43; favored by law, 182; as trust beneficiaries, 138

Remote kin as claimants, 29–30

Republican Party, opposition to estate taxes, 177

Revocable trusts, 104–5

Revocation of wills, 68–70, 197n41, 197n45

Rhode Island: abolition of rule against perpetuities, 131; charitable bequests in wills, 141

Rice, William Marsh, 86

Robber barons, 133, 134

Robert Schalkenbach Foundation, 142–43

Robson, Reginald A., 40, 41

Rockefeller, John D., 133, 134, 169, 175, 176

Rockefeller Foundation, 150

Romans, Lorraine E., 72

Roosevelt, Franklin D., 133

Rosenwald, Julius, 153

Rosenwald Foundation, 153

Rothko, Mark, 198n63

Rule against perpetuities, *see* Perpetuities law

Russell Sage Foundation, 142

St. Luke's–Roosevelt Hospital Center, 162

Salmon, Marylynn, 5

Same-sex marriage, 53, 193n100

Same-sex partners, 12, 50, 51, 52, 53, 54, 97

San Bernardino County, California, will study, 65, 82, 84, 100, 112, 141

San Francisco Foundation, 159

Schwerzler, Robert, 54

Scott, Henry, 34

Scott, Shirley E., 34

Scudder, Henry Martyn, 86

Searles, John, 62

Sears, Roebuck, & Co., 153

See, Francis V., 29–30

Self-proved wills, 179, 195n7

Seton Hall College of Medicine, 157

Sex discrimination, 157–58

Shameia, Saba George, 198n65

Shammas, Carole, 5

Shanks, John, 92–93

Shannon, Patricia, 66

Shaw, Carolyn and Lloyd, 31–32

Shaw, George Bernard, 143

Shriners' Hospitals, 72, 138–39

Siblings, will contests between, 95, 96. *See also* Children

Simpson, O. J., 190–91n50

Sisters of Mercy of Arizona, 153

Slavery, 8, 21, 27, 55–56, 96–97, 154

Smithers, Adele, 162

Smithers, R. Brinkley, 162

Smithers v. *St. Luke's–Roosevelt Hospital Center*, 162
Smith v. *Nelson*, 61–62
Snide, Harvey and Rose, 79
Social classes, *see* Classes
Social Security survivors' benefits, 47, 49
Soldiers, oral wills, 59, 195n5
South Dakota: escheat cases, 45–46; intestacy law, 34; trust business, 133; will contests, 94
Southern United States: plantations, 21; primogeniture, 21; slavery, 8, 21, 27, 55–56
Sparks, John, 95
Spendthrift trust doctrine, 116–18, 121, 122, 123, 132, 182
Spouses, *see* Marriages; Widows and widowers
Stanley v. *Illinois*, 55
State laws: abolition of dower, 24; acceptance of holographic wills, 65; adoption, 188n10; changes to attract trust business, 132–33, 134; charitable trusts, 145; civil unions, 51, 52, 53, 193–94n104; community property, 16–17, 26, 31, 109; enforcement of charitable trusts, 162–63; estate and inheritance taxes, 174, 175–76; intestacy, 27–35; marriage, 48–51, 53, 193n92; mortmain, 70–73, 149, 189n30. *See also* Trust law; *and individual states*
States: attorneys general, 162–63, 167; competition for trust business, 132–33, 134; efforts to retain charitable trust assets, 166–67; legislatures, 134
Stephen, Francis, 91
Story, Joseph, 147
Straisinger, Maude, 84, 200n5
Straus, Ferdinand, 25–26, 31
Strittmater, Louisa, 98
Succession: asset amounts in United States, 4; social importance, 4–5, 14; societal rules, 7. *See also* Law of succession
Suicide notes, as wills, 67
Sullivan, Helen, 74
Support trusts, 121
Supreme Court, Pennsylvania, 71–72
Supreme Court, U.S.: correction of mistakes in wills, 78; rulings on charitable trusts, 145, 146–47; *Stanley* v. *Illinois*, 55
Surviving spouses, *see* Widows and widowers

Taft, Lorado, 165
Taxes: charity exemption, 143, 151; in England, 122; on generation-skipping transfers, 131–32, 173–74; gift, 113, 172, 173; income, 16–17, 137; inheritance, 171, 174, 175–76; on trusts, 112–13, 137. *See also* Estate taxes
Tennessee: charitable trusts, 167; Davidson County, 82, 84, 88; will contests, 82
Terra Museum, 167
Testamentary trusts, 112
Testaments, 19–20
Texas: adoption law, 56; ambiguities in wills, 68, 76; community property, 16, 26; estate tax abolition, 175; holographic wills, 67; perpetuities, 138; Probate Code, 10
Thatcher, Margaret, 90
Thelluson v. *Woodford*, 136
Thellusson, Peter, 136, 137
Thompson, Frederick M., 153
Thompson, W. P., 96–97
Tichborne, James, 28
Tilden, Samuel, 147–48, 149
Tocqueville, Alexis de, *Democracy in America*, 8
Torregano, Ernest J., 84–85
Totten trusts, 107–8, 109, 180

Transsexuals, 42
Truax v. *Southwestern College*, 108
Trust companies: history, 134; lobbying by, 131–32, 134, 182. *See also* Prudent investor rule
Trustees: of caretaker trusts, 114; duties, 102, 104, 107; of dynastic trusts, 114; fees, 107; professional, 114–16, 123–24, 131–32, 134, 182; prudent investor rule, 114–15, 116, 120, 123
Trust law: changes, 121–22; charitable trusts, 145–52; Claflin doctrine, 119–20, 121, 206n24; default rules, 113; development, 102, 124; English, 101–3, 121, 122, 123, 145; future of, 136, 182–83; role of state legislatures, 134; spendthrift trust doctrine, 116–18, 121, 122, 123, 132, 182; trustee duties, 102, 104, 107; Uniform Prudent Investor Act, 123–24; Uniform Trust Code, 121, 161. *See also* Perpetuities law
Trusts: accumulating, 136–39; for animals, 144, 211n20; asset protection, 132–33; beneficiary rights, 102–3, 119; caretaker, 113, 114, 115; in common law systems, 101–3; definition, 101; discretionary, 104, 117; documents, 103; evolution, 103, 120–23, 124; future of, 121–22, 182–83; income taxation, 137; investment policies, 114–16, 120, 121, 123–24; irrevocable, 104, 112–16; lifetime trusts for spouses, 41; living, 104–7, 180; marital deduction, 112; modification, 122, 154–61; perpetual, 131, 135, 136, 137, 182–83; professional asset management, 105; protective, 123; purposes, 103–4, 113–14; revocable, 104–5; support, 121; tax consequences, 112–13; termination, 119–21, 206n24; testamentary, 112; time limits, 130, 208n20; Totten, 107–8,

109, 180; for widows, 41, 111–12. *See also* Charitable trusts and foundations; Dynastic trusts

"Unborn widow" case, 128
Undue influence claims, 2, 88, 93–97, 202n41, 202n43
Uniform Probate Code, 30, 31, 80, 196n24, 200n4
Uniform Prudent Investor Act, 123–24
Uniform Statutory Rule Against Perpetuities, 130, 207n1
Uniform Trust Code, 121, 161
United Kingdom, *see* England
United States v. *Burns*, 33
United States v. *Cerio*, 160–61
"Unnatural" wills, 93, 96, 98, 99
"Uriah Heep" cases, 95

Vasquez, Frank, 54
Vermont: civil unions, 52; trust law, 120
Vidal v. *Girard's Executors*, 146–47
Videotaped wills, 67–68

Waggoner, Lawrence, 51
Walker, Charles, 138
Walker, James, 78
Ward, Edward H., 100
Washington Legal Foundation, 169
Washington state: domestic partnerships, 53; King County, 141; marriage laws, 52; trust law, 131; will substitutes used, 106–7
Water, 17–18
Wealth: attitudes toward, 14, 120–21, 133–34, 174–75, 176–77, 181; in developed countries, 7; of dynastic families, 5, 174–75; inequalities, 135, 178, 182; inherited, 174–75; of robber barons, 133, 134; in United States, 122–23,

133–34, 135, 176; will contests for large estates, 84, 89–90. *See also* Charitable trusts and foundations; Estate taxes; Trusts

Weiss, Walter A., 97

Wendel, Georgiana, 29

White, Mrs. E. J., 66

White, Helen L., 69

Widowers, curtesy rights, 22–23, 188n21

Widows: dower rights, 22, 23, 24–25, 188n21; social status, 17–18

Widows and widowers: of common law marriages, 48–51, 52; disinheritance of adulterous, 33, 191n53; duration of marriage before death of spouse, 31; effects of remarriage, 18, 41, 111–12; estate tax exemption, 112; homestead benefits, 36; inheritance rights, 11, 12, 35–36, 180–81, 189n23, 189n25; intestacy law provisions, 19, 22–27; restrictions on disinheritance, 18–19, 25–26, 31–32; rule of perpetuities and, 128; trusts for, 41, 111–12

Will contests: charitable trusts disputed by relatives, 38–39, 147, 148; by children of previous marriage, 42, 85, 94, 95; costs, 83; estate sizes and likelihood of, 84; forgery claims, 86–87; fraud claims, 87–88; grounds, 85–99; heirs as contestants, 29–30, 45–46, 84–85; hurdles, 83–84; lack of capacity claims, 88, 89–93, 97–99; no-contest clauses, 83, 85, 200n4; procedures, 82; rarity, 82–83; results, 92, 99; between siblings, 95, 96; social context, 96–99; standing of heirs, 83–84, 200n5; undue influence claims, 2, 88, 93–97, 202n41, 202n43

Wills, 4; ambiguities, 74–76, 78, 199n68, 199n74; audio recordings, 196n35; changing, 104–5; charitable gifts in, 70–73, 140–41; in colonial period, 62–63; conditional, 61; customary language, 63; declining formality, 64–65, 69, 80–81, 179–80; declining importance, 13, 77; defining, 58; destroying, 68–69; electronic, 68, 197n40; filing, 9; formal written, 58–65; freedom of testation, 19, 44, 46–47, 96; holographic, 59, 61, 65–67, 179, 196n24; intentions, 59–60, 61–62, 76–77, 79; legal requirements, 59–60, 80, 88; of married people, 41, 79; minimum age, 89; mistakes in, 62, 74–77; mortmain laws, 70–73, 149, 189n30; objections to, 82–83, 85; oral, 59, 195n5; proportion of population with, 60, 100; respect for, 62; revocation, 68–70, 197n41, 197n45; rights of married women, 27; self-proved, 179, 195n7; signatures, 59, 63–65, 69, 79, 196n18, 197n40; unnatural, 93, 96, 98, 99; videotaped, 67–68; witnesses, 59, 61–62, 63–64, 80, 195n6. *See also* Disinheritance; Intestacy laws; Probate

Will substitutes, 13; acceptance, 110, 180; annuities, 110; community property system as, 109; declarations of trust, 109; effect of divorce on, 70; growing use, 100–101, 110, 180; joint tenancy, 109–10; life insurance, 110; living trusts, 104–7, 180; oral promises, 101; pension plans, 110; P.O.D. (payable on death) accounts, 108–9; Totten trusts, 107–8, 109, 180. *See also* Trusts

Wisconsin: enforcement of charitable trusts, 162; marriage law, 193n92; mistakes in wills, 78–79; proportion of probate estates, 100; will contests, 82, 92–93

Wives, *see* Marriages; Widows
Women: married, 8, 17, 23, 26–27; property rights, 17; proportion with estates, 60; social status, 8, 11. *See also* Widows

Wood, Ida, 28
Wright, Lorenzo D., 98–99
Wyoming trust law, 131, 209n23

Young v. *McCoy*, 117

The authorized representative in the EU for product safety and compliance is:
Mare Nostrum Group
B.V Doelen 72
4831 GR Breda
The Netherlands

www.ingramcontent.com/pod-product-compliance
Lightning Source LLC
Chambersburg PA
CBHW020754160426
43192CB00006B/327